BEYOND DOUBT

Beyond Doubt

A DEVOTIONAL RESPONSE
TO QUESTIONS OF FAITH

Cornelius Plantinga Jr.

ILLUSTRATIONS BY PAUL STOUB

BIBLE WAY
Grand Rapids, Michigan

© 1980 by the Board of Publications of the Christian Reformed Church
2850 Kalamazoo SE
Grand Rapids, MI 49560

Printed in the United States of America

Library of Congress Cataloging in Publication Data

Plantinga, Cornelius, 1946-
    Beyond doubt.

    Bibliography: p.
    Includes index.
    1. Meditations.   2. Theology—Miscellanea.   I. Title.
BV4832.2.P54   242   80-10647
ISBN 0-933140-12-6

Q. WHAT THEN MUST A CHRISTIAN BELIEVE?

A. Everything God promises us in the gospel.
   That gospel is summarized for us
   in the articles of our Christian faith—
   a creed beyond doubt,
   and confessed throughout the world.
                        —Heidelberg Catechism,
                                    Q & A 22

Contents

Author's Preface

Beyond Doubt is the second-year course in the Truth for Life division of the adult curriculum published by the Christian Reformed Church's Education Department. In planning, editing, illustrating, publishing, and distributing, this course is a staff project. It is offered by the church for the church.

Still, someone had to write it. Accordingly, I have asked for space here to describe the course's shape and aim and to make some acknowledgments.

Beyond Doubt consists of one hundred fifty meditations and about one hundred associated questions and answers. All this material is divided into six units of three to eight "weeks" each. The units correspond to traditional areas of theological investigation: the doctrines of God, humanity, Christ, salvation, church, and last things. Each of the weeks within a unit presents five meditations and three to five Postscript questions. In the separately published leader's guide, I propose my answers to these questions.

Readers will notice at once that the weeks themselves pose *questions*—questions about God (e.g., How do we know God?), about humanity (e.g., How should we see ourselves?), and so forth. The staff and I have tried to limit ourselves in each area to the sorts of questions actually being raised in the church today. To help, a number of thoughtful pastors took considerable time to list for us the acutest and most persistent questions now being asked in their own congregations. Gathering their questions and our own under the several heads of doctrine, we arranged a topical scheme for the course. It then remained for me to fill in the meditations and Postscript questions and answers.

The meditations are headed by a relevant biblical text and, with a few exceptions, a short passage from one of the

Reformed confessions. They are followed by a prayer, hymn, or recitation. In nearly every case the hymns may be either sung or said as prayers. Though they present a few sensitive subjects (especially in week eleven), the meditations are intended to be suitable for family devotions and the Postscript questions helpful in stimulating group discussions.

The first year companion to this present course (*A Place to Stand*) is organized historically and confessionally. This time the staff and I chose the weekly topic questions more for current liveliness than for historical or theological importance. Of course many questions are both lively and perennial. But where we had to choose between, say, two sorts of questions in the broad area of salvation doctrine— a traditional technical question (e.g., What about supra- and infra-lapsarianism?) and a forceful contemporary moral question (e.g., How shall we handle our wealth?)—we chose the latter sort every time.

The result is a sort of hybrid. The course is meant to address important issues arising from our contemporary experience as believers in Jesus Christ. At the same time, we have used a traditional theological structure and have stubbornly attempted to exercise firm biblical control throughout. Thus we offer neither a miscellaneous collection of meditations nor a short systematic theology but rather what we trust is a book of faithful existential devotions with a biblical, theological spine.

The style is meant to be plain and as widely understandable as possible. Alert readers will detect an alternation in the use of third person pronouns between masculine and feminine forms. The result may appear cute; it is intended to be fair.

To leaders who must deal with my proposed answers to Postscript questions, I apologize. I attempt to answer, and to answer briefly, questions many of you have for years been pondering more deeply than I. If my answers appear presumptuous or wrong, or if you are older and wiser than I, please forgive. Use what you can and let the rest go. Correct, revise, alter, adapt! Make up your own questions and answers. It would be foolish for me to pretend I do not think my answers right. But it would be even more foolish to assume they cannot be greatly improved upon.

Finally, I want to thank a number of people who have joined in the production of this course: the pastors who submitted questions; the Christian Reformed Church's Education staff with whom it is a joy to work; Paul Stoub, whose artistry seems to me a thing of delight and wonder; and, especially, three people who have aided me in writing. To A. James Heynen, for conceiving the format of the course and often suggesting organizational improvements; to Clarence Boomsma, for many keen insights into the faith and mature observation of trends in the church; to Douglas E. Nelson, who is the primary, if hidden, author of a sizable share of this material—to these three wise men I offer hearty thanks.

To Dr. Nelson I owe a particular debt. His thoughts, phrases, stories, and examples are liberally scattered through these materials—often, but not always, with acknowledgment. He has modestly granted me this freedom; now an even greater modesty must prevent him from admiring this course. I wish here to acknowledge his contribution and to thank him for his many years of deeply probing and caring ministry at the First United Presbyterian Church of New Haven, Connecticut. Dr. Nelson first taught me that the Christian believer seeks understanding very often in the interrogative mood and that a faith beyond doubt is not yet beyond question.

To him I dedicate this work with the deepest gratitude and respect.

Cornelius Plantinga Jr.
Reformation Day, 1979

Week One

How Do We Come to Know God?

The most important question in the world is the question about God. Are we—we human beings who hope and laugh and fear—*alone* in the universe? Or are we at this very moment in the unspeakable presence of him who is both a terror to our sin and a loving Father to all his children? How do we know?

For six weeks let us ask our questions about God. Of course, we have to ask our questions as believers. That is what most of us *are.* We cannot, and may not, try to jump out of our skin and ask the skeptic's question, How do you know? Instead, from our place in Christ we ask, How do we come to know God?

Scripture
" 'Gather the people to me, that I
may let them hear my words, so
that they may learn to fear me all
the days that they live upon the
earth, and that they may teach
their children so.' "
Deuteronomy 4:10

Confession
Children are to be brought up by
the parents in the fear of the
Lord.
Second Helvetic Confession,
Chapter XXIX

1

Most children come to know about God
through parents. A child learns that there is a
sort of person named God. We cannot see this
person, but he can see us. And we can talk to
him. He is good. He is great. He is extremely
high. He has something to do with another person by the name of Jesus. Either may be called
"the Lord."

It is not long before a child reflects on these
things. Then he asks wonderful questions: How
can God see us if he has no eyes? What does he
look like? Is God stronger than Superman? Is
Jesus the same person as God?

Parents do their best with such questions.
Meanwhile, the child notices that just as he is
fastened to his parents by need, love, and obedience, so they are fastened to God. Surprising-
ly, parents turn out, in a way, to be children
too—children of God. This impresses a child.
He notes that all the really basic rules for right
living seem to come not from, but through, his
parents.

More and more, he gets worked into the
family way of life. At the heart of it is a set of
attitudes and practices which ties the whole
family to God. It is called religion. The main tie
or bond in true religion is what the Bible calls
"the fear of the Lord." It is an attitude of mixed
reverence and love. And it has less to do with
knowing *about* God than with knowing God
himself.

Parents attempt to teach their children this
fear of the Lord. As our passage shows, they
are thus obedient to the Lord himself. But often
this profound attitude is not so much taught as
caught. A child catches it from his parents'
reverent tone of voice when they mention God.
He is deeply impressed by a glimpse of his
parents praying on their knees. When his
mother says to his father, "Henry, we *cannot* do
it! It simply is not right!" the child perceives
that this too has something to do with the fear
of the Lord, even though the Lord has not
been explicitly named.

So it goes in untold numbers of families down
the ages. We see it begin among the Israelites.
They *learn* to fear the Lord "that they may
teach their children so."

A Prayer
God our Lord, we know you are kind and good. Yet let us
reverently fear you for your power and holiness. We know you
are strong and holy. Yet let us love you for your kindness and
goodness. In Jesus' name, Amen.

Scripture
God also said to Moses, "...Go and gather the elders of Israel together, and say to them, 'The Lord, the God of your fathers, the God of Abraham, of Isaac, and of Jacob, has appeared to me saying, "I have observed you and what has been done to you in Egypt; and I promise that I will bring you up out of the affliction of Egypt." ' " Exodus 3:15-17

Confession
We believe that the Holy Scriptures fully contain the will of God, and that whatsoever man ought to believe unto salvation is sufficiently taught therein.
Belgic Confession,
Article VII

2

We come to know God through his Word. Already as children we may have heard stories and other biblical accounts of God's doings and his ways. Now, too, somebody reads at the dinner table. Possibly there is a Bible story before bed. Many of these readings reveal that God rescues his children. Most are interesting. Some are sad. A few are quite funny. Several are, frankly, quite terrifying.

The Bible tells us what God says. That is why it is called God's Word. God's Word comes to us by way of certain human beings. These people are God's messengers or ambassadors. They are *sent*. They represent the sender and speak on his behalf. And when they speak, *God* may truly be said to speak. So Moses is sent to the Israelite slaves in Egypt. "Go and say to them," says God. That is always the twin command: "go and say." "Go and say to them, 'I see your trouble and I will save you.' "

The Israelites came to know God through his Word. In this case Moses brought it. He brought it into their trouble.

That is where we find God's Word. In trouble. Always God's Word is addressed to us in our fallenness. It talks of liberation for slaves, health for the diseased, hope for the depressed. The Bible is meant to lead confused and blinded people up and out into the light. Then it means to set them to work.

Sometimes people get confused about this. They talk as if the Bible is intended mainly to give us information about God. Apparently that is not true. The main thing God wants to do with the Bible is not to satisfy our curiosity about his nature, but rather to point the way out of our predicament. It is not as if God says: "I see that you are curious about me. I can fix *that*. I promise to tell you all you want to know." It is rather that he says, "I see that you are badly fallen and hurt. I promise that I will lift and heal. Now here is what you must do."

God wants to make us wise—"unto salvation." Our main problem, as he sees it, is not so much ignorance as sin.

A Prayer
O Lord our God, send your Word past our defenses and into our hearts and homes. Rescue us from all which displeases you and drags us down. Through your Word, let us know you as our deliverer. For Jesus' sake, Amen.

Scripture
And the Word became flesh and dwelt among us, full of grace and truth....No one has ever seen God; the only Son...has made him known.   John 1:14,18

Confession
[Christ] has been ordained by God the Father and has been anointed with the Holy Spirit to be our chief prophet and teacher who perfectly reveals to us the secret counsel and will of God for our deliverance.
Heidelberg Catechism,
Answer 31

3

A child who once sees real fear on the face of a parent may never forget it. He does not expect to see fear there. It registers. From then on, whenever he thinks of fear, he may recall that terrible *look.*

That is the way with ideas which are most real to us. They must come alive. They have to take on some of the blood and smoke of real existence. And then they often surprise us. So we say, "I never *knew* real jealousy till I met him!" Or, "You think *that's* honesty? You don't know the meaning of the word."

That is true. We do not know the meaning of a word till it takes flesh among us. Nor did God's ancient people. So when the time was ripe, God finally sent his Word not merely by a person but *as* a person. Here is God's Word—with a name and address, with his own clothes and habits and hungers and fears.

We come to know God through his Word in the flesh. In so many ways it is a surprising Word. Who expected the Word of God in diapers? Who would have searched in a feedbox among peasants?

But let us again try to be clear: the Word is not sent mainly to reveal the surprising turns in God's character. This Son who comes as gospel into our desperation is not merely trying to get us to say, "Aha! So *that's* what God is like!"

No. His business is more urgent than that. True, he does show us what deliverance is like. We see him dealing with a dirty woman, or dining with a wormy-souled little scoundrel, or bringing to some hopeless cripple an almost hilarious freedom to leap and walk. We see it and never forget. So *this* is deliverance!

But the Word is not just showing deliverance. This Word is delivering. And he keeps measuring for deliverance such shoddy or shattered ones as we.

His method may not suit us at all. Whatever made us think we would *like* having the Son of God pitch his tent in our camp? Who can *endure* the day of his coming? What if he wants to change our setup? What if he wants to pull up all our stakes? Suppose he decides to feed the poor and to send the rich away empty!

Blessed are the pure in heart, for in him they shall see God.

A Prayer or Hymn
Come, thou long-expected Jesus,
Born to set Thy people free;
From our fears and sins release us;
Let us find our rest in Thee.

—"Come, Thou Long-expected Jesus"

Scripture
O Lord, our Lord, how majestic is thy name in all the earth! Thou whose glory above the heavens is chanted by the mouths of babes and infants....
Psalm 8:1, 2

Confession
We know Him...by the creation, preservation, and government of the universe.   Belgic Confession, Article II

4

Douglas Nelson somewhere recalls the preface to Whittaker Chambers's book *Witness*. Chambers tells of watching his baby one day as she meditatively dribbled pabulum over the tray of her high chair. Chambers was a convinced Communist and an embittered atheist. He found himself staring with fascination at his daughter's tiny, intricate ear. It seemed to him a marvel. Only a *planner* could have planned that ear. It set Chambers on the road to belief.

Believers are themselves often overtaken by creative signs of God. A surprise crocus in March, the angle of an autumn sun across a field, tree sounds and small animal noises in some wooded place, the pattern traced by a desolate bird in flight—these things, and so many others, speak to a believer of God.

We know God, or know him better, through creation. But we also know him through his providence. A treasured child is rescued; a loved one recovers; a marriage is fastened for good. So many rich gifts whisper God's name to an alert soul. Music can do it powerfully. So can a nourishing friendship. Even the smell of slow, savory cooking can remind a Christian how good it is to have someone to thank.

We know that sometimes God's providence must hold us in trouble. Someone's child is not rescued; a loved one does not recover; a marriage comes unglued. Christians have to come to terms with suffering.

Yet even then many believers are deeply moved by a sense of God's care. A lost hiker shivers miserably through a cold night; yet he has never been surer that God is with him. Sad and thoughtful parents visit the scene of their children's airplane crash years after it happened. They are startled by a sudden shaft of sunlight which reminds them strongly that God holds their children. Elizabeth Gray Vining writes of a time when grief had frozen her heart and locked every door in her against any hope. One morning she woke, dull and leaden as usual, to hear what sounded like rain on the porch roof beneath her window. When she got one eye open enough to look, she saw sun streaming in. The patter was not rain but the soft fall of locust blossoms from the tree beside her house. So many of them that the roof was white! Then and there the ice in her soul began to break up.

A Prayer
O Lord, our Lord, how majestic is thy name in all the earth! Thou whose glory above the heavens is chanted by the mouth of babes and infants, thou who hast made the heavens and established the moon and stars; O Lord, our Lord, how majestic is thy name in all the earth!   —from Psalm 8

Scripture
When we cry, "Abba! Father!" it is the Spirit himself bearing witness with our spirit that we are children of God.
Romans 8:15,16

Confession
What, therefore, neither the light of nature nor the law could do, that God performs by the operation of the Holy Spirit through the word or ministry of reconciliation; which is the glad tidings concerning the Messiah....
Canons of Dort III-IV, Article 6

5

It is remarkably hard to answer the question, "Why do you believe in God?" So many answers do not seem quite final. You might say, for example, "I believe because my parents taught me." But that is not a final answer. Even wise parents are wrong about some things. They might have been wrong about God.

You might say, instead, "I believe in God because of the Bible and what it says about him." But, again, how do you know the Bible is right? Other books disagree with it.

Perhaps you could say, "I believe because God has actually sent his Son among us." But, once more, that answer seems unsatisfactory. After all, you learned about Christ from the Bible—and the Bible has been set aside for the moment.

Well, then, suppose you say, "I believe because I can see evidence of design and providence in the world." That will not quite clinch the matter either. Perhaps the universe was designed by a beginning team of designers. They were pretty good. For example, they outfitted many creatures with an ingenious, built-in pump called a "heart." But they did not perfect it. So some creatures have heart failure.

When it comes right down to it, we are hard put to say how we know God. Yet we do. With all our heart we are convinced of God and his love and his determination to put things right in a world gone wrong.

How do we know? Perhaps the plainest thing to say, first, is that we have a strong inner conviction. We are *convinced* of God. And we discover that the Bible knows about this strange, unshakable conviction. It calls it the witness of the Holy Spirit.

As it turns out, the Spirit is the hidden persuader in all of our otherwise doubtful sources. It is the Spirit who stimulates childlike faith in what our parents say and do about God. The Spirit witnesses to the truth of the Scriptures, telling us in our hearts that "they are from God." The Spirit sparks faith in Jesus Christ, the Son of God. It is even the Holy Spirit who is brooding over our deep places when we ache with the sense of God in nature.

When in some moment of recognition we call God's name; when after years of prayerless life we begin again; "when we cry, 'Abba! Father!' it is the Spirit himself bearing witness with our spirit that we are children of God."

A Prayer or Hymn
Creator Spirit, by whose aid
The world's foundations first were laid,
Come, visit every pious mind;
Come, pour thy joys on human kind;
From sin and sorrow set us free,
And make thy temples worthy thee.
—"Creator Spirit, by Whose Aid"

Postscript

1. Deuteronomy 6 contains a basic and famous passage which has to do with training children in the knowledge of God. The context is clearly covenantal. Listen:

   And these words which I command you this day shall be upon your heart; and you shall teach them diligently to your children, and shall talk of them when you sit in your house, and when you walk by the way, and when you lie down, and when you rise. (Deut. 6:6,7)

   Some parents take this sort of thing very seriously—and very literally: "Jesus wants you to eat your cereal!" "God doesn't like it when little boys hit their sisters." "Do I have to get out the 'Jesus-Spanker' again?"

   How about that? Is the knowledge of God best handed on to our children by constant repetition of the Lord's name? Is it wise to include some reference to "God," to "Jesus," or to "the Lord" in connection with most of our daily pursuits?

2. Distinguish between the following two statements:
   a) The Bible is the answer.
   b) The Bible has all the answers.
   Which statement seems closer to the truth?

3. Is the Bible concerned with the existence of God? What are the clearest passages in which the Bible proves God's existence?

4. Is creation or providence enough to convince an unbeliever of God? How do these affect a *believer's* knowledge of God? Is there a basic difference between the way a believer and an unbeliever look at stars and constellations, for example?

5. What can one say in answer to the straight question, "Why do you believe in God?"

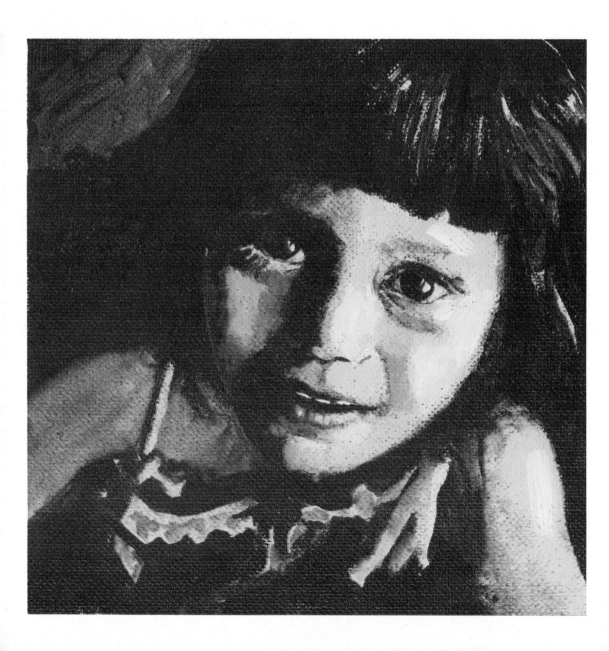

Week Two

What Is God Like?

At the same time we come to know God, we also come to know something about what he is like. Of course, we cannot thoroughly understand or see through him whose greatness unimaginably transcends our littleness. Nor are we allowed to sit around and casually "discuss God." He is, after all, our Father and holy Lord. And he calls us not so much to discuss him as to obey him. Yet we may reverently ask who this is who lays his claim on us. What is God like?

Scripture
Ephraim is joined to idols, let him alone....Yet it was I who taught Ephraim to walk, I took them up in my arms.
Hosea 4:17; 11:3, 8, 9

Confession
The eternal Father of our Lord Jesus Christ...is my God and Father because of Christ his Son.
Heidelberg Catechism,
Answer 26

6

Many couples choose not to have children. It is not that they dislike children particularly. They just do not want any in their homes and lives. Children need time and take pains. You have to risk and spend yourself for children. You can get attached to children, and they can break your heart.

God has chosen to have children. God is fatherly. In Hosea, God's child is called Ephraim. Ephraim stands for Israel and all God's children. God loves Ephraim. But Ephraim has gradually been breaking his father's heart. A careless and stubborn prodigal son, Ephraim has been wasting his father's gifts, blackening the family name, and smearing over his own soul with an ugliness which years cannot erase.

There have been numerous fatherly warnings from God. "Don't do that, son! *Look* at how you have come to live! You are sick and hurt and desperately wrong. You are feeding on sin. Come home!"

But Ephraim will not listen. At times it seems he cannot listen.

Finally God lets Ephraim go. He does not get even. He just gets out. Here is the ageless picture of a hurt, angry, and deeply disappointed parent. He has said everything there is to say. He has tried everything he can think of. None of it has worked. Now it is time for silence and restraint. "Ephraim is joined to idols; let him alone."

Here is God our Father, as someone put it, "pacing the room, biting his lip, hands gripped tightly behind his back." He forces himself to let us go, let us hit bottom, let us see what life is like in the darkness. If we want to destroy ourselves—well, all right.

And yet, he cannot do it. He cannot let us go. Isn't he the one who lifted and held us when we toddled into trouble? Isn't he the one who bent to feed our hunger with child-sized bits of food? Has he not sat with us many times through the watches of the night?

How can I give you up, O Ephraim!
How can I hand you over, O Israel!...
I will not execute my fierce anger...
for I am God and not man.

"For I am God and not man." In those words lies the only hope for children who would otherwise make themselves fatherless.

A Prayer
Our Father who art in heaven, hallowed be thy name.
Thy kingdom come, thy will be done, on earth as it is in heaven.
Give us this day our daily bread; and forgive us our debts,
    as we also have forgiven our debtors;
and lead us not into temptation, but deliver us from evil.
For thine is the kingdom, and the power, and the glory, forever.
Amen.
—The Lord's Prayer

What Is God Like?

Scripture

To whom then will you liken God, or what likeness compare with him?...Have you not known? Have you not heard? The Lord is the everlasting God, the Creator of the ends of the earth. He does not faint or grow weary, his understanding is unsearchable.
Isaiah 40:18, 28

Confession

We all believe with the heart and confess with the mouth that there is one...God; and that He is eternal, incomprehensible, invisible, immutable, infinite, almighty.
Belgic Confession, Article I

7

As we were reminded in meditation 6, God is our Father. For many people that is a sobering thought. Some of our fathers are, after all, not very godly. A number of them are not even very fatherly. God is like *them*? God is like that friendly, confused man at the end of the table?

No, not very much. But we have to say something about God, and, with Calvin, we stammer as best we can. We know all of our human comparisons fall short. God is unimaginably greater than we can think. J. B. Phillips, in fact, once traced the cause of meager faith to our shriveled ideas of God. *Your God Is Too Small*, said Phillips. Your notion of God is thin and cramped.

So it is. Sometimes it is also absurd. We think of God as a smothering parent or an aging grandfather in his skychair. We imagine a meek and mild lover of our pranks and winker at our mischief. We picture him as a harassed switchboard operator, trying to handle all the incoming prayers. Or we may find God a blight, a drag on our fun and games, an old-fashioned person trying to hold us back. Our ideas of

God are pinched and little. Some are almost blasphemously so. We forget that God is incomprehensibly *great*.

The biblical writers did not forget it. They knew that the Lord is great and greatly to be praised, and that his greatness is unsearchable. They knew, in Phillips's words, that God is a being both of "terrifying vastness and of minute attention to microscopic detail." God numbers both the galaxies and the hairs of our heads. He is equally concerned with a falling star and a falling sparrow—and a fallen sinner.

To whom then will you liken God?...

Have you not known? Have you not heard?

The Lord is the everlasting God,

the Creator of the ends of the earth.

The remarkable thing is that this great God is also our Father. It is not that he is either great or else our Father. He is both. The psalmists are always talking of God's cosmic greatness one moment, and the next moment marveling at his patience with an individual's single sin and private shame. God and Father. Both.

A Prayer

There is none like thee among the gods, O Lord,
  nor are there any works like thine....
For thou art great and doest wondrous things,
  thou alone art God.
Yet thou art *my* God;
  be gracious to me, O Lord.
I give thanks to thee, O Lord my God, with my whole heart,
  and I will glorify thy name forever.
For great is thy steadfast love toward me. Amen.
—from Psalm 86

Scripture
Then Jacob awoke from his sleep and said, "Surely the Lord is in this place; and I did not know it." And he was afraid, and said, "How awesome is this place!"
Genesis 28:16,17

Confession
[God] is most holy in all his counsels, in all his works, and in all his commands.
Westminster Confession, Chapter II

8

An American preacher recalls in one of his sermons that long before the stories of Abraham, Isaac, and Jacob were written down, Israelite fathers told them to their children. A good storyteller could make those stories live. He would tell about Abraham and Sarah at Gerar—how Abraham once tried to save his own skin by passing Sarah off as his sister. Sarah never forgot. There was always a certain look in her eye after that. There would be stories of blind old Isaac with his senile cackle, of a blustery Esau, always waving his big, hairy fists around. Then there were the Jacob stories. Everybody liked those stories. What a character! What an agile, wheeler-dealer of a fellow Jacob was!

But one particular story always seemed to catch people by the heart. It is the story of Jacob at Bethel. The story has in it that strange, eerie feeling of waking from sleep and being afraid. Jacob has felt a *presence*. And he is afraid not because this presence hurts him, but because it haunts him. Jacob has an awesome sense of someone from beyond, someone utterly alive and yet wholly unhuman—someone wholly *other*. Jacob has been in the unspeakable presence of a holy God.

It is a great tragedy that in an age of instant pals and popular democracy many Christians are losing the sense of God's holiness. We pray against television background noise. We come into a sanctuary and yak and grin and clap our friends on the back. Our sense of God's holiness has become so weak that we are able to speak familiarly of "the Lord" while stretching our limbs and chewing our gum.

For Jacob there can be no morning worship until he has known the fear of the Lord. He has a hard night on his stone pillow, a night full of dreams and whisperings and old memories. It is an unholy night until Jacob begins to dream. For this shifty, tainted man, it may have been the turning point. It is not that Jacob is able to climb up and lay hold on God. Not at all. He never could. Jacob's God is far above Jacob's ladder. Yet, by this dream and by this ladder the Holy One of Israel descends to reach for one of his sons.

Then Jacob awoke from his sleep and said, "Surely the Lord is in this place; and I did not know it." And he was afraid, and said, "How awesome is this place!"

A Prayer
O Lord God, you are holy beyond our thinking and here with us beyond all knowing. Even in darkness your light shines and even in our confusion your truth is made known. Surely you are with us even when we do not know it. Through Jesus Christ our Lord, Amen.

Scripture
He is the image of the invisible God....For in him all the fulness of God was pleased to dwell.   Colossians 1:15,19
"He who has seen me has seen the Father."   John 14:9

Confession
We believe that Jesus Christ according to His divine nature is the only begotten Son of God...co-essential and co-eternal with the Father, *the very image of his substance and the effulgence of his glory.*   Belgic Confession, Article X

9

There is a story which has been told by Scottish Presbyterians for years. As Douglas Nelson tells it, somewhere back in the early eighteen hundreds a young boy in Scotland went with crowds from all the nearby villages to see a hanging. Two laboring men had quarreled with a third man, and had then followed him across a pasture and slipped a knife between his ribs. After some time the two killers were caught, tried, and condemned to be hanged. On a lovely May morning the troops paraded to the very place where the murder had been committed. There the gallows stood—black crossbeam and two empty nooses. The ashen-faced criminals were led up the steps and the grisly preparations were made. Then the infantrymen presented arms, the cavalrymen drew their swords, and the drummers lifted their sticks to start the rogues' tattoo. For just that instant there was complete silence across the field and through the crowd. And then, in that hush, a startled lark suddenly soared up from the foot of the gallows. Straight up it shot, as larks do, and the cascading joy of its singing seemed to come from nowhere but heaven. The young Scottish boy who was watching later said he could never forget that picture—the pure burst of loveliness in the May sky and, down below, two men kicking and twisting at the end of a rope.

We have seen that same mixture of glory and death before. The disciples who see in Jesus Christ the image of God also see him humiliated by clods and beaten up by thugs. They see the face of God's glory blackened, puffy, and running with other men's spit. They see God's Son weak and drained of blood and hope. They see him dead.

"He who has seen me has seen the Father," said Jesus. In their astonishment and pain, the disciples at the foot of the cross must have wondered about that. Only later, only after the first Easter, were they ready to see that God makes life by this death, strength from this weakness, "peace by the blood of his cross."

The "fulness of God" is full enough to take in such suffering and turn it to glory.

A Prayer
What wondrous love is this, O Lord our God, which comes with light into our darkness and with the Son of heaven into our hell. For the Christ in whom we see you, and know you, and come to peace with you, we give you humble thanks. Amen.

Scripture

The grace of the Lord Jesus Christ and the love of God and the fellowship of the Holy Spirit be with you all.

II Corinthians 13:14

Confession

Since there is but one God, why do you speak of three: Father, Son, and Holy Spirit?

Because that is how God has revealed himself in his Word: these three distinct persons are one, true, eternal God.

Heidelberg Catechism, Q & A 25

10

What is God like? He is fatherly, great, and holy. He is like Jesus Christ his Son. God is, finally and everlastingly, triune.

For centuries before Christ the people of God daily separated themselves from their neighbors who believed in many gods. The Jews solemnly reminded themselves that God brooks no rivals: "Hear, O Israel: The Lord our God is one Lord" (Deut. 6:4). But with Christ has come a new understanding of God's oneness. Christians have come by divine revelation to believe in the holy Trinity.

To this day, Jews believe that Christians have therefore slipped into heathen polytheism. An important Jewish novelist speaks for many Jews when he says, "The concept of Jesus as man-God is incomprehensible to the Jewish mind. That concept is pagan. . . . The Jesus whom Christians talk about—the Jesus who is worshiped—is the Jesus Jews don't understand."

Here is the root of the doctrine and the problem of the Trinity. Many Jews "do not understand" a "Jesus who is worshiped." But some Jews did. That is the way the Christian faith began. Following Jesus Christ's own words and deeds, a small circle of Jewish disciples came to see that this person was to be called Son of God, that he was divine, and that he was to be *worshiped.* It is a Jew—born under the law, circumcised on the eighth day, trained in the traditions of the Jewish fathers—who calls Jesus Christ "the image of the invisible God." It is a number of sons and daughters of Abraham who first confess Jesus as the Christ and the Son of God. Salvation is from the Jews. Our Lord was himself Jewish.

So some Jews *did* understand the God-man. From them we have come to know that there is one God—*and* one Lord Jesus Christ. He too is to be worshiped and adored. And this Christ himself speaks of sending the Spirit of Truth—yet another divine person. Thus for centuries Christians have worshiped, educated, lived, and hoped in the name of God the Father, Son, and Holy Spirit.

What is God like? God is a holy and everlasting Trinity of three persons. We remind ourselves of it every Sunday when the benediction is said.

A Recitation
The grace of the Lord Jesus Christ and the love of God and the fellowship of the Holy Spirit be with you all.
—II Corinthians 13:14

Postscript

1. The Bible frequently speaks of God as our Father. The God *of* our fathers, Abraham, Isaac, and Jacob, turns out to be God our Father. To his disciples Jesus spoke of "my Father" and "your Father." One day he taught them to pray "our Father."

   What are some implications of the idea that God is our Father? For example, does this image imply that God is male? Would God have been a father if he had not created us? What are some characteristics of fatherhood which God perfectly exemplifies?

2. Consider the "too small" ideas of God in the third paragraph of meditation 7:

   > smothering or tyrannical parent
   > aging grandfather
   > meek and mild (especially in regard to Jesus)
   > indulgent lover and winker
   > God-in-a-box (God is Lutheran, or Reformed, or . . .)
   > God as a Deist (removed, aloof, uninvolved)
   > God as a harassed switchboard operator
   > God as the "pale Galilean" (a blight on fun)

   Where do such ideas come from? What are the biblical correctives for them?

3. In Genesis 28:17 we find one part of the Bible's picture of God's *holiness*. The other part may be found in such a passage as Isaiah 6:1-5. In the Genesis passage, God is the transcendent Creator who arouses powerful feelings of our smallness and creatureliness. What additional dimension of God's holiness is found in the Isaiah passage?

4. Optional: Are we losing the sense of God's holiness in our worship and in our lives?

5. Meditation 9 raises the question whether we can truly see God in the life and work of one who suffers as Jesus does. For both Jews and Greeks, the fact that Christ was *crucified* was conclusive proof that he was not divine. In a number of ways Paul wrestles with the fact that the cross is "a stumbling block to Jews and folly to Gentiles."

   But Paul is also concerned to apply the paradox of God's weakness being "stronger than men" (I Cor. 1:25) to the lives of believers. Look at II Corinthians 12:1-10. There is the same paradox again. *Can* we find the strength of God in weakness? How?

6. Why does the doctrine of the Trinity matter at all? Why is it more than merely a theologian's puzzle?

Week Three

If the Lord Is With Us, Why Do We Suffer?

A Christian philosopher once addressed an overflow crowd at an Ivy League university. He spoke about whether it makes sense to believe in God. After the speech, a young Jewish student stood up and demanded to know how anyone could believe in God after Auschwitz. "How can a good and powerful God allow such horrors? There *is* no God!"

We believe there is. We have come with all our heart to know God and what he is like. But, as honestly as possible, we have to face the first question asked by those who have suffered or been impressed by suffering: why does God allow suffering? To tell the truth, there are times when it is the first question believers *themselves* ask: If the Lord is with us, why then has all this befallen us?

Scripture
And the angel of the Lord appeared to him and said to him, "The Lord is with you, you mighty man of valor." And Gideon said to him, "Pray, sir, if the Lord is with us, why then has all this befallen us?"
Judges 6:12,13

Confession
We can be patient when things go against us, thankful when things go well, and for the future we can have good confidence in our faithful God and Father that nothing will separate us from his love.   Heidelberg Catechism, Answer 28

11

An expert on death and dying reports an incident many of us will understand. A woman came out of a sickroom where a loved one was dying and asked in a tightly controlled voice, "Is there a room anywhere in the hospital where I can go to scream?" A doctor directed her to a place and later mused over the idea that every hospital—maybe every office and home—ought to have a screaming room.

The human voice which calls to God out of suffering often rises to a scream. C. S. Lewis lost his wife to cancer. Just after she died, he wrote down some of the torture of his thoughts:

Not that I am...in much danger of ceasing to believe in God. The real danger is of coming to believe such dreadful things about Him. The conclusion I dread is not "So there's no God after all," but "So this is what God is really like. Deceive yourself no longer."   (*A Grief Observed*)

Lewis mentions the time he and his wife had prayed for a cure, for the miraculous grace of recovery. There were false diagnoses, false hopes, strange remissions, and even one astonishing recovery. But it was only temporary, and the God who held Joy Davidman Lewis in his hands did fearful things with those hands:

Step by step we were led up the garden path. Time after time, when He seemed most gracious, He was preparing the next torture.... I wrote that last night. It was a yell rather than a thought.

A yell rather than a thought. You do not think clearly when you are racked, humiliated, betrayed, or bereaved. You scream.

And it is not unbelief which shouts its hurt or bewilderment at God, but belief. Unbelievers shout their fury at the blind, dumb workings of fate. But believers have to speak somehow with a "faithful God and Father" who seems at times so absent, so willing to tolerate horror, so far from helping. Generation after generation, believers turn toward heaven to shout their one great question: "*Why?*"

"Why dost thou stand afar off, O Lord?"

"If the Lord is with us, why then has all this befallen us?"

"My God, my God, why hast thou forsaken me?"

A Prayer
O my God, I cry by day, but thou dost not answer; and by night, but find no rest. Be not far from me, for trouble is near and there is none to help. Amen.   —from Psalm 22

If the Lord Is With Us, Why Do We Suffer?

Scripture
For my thoughts are not your thoughts, neither are your ways my ways, says the Lord. For as the heavens are higher than the earth, so are my ways higher than your ways and my thoughts than your thoughts.

Isaiah 55:8, 9

Confession
And as to what He does surpassing human understanding, we will not curiously inquire into farther than our capacity will admit of; but with the greatest humility and reverence adore the righteous judgments of God, which are hid from us, contenting ourselves that we are pupils of Christ.

Belgic Confession, Article XIII

12

Our suffering questions are *why* questions. Why did God permit the fall if he knew what evil would come from it? Why does he allow this, or this much, pain? Why here and now? Why does he permit *children* to suffer? And why do the righteous suffer? Why does Beethoven lose his hearing while punk rock freaks manage to keep theirs? Why does this pious, gentle soul have disease while that selfish, careless clod has health?

Some believers, like Job's friends, think they have answers to such questions. God is testing you, they say. God is punishing you for cheating. God is fattening that unbeliever for slaughter. God foresaw that if your child had lived longer, she would have been a covenant breaker.

The truth is we seldom know any of these things. We may know a little. We may know why a person has a hangover. We may know how a person gets venereal disease. We may know why a liar cannot get anybody to trust him. But even here there are surprises. Some liars become presidents. Some rakes stay healthy. Some drunks rise and shine.

The most truthful answer to our *why* questions about suffering is that we do not know. We commit ourselves to a God who loves and cares, and by his grace the commitment stays fastened though the mountains shake and the earth be moved. We know that in all things God works for *good*.

But let us face two facts. One is that we often do not know what good that is. We cannot see it or tell it. God has his reasons for allowing *this* crushing humiliation or *that* demonic target-practice, but we do not know what his reasons are. It often seems that we are given a little courage rather than much knowledge.

But let us also face another fact. On the day when he died, our Lord shouted, "My God, my God, why hast thou forsaken me?" Two days later he appeared to his disciples and said, "Peace be with you."

A Prayer
O Lord our God, we see in a mirror darkly. But we see there the face of your Son who suffered with us and for us. Though faith fails and hearts sink, we know that he has led the way through suffering and death to a peace which passes understanding and a victory which can never be undone. Through Jesus Christ our Lord, Amen.

If the Lord Is With Us, Why Do We Suffer?

Scripture
We are children of God, and if
children, then heirs, heirs of God
and fellow heirs with Christ, provided we suffer with him in order
that we may also be glorified
with him.   Romans 8:16,17

Confession
By ourselves we are too weak to
hold our own even for a moment.
And our sworn enemies—the
devil, the world, and our own
flesh—never stop attacking us.
And so, Lord, uphold us and
make us strong with the strength
of your Holy Spirit, so that we
may not go down to defeat in
this spiritual struggle.
                    Heidelberg Catechism,
                    Answer 127

13

People often suffer because of their own sin
and folly. Perhaps more often they suffer from
the sin or folly of others. "Others" include not
only human others, but also the evil one and
his hosts.

Christians are repeatedly told in the New
Testament to expect suffering at the hands of
others because of the gospel, or for the sake of
Christ. The world is terribly fallen and bent.
Anyone who tries to live in a straight and
upright way will sooner or later be opposed. If
we do right, we may suffer for it. Thus we must
not talk too easily of "Christ, our example." At
least we must not forget the context of I Peter
2:21:

> For to this you have been called, because
> Christ also *suffered* for you, leaving you an
> example, that you should follow in his steps.

A few Christians have followed in his steps
with the sort of strength which leaves the rest
of us in the dust. A pastor tells of Father
Damien, the saintly missionary to the leper colony on the island of Molokai. Damien was
much loved by the festering people who had

been sent there to get on with their dying. But
one Sunday a whole new world reached out
and took them in. It happened when, for the
first time, Father Damien opened his sermon
with the words, "We lepers." For now, under
his robes, was a body dying with their disease.
And now, in his words, these people heard the
voice of Christ.

How badly our lives suffer by comparison! We
want not suffering, but success. We identify not
with those who are low and hurt, but with
those who are snug and proud. We do not like
lepers or losers very well. We prefer climbers
and comers. For Christians, the temptation to
be conformed to this world is desperately sweet
and strong.

Yet, says Paul, we are children of God *provided* we suffer with Christ. No doubt few of us
can follow where Father Damien walked. God
does not give his hardest assignments to his
weakest children. But a life with no suffering,
no embarrassment, no inconvenience for the
sake of Christ is not a Christian life.

What, then, must we do?

A Prayer
Lord God, we have sought our comfort in things which perish
and our security in that which cannot hold. Correct, chasten,
and heal us for the sake of Jesus Christ our Lord. Amen.

Scripture
Suffering produces endurance, and endurance produces character, and character produces hope, and hope does not disappoint us, because God's love has been poured into our hearts through the Holy Spirit which has been given to us.
Romans 5:3-5

Confession
Through Christ's death our old selves are crucified, put to death, and buried with him, so that the evil desires of the flesh may no longer rule us.
Heidelberg Catechism,
Answer 43

14

The most general biblical answer to the question of suffering is that we do not know why God permits it, nor why he permits it in a given case. Yet we do know that Christians must suffer for the sake of the gospel. Father Damien knew it too. The Bible also says that we may suffer from the terrible love of God. Like Jacob, all of us have to wrestle with God. And, like Jacob, we may come out limping. In the severe mercy of God we are scrubbed, changed, trained, wrestled into shape. We may not enjoy it. But there is no doubt that we are in for it, one way or another.

Kathryn Lindskoog writes about this in describing her nephew John:

My little nephew John was born with a defective heart. This summer he was six, and went to Mercy Hospital for surgery.

"You'll feel stronger and grow bigger after your operation," they told him. In four hours they successfully patched a hole the size of a quarter and put him into intensive care.

A few days later in his oxygen tent with tubes here and there, the incision still healing, and a nagging thirst that could not be quenched because of fluid regulation, John looked at his mother ruefully with large brown eyes and said simply, "Mommy, I felt better *before* the operation!"

I think John said it for us all. We were all born with defective hearts....

(*Eternity*, August 1976)

So we were. Conversion is a change of heart. And in some ways we feel better before the operation. The cure is often slow and nearly always painful. Pride must be whittled down. Offenses must be repented of to people we do not like. Certain luxuries and flings have to be abandoned. Self-pity must be fought off. Work must be done the right way even if there is less praise for it that way.

None of us likes this sort of thing. Yet without it we are lost. The confessions call such a process *mortification*. It means "dying off." It is no fun. We are going to be put right if it kills us. God has a model from which he works as he keeps on rubbing, cutting, twisting, and molding his children. He has in mind a certain image of how we ought to look. And, as C. S. Lewis says, God pays us the "intolerable compliment" of working us till we fit the image.

We know who his model is. We know who is the image of the invisible God. And we know that, strangely, even this Lord Jesus Christ *learned* obedience through suffering. Even he had to die before he could rise again.

We are only pupils of Christ. But it is the same Christlike pattern which we have to trace. There is going to be pain in it before there is glory.

A Prayer
Rule us, O Lord, by your Word and Spirit in such a way that more and more we submit to you. Help us and all others to reject our own wills and to obey your will without any back talk. Your will alone is good. Through Jesus Christ, Amen.
—from Heidelberg Catechism, Answers 123, 124

Scripture

We know that in everything God works for good with those who love him, who are called according to his purpose.

Romans 8:28

Confession

I trust him so much that I do not doubt he will provide whatever I need for body and soul, and he will turn to my good whatever adversity he sends me in this sad world. He is able to do this because he is almighty God; he desires to do this because he is a faithful Father.

Heidelberg Catechism,
Answer 26

15

Believers seek not to explain, but to live with, the presence of evil. Even in *this* God works for good. It is a matter of trust. Just as children trust their parents' judgment that this dental repair, this doctoring, or this discipline will in the long run do them good, so children of God view the strange ministrations of a Father's love.

There are times when we think we can see what God is doing. Usually it is in retrospect. In that defeat he was breaking our grip on things which perish. By that pain he was making us humbler and abler to weep with those who weep. In these scary circumstances he may right now be outfitting us with courage. No doubt he sometimes lets us suffer vicariously, as Christ did, not so much for our own good as for the good of others. Could it be that saints are sometimes called upon to bear a fearful disease with grace so as to encourage those of us who are weak? A saint is "a person who makes it easier to believe in God." Perhaps a few words of quiet faith from the lips of a wasted and dying person can do more good than all the easy clichés of some thoughtless comforter.

But let us be honest. God's good is often hard for us to understand. Good is in many cases hard to *measure*. As Ernest Campbell remarks, nobody comes on TV at suppertime to report on the day's gains and losses in good. Nobody says, "Kindness was up two points today. Courage was off a half. Faith stayed the same." Nobody does that. We have to discern good, where we can, with the eyes of faith. There are times when we strain our eyes to see it.

But it is there! It must be. In strange places and where nobody expects it, in sickness and handicap, in the gray reaches of ordinary life, and in the sharp agonies in which God shouts at us—it is there.

Douglas Nelson tells of visiting a terrible little cell in the dungeon of an old English castle. No light had ever come there from outside. On one wall the stone had been worn into the shape of a hand, for men dying of thirst leaned there while they licked the filthy moisture which leaked from the moat through one small crack. In that blackness someone had scratched—with a belt buckle, perhaps—the old words of Jacob: "The Lord was in this place and I knew it not."

Even here. Even in this. The Lord is with us—for good.

A Recitation

I am sure that neither death, nor life, nor angels, nor principalities, nor things present, nor things to come, nor powers, nor height, nor depth, nor anything else in all creation, will be able to separate us from the love of God in Christ Jesus our Lord.

—Romans 8:38, 39

Postscript

1. Believers almost unconsciously assume that if the Lorde is with us, no evil will befall us. Tyndale's translation of Genesis 39:2 puts this assumption quaintly: "And the Lorde was with Joseph, and he was a luckie felowe."

   What do you make of such an assumption? What is its basis? Is it a valid assumption?

2. Some people say we ought to thank and praise God for suffering. They say the only way we can triumph in painful circumstances is by saying, "Praise You, O Lord, for my daughter's divorce. Thank you for my lung cancer!"

   What do you think about this?

3. What do you think of the attempts people sometimes make to explain another person's suffering? May we dare to say to a sufferer: "God saw that your marriage had gotten as far as it could without going over the hill and slipping down. That is why he took your wife"? (See meditation 12.)

4. Meditations 13 and 14 suggest that genuine Christians may *expect* to suffer—either because the world opposes them, or because God is tempering them into sharp tools, or because of some combination of these things.

   But the fact is there are plenty of Christians who do not seem to suffer very much. Should we be worried if things go well for us? Does that mean God thinks we are too weak to be trusted with a dangerous mission? Does it mean, as in Hebrews 12, that we are being neglected as bastards instead of being disciplined as children? Explain.

5. Does God send us things like murder, multiple sclerosis, and tornadoes? When a young man dies in an accident, we say, "The Lord took him." Did he? What is God's role in these things?

Week Four

How Does God Act?

A number of ancient and modern philosophers believe God is unemployed. He does
not do anything. In reality he is not an
actor, but only a *factor.* He is distant,
removed, turned in on himself, shut out of
our world by the inexorable laws of
nature.

The Bible makes straight such crooked lines
of thought. From beginning to end the
Bible speaks of a God who *acts,* and who
acts in history, and who acts in *our*
history. So we naturally want to know,
How does God act?

Scripture

Not one [sparrow] will fall to the ground without your Father's will...even the hairs of your head are all numbered. Fear not, therefore. Matthew 10:29-31

Confession

Providence is the almighty and ever present power of God by which he upholds, as with his hand, heaven and earth and all creatures.

Heidelberg Catechism,
Answer 27

16

Children are sometimes afraid. Adults are too. But children are often afraid of different things than adults are. Children are afraid of large, friendly dogs who can knock a small person over with a single, hairy paw. Children fear thunder and blood and such wierd storybook creatures as "ghosties and goblins and things that go 'bump' in the night." Most children are afraid of the dark, of dark closets, and of those dark places "where the wild things are." When a child is lost, she is not merely annoyed or confused. She may be terrified. When a child lives among broken and irresponsible people, he may be desperately afraid he will be abandoned.

Jesus speaks to all God's children about a Father's providence. And he speaks to our fear. He speaks to our early, childlike awareness that in so many ways the world is a fearful place. In such a place the Father knows, loves, and cares for his children.

A theologian who wished to speak of the acts of God might begin with creation. But a child begins with providence. In homes where there is knowledge of God, a child first learns that God keeps and provides. A child comes to know with a wonderful, childlike certainty that even when he is hurt, or lost, or afraid, he is not alone. So in many homes a child lays himself down to sleep, entrusting his very soul to the God who keeps him in the dark and through the night.

God acts in his providence. Even a child knows that. But soon a child knows something else. Soon he knows that people sometimes interfere with God's providence in wicked ways. Take food, for example. God gives daily bread for his creatures. Every harvesttime God gives food—and skillful farmers to gather and market that food. But, strangely enough, the food seldom reaches those who are hungriest for it. Some people keep huge stores of food for themselves, often throwing much of it away. Other people have to get along with very little.

God acts and God provides. But he uses *us* to do it. We must never fear that God will forget to provide. What we must fear is that some of us might get in the way.

A Prayer
God our Father:
Do take care of all our physical needs so that we come to know that you are the only source of everything good, and that neither our work and worry nor your gifts can do us any good without your blessing. And help us to work faithfully so that we may share with those in need. Through Jesus Christ our Lord, Amen. —from Heidelberg Catechism, Answers 125, 111

Scripture

In the beginning God created the heavens and the earth.

Genesis 1:1

Thou didst form my inward parts, thou didst knit me together in my mother's womb. **Psalm 139:13**

Confession

The eternal Father of our Lord Jesus Christ...out of nothing created heaven and earth and everything in them.

Heidelberg Catechism, Answer 26

17

Children ask "Why?" nearly as often as philosophy students do. A curious four year old can drive you to a confession of the doctrine of creation with about four "Whys":

Why is our car green?

That's the color they painted it at the factory. Why?

Some people ordered green cars. Why?

Green is their favorite color. But why?

That's the way God made those people. Oh.

It is good to be able to say, "That's the way God made those people" instead of, "I don't know." God has acted in his creation, and many of our "Why?" questions about the curious and interesting features of our world find their answers somewhere in God's creative plan.

But why did God choose to create at all? Why didn't Father, Son, and Holy Spirit enjoy their trinitarian fellowship without taking on the task of creating and the burden of caring for an *outside* world? And why, in that world, did God find room for the likes of you and me?

Creation is a fruit of God's love. Father, Son, and Holy Spirit lacked nothing, and yet freely chose to make powers and persons outside themselves. This is a mark of unselfish, outgoing, overflowing love. This is the remarkable love which does not merely recognize, but actually *creates* persons with their own freedoms, hopes, fears, and joys. God creates because he is a loving, fellowshipping God.

There are times when the greatness of God's creation comes home to us. On Christmas Eve, 1968, Apollo 8 was returning from history's first flight around the moon. The pictures and accounts of earth as seen from the very heavens powerfully impressed many who saw and heard them. At the close of the second telecast, Commander Frank Borman announced that he and the other astronauts had a message for us. With the stupendous view of the revolving earth before him, Borman began to read the first verses of Genesis: "In the beginning, God created the heavens and the earth." The other astronauts took up the reading, and Borman finally finished where God finished his creation: "And God saw everything that he had made, and behold, it was very good."

God still creates. In some wonderful way, he has seen fit to create you and me. It means that from the beginning we are not our own.

A Confession

In the beginning God created the heavens and the earth, and the Word was with God, and the Word was God. All things were made through him, and without him was not anything made that was made. The earth was without form and void, and darkness was upon the face of the deep; and the Spirit of God was moving over the face of the waters.

—from Genesis 1 and John 1

Scripture
Now Jesus did many other signs in the presence of the disciples, which are not written in this book; but these are written that you may believe that Jesus is the Christ, the Son of God, and that believing you may have life in his name.　John 20:30, 31

Confession
All men wondered to see the water turned into wine. But every day the earth's moisture, being drawn into the root of a vine, is turned by the grape into wine, and no man wonders. Full of wonder then are all the things which men never think to wonder at.　St. Gregory the Great, *Morals on the Book of Job*

18

God's acts in creation and providence are regular and orderly. We can find natural patterns in them. We describe these acts with what we call the "laws of nature." We depend on this rhythm and orderliness of God's acting. It lets us make plans. It lets us do science. It lets us stay sane. We note that the planets stay in their orbits. Cannonballs, and even feathers, fall *down* when we drop them. If you go out to the airport and run down a vacant runway, flapping your arms, you will not take off. You don't have nearly enough wingspan. And you cannot count on God's making an exception, just this once, because you are late for your meeting.

But sometimes God, or God's agent, does do something unusual. Sometimes an act is performed which cannot be explained according to the laws of nature. When God does an extraordinary act, we call it a miracle.

Miracles are closely connected with God's other acts. The Bible seldom makes sharp distinctions between God's providence and God's "special" providence. In fact, as Gregory the Great, C. S. Lewis, and others have pointed out, many of Jesus' miracles are small,

fast examples of the big, slow acts which God performs all the time. Every harvest God feeds the multitudes with many loaves multiplied from a few grains. Every summer, along the sunny hills, God turns water into wine. Jesus does the same thing fast and on a small scale. He just does what he sees the Father doing. There is, as Lewis put it, a kind of "family style."

But God's family never does miracles just for the fun of it. Miracles are not mere magic. God's Son does not care simply to dazzle people who gape and gawk. No, miracles are "signs." Miracles attest the power of God and the presence of his Son. Miracles tell us in miniature and in brief what is always true on a grander scale. Miracles tell us that God is at work. Miracles get desperately needed *work* done in a fallen world.

Miracles are serious things. They are done, one way or another, for our redemption. Think of the exodus. Think of the resurrection. Think of the fact that Jesus did many other signs *so that* we may believe and "have life in his name."

A Prayer
O Lord our God, we know you are not only good, but also great. We know you are able to do strange and wonderful things. Let us not be so skeptical that we fail to see them. But neither let us be so greedy for signs that we fail to see the slow, steady wonders of creation and providence all around us. In Jesus' name, Amen.

Scripture
But when he came to himself he said..."I will arise and go to my father, and I will say to him, 'Father, I have sinned....'"
Luke 15:17,18

Confession
[Regeneration] is evidently a supernatural work, most powerful, and at the same time most delightful, astonishing, mysterious, and ineffable....
Canons of Dort III-IV, Article 12

19

A recent writer recalls the story G. K. Chesterton tells about a boy who left his home on an English mountainside. The boy was searching for a remarkable thing he had heard about since babyhood. It seems that somewhere, outlined on distant hills, was the huge shape of a giant man. It was a kind of miracle, people said, how the giant had taken shape in the rock of the hills. The boy decided he must see that shape. He must discover that giant if it took all his life. Across the valley he trudged, hoping to see the miracle on the next row of hills. It was not there. But, as he turned to get his bearings, he looked back. And there, where he had come from, the white limestone rocks formed the outline of a giant. In the heart of this giant shape was the house he had left. He had been too close to see it.

The greatest act of God's providence happens close to home. It happens so close to home we may not see it. God's great miracle is to breathe new life into our own collapsed lives. Theologians call it regeneration. Jesus calls it being born again.

Adam left the garden. The prodigal son left home. We have all tried somehow to break out of the Father's embrace and the Father's house to seek our happiness in a far country. We have been told of wonders and pleasures there.

But it is not true. Life in the far country is futile and unhappy. Its days are empty and its nights are cold. It is only in turning and looking back that we discover what we have been seeking. We have left the only place where greatness dwells and the only home where sons and daughters are really loved. But it takes pains—something like birth pains—to get out of the far country and back home to the real world.

Unless one is born anew, said Jesus, he cannot even *see* the kingdom of God. No doubt the prodigal son began to see it for the first time when he said, "I will arise and go to my father, and I will say to him, 'Father, I have sinned.'"

A Prayer
What wondrous love is this, Lord God, which seeks us when we are runaways from home and draws us back to live and feast with all your other children! Rescue us from every impulse to seek our fortune in empty places and among hopeless people. Spark us to new life by your Spirit and equip us to serve you with energy and devotion. Through Jesus Christ our Lord, Amen.

Scripture
But according to his promise we wait for new heavens and a new earth in which righteousness dwells.   II Peter 3:13

Confession
Finally, we believe, according to the Word of God, when the time appointed by the Lord...is come and the number of the elect complete, that our Lord Jesus Christ will come from heaven...to declare Himself Judge of the living and the dead....
Belgic Confession,
Article XXXVII

20

In December 1978 *Redbook* magazine carried a story of a woman by the name of Janet Zorick. Mrs. Zorick lost her husband in a terrible fire in a crowded building. She too had been in the fire, but her husband had lifted her over his head and thrown her forward toward the exit. Though badly burned, she escaped. Her husband did not.

For months afterward she could not sleep well. She remembered in ghastly detail the sight of people on fire, of husbands who "just kept going when their wives were knocked down," of her own husband's look of horror as he picked her up. She remembers him gasping, "One of us has to get out for the kids." She recalls how she felt when his blackened watch was returned to her, and what a numbing indignity it seemed to her that he was found with only one shoe on.

Later, Mrs. Zorick tried to sort through some of the agony of her thoughts. Though she and her husband were both strong, church-going Lutherans, she had, for a time, great difficulty believing in God. How could he have allowed such a tragedy?

Finally, though scarred and shaken, her faith came back. Again and again she concluded that she *had* to believe in God—and in the life to come. God had reached for her husband in a horrifying way, but it must have been God into whose presence her husband was received. Else, she concluded, nothing means anything. "There has to be a hereafter or what's the use of anything?"

At the borders and crises of life Christians have always looked for anchorage to the great biblical truth that our little careers are not the whole story. As a huge, sweeping conclusion to his great work of creation, providence, and redemption, God finally brings all history to a climax and ushers in a new heaven and a new earth. This is the last and most splendid of his acts. Part of its glory is that all God's children shall be gathered to his city for communal feasting and rejoicing. Of this community we are, *and always shall be*, living members.

We must not let this vision hinder or stop us from doing our work. But it is not wrong to let the hope of God's consummation come to mind now and then. In fact, there are times, as for Janet Zorick, when it seems our only hope.

A Recitation
I believe in the Holy Spirit; ...the communion of saints; the forgiveness of sins; the resurrection of the body; and the life everlasting, Amen.   —from the Apostles' Creed

Postscript

1. People often describe narrowly missed accidents or unusual escapes from embarrassment or trouble as "providential." Are they? How do we know? And what good is it to believe in providence?

2. How likely is it, in your estimation, that God has created not only our world and its people, but also other worlds of intelligent creatures? Suppose there were worlds of other creatures. What sorts of adjustments in our own thinking about God's relationship to us would follow from the knowledge of such worlds?

   By the way, is it wrong or useless to speculate about these things? Why or why not?

3. If God could not create everything just the way he wanted it, why do we say he is almighty? If he *did* create everything the way he wanted it, why is it necessary for him now to doctor, or tinker with, his creation by means of miracles?

   Aren't the biblical miracle stories simply the mythological trappings of the *real* Christian message—that we ought to love one another? Explain.

4. Critics who report on somebody's "getting religion" sometimes talk deprecatingly about the need for security, or the crawling back into the womb, or the deep desire to believe in a loving father figure. Regeneration, they say, can easily and best be explained psychologically. For that reason we have no need to postulate "Holy Spirits" or anything of the sort.

   What would you be inclined to reply to such a person?

Week Five

Why Pray?

A Christian graduate student invited his professor home for dinner. As was his family's custom, the student offered a prayer before the meal. Afterwards, the professor said, "You might as well have whistled."

Was the professor right? Is prayer a kind of whistling in the dark which nobody hears but we ourselves? Christians wish to speak with him who has acted in their lives. Can we? Does it do any good? Why pray?

Scripture

Rejoice always, pray constantly, give thanks in all circumstances; for this is the will of God in Christ Jesus for you.

I Thessalonians 5:16-18

Confession

Why do Christians need to pray?

Because prayer is the most important part of the thankfulness God requires of us.

Heidelberg Catechism, Q & A 116

21

In one of his books, John Baillie tells of a time he attended a religious service conducted by a humanist. The service included a sort of prayer of thanksgiving, "except that each phrase, where we should ordinarily say 'We thank Thee, O God,' was introduced rather by the words 'We are thankful.' "

It must be an odd feeling to be thankful to nobody in particular. Christians in public institutions often see this odd thing happening at Thanksgiving. Everyone in the institution seems to be thankful "in general." It is very strange. It is a little like being married in general.

Christians are thankful to God. Prayer is the most important way of saying so. For centuries, godly people have observed and been helped by the great acts of God in history. God has created, redeemed, and provided both food and deliverance for his people. The apt response has always been thanksgiving. So the psalmists, in the rich context of the covenant community, take note of God's deeds and then urge thanks. *First* one gives thanks; *then* one brings requests (Ps. 50:14,15).

For what do we thank God? For all his gifts. For specific things we deliberately name. For his saving acts, his mighty rescue of self-destructive people. For water which cools, cleans, and quenches; for these friends; for that old memory; for this splendid sunshine after rain. Kids thank God too: for sports, for family, for wonderful things to toy with. The whole Christian community gathers each week to thank God for recovery from sin, for kindness which has broken through our shame, for forgiveness which restores to us the joy of our salvation.

In all circumstances, says St. Paul, give thanks. Not *for* all circumstances; *in* all circumstances! So we give thanks for health and in sickness; for happiness and in depression; for family and friends and in those times when it has pleased God to take to himself someone we love.

Why pray? Because prayer is the most important part of the thankfulness God requires of us. Why give thanks? It is the will of God in Christ Jesus.

A Prayer of Thanks

God of Life, who hast loved us into life, Thy shepherding care guides and sustains us. Thou hast nourished us with bread of fields, bread of friendship, bread of Providence, and the living Bread of Christ. How can we thank Thee as we ought? We would be thankful in prayer and deed and inmost spirit; through Jesus Christ our Lord. Amen.

—from The Book of Common Prayer (Episcopal)

Scripture
I know, O Lord, that the way of man is not in himself, that it is not in man who walks to direct his steps. Correct me, O Lord, but in just measure; not in thy anger, lest thou bring me to nothing.   Jeremiah 10:23, 24

Confession
What is your only comfort in life and in death?
That I am not my own, but belong—body and soul, in life and in death—to my faithful Savior Jesus Christ.
Heidelberg Catechism, Q & A 1

22

At the heart of human corruption is a deep tendency to be deceived and especially to be self-deceived. This tendency is as old as the Garden of Eden. It is still with us. We see it showing through in many of the things we say and suppose. We say we have no sin. We tell ourselves we have always tried to live a good life. We say we will have time *later* to spend with our children. We insist that this is our last cigarette. We suppose that self-help schemes may bring us first aid. Like some tragic Samson we rise up to do battle, counting as usual on our own strength—unaware that the Lord has left us.

None of it is any good. "We deceive ourselves and the truth is not in us." After bringing thanks to God, the Christian generations have always had to sink to their knees for frank and painful *confession*.

We confess our sin. We have ignored God for weeks at a time. We have tied our feelings of self-worth to success on the job rather than to the grace of God. We have spent more money in one week for fun and games than we spend in a whole year for feeding the poor. We have loved handsome people and given them gifts. Meanwhile, we have sent the lonesome ones away empty. We cannot be bothered, inconvenienced, distracted from business as usual. Truly there is no health in us.

There is more. We confess our dependence. Jesus taught us to pray "Our Father." He reminds us that we are children. We did not make ourselves, will not help ourselves, cannot forgive ourselves. We have no adequacy of our own. For all those gifts we imagined to be self-given we are dependent on the goodness of our Father.

There is still more. Especially as we age, we confess our failure. Life has not turned out as we had hoped. In so many ways we have not measured up even to the modest expectations of others—let alone to our own youthful dreams. Other people have gone further than we have and we know it. Our marriages, careers, hopes, and plans have so often very quietly and earnestly died.

In confession we look for mercy, assurance, and the profound consolation of knowing how far God was willing to go to have and keep us.

A Prayer of Confession
We know, O Lord, "that the way of man is not in himself, that it is not in man who walks to direct his steps." Correct us, O Lord, but in just measure; not in thy anger, lest thou bring us to nothing. Amen.

Scripture
Men shall proclaim the might of thy terrible acts, and I will declare thy greatness. They shall pour forth the fame of thy abundant goodness, and shall sing aloud of thy righteousness
Psalm 145:6,7

Confession
Christ by his Spirit is also renewing us to be like himself, so that in all our living we may show that we are thankful to God for all he has done for us, and so that he may be praised through us.
Heidelberg Catechism, Answer 86

23

Some people are never satisfied. They think others drive too slow and eat too fast. They're convinced government is no good, the schools are no good, and the church is full of hypocrites. Something is wrong with every sermon these people hear, every program they see, every dish of food they are willing to try. Such people seem to spend the whole of their sour little lives in front of a complaint window. They are like the pessimistic farmer who had six chickens hatch one morning. He was inconsolable. When someone asked him what was wrong, he replied bitterly: "I had six chickens hatch this morning, and now all of 'em have died on me but five."

Open, grateful human life resounds not with complaints but with praise. The healthiest people are the ones who praise the most. Family, friends, books, sports, music, nature—all these things draw *praise* from healthy people: "Did you see *that*? Wasn't it great!" "Did you hear what she did for her sister? Isn't she a generous person!"

But Christians reserve their highest praise for the goodness and greatness of God. The Psalms ring with it: "The Lord is great and greatly to be praised! Praise the Lord!" At creation, says the book of Job, "the morning stars sang together, and all the sons of God shouted for joy."

Praise is a way of expressing awe and admiration for the stunning greatness of God and his deeds, and for the ingenious ways in which God keeps fitting his help to our need. Our prayers ought to include some hearty praise. But whether in prayer or other speech, the praise of God may never be glib. Some people say "Praise the Lord" with all the care and reverence they lavish on "Pass the milk!"

Not that. Our praise must be both candid and thoughtful. Praise of God is the very music of heaven.

A Prayer of Praise
God of Grace and God of Glory, great Thou art and greatly to be praised. Kind art Thou and deeply to be loved. We adore Thee, before whom angels hide their faces. Thou art Life and Light. Thou art Journey and Home. We bow before Thee asking nothing, save that our life may be Thy flame. Glory be to Thee, O Lord most high! Through Jesus Christ our Lord, Amen.
—from The Book of Common Prayer (Episcopal)

Scripture
And Jesus said, "Father, forgive them; for they know not what they do." Luke 23:34
And [Stephen] knelt down and cried with a loud voice, "Lord, do not hold this sin against them." Acts 7:60

Confession
Because of Christ's blood, do not hold against us, poor sinners that we are, any of the sins we do or the evil that constantly clings to us.
Heidelberg Catechism, Answer 126

24

Someone has thought of a way to teach children to pray for others. You look at your hand. The thumb is closest to you; it reminds you to pray for those who are nearest—for family, loved ones, and neighbors. Your index finger is used to point; it expresses authority. It reminds you to pray for teachers, police, and parents. The middle finger is the highest finger. It reminds you to pray for presidents, prime ministers, and "all who are in *high* authority." (In some cultures the middle finger has to remind Christians to pray for enemies.) The ring finger is the weakest, as all pianists know. It reminds you to pray for those who are poor, oppressed, afraid, and sick. Finally, there is the little finger. It reminds you to pray for yourself, that God may have his way with you. You come last.

Four out of five prayers make requests for others. We call such prayers *intercessions*. In intercession we play the part of priests, going into God's presence for the sake of another. Intercessions are especially fragrant and loving prayers.

The bright pattern of intercession runs through the Bible. Moses pleads for the children of Israel; Paul for his young churches; our Lord, and Stephen after him, for enemies. Here, as someone has said, is prayer in a major key. Here is prayer that is twice blessed. When God hears and answers such prayer, he blesses those for whom we pray. But simply by praying such prayers, we too are blessed. For it is almost impossible to remain self-absorbed, angry, or proud when you are humbly praying to almighty God for the good of others. Intercession crushes our selfishness.

But does God in any way rest our neighbors' good on *our* prayers? Why not? After all, God often rests our neighbors' good on our thoughtfulness and work. Perhaps it is also so with our prayers.

It is an awesome thought.

A Prayer of Intercession
God of the Common Good, who hast bound us in one bundle of life, we plead our neighbor's need. For the nations we pray: give peace in our time. For the workers of the world we pray: gird them and us that none may lack bread, since Thou hast given enough for all. For the sorrowing and the sick we pray: make their shadow the secret way of Thy coming. For our friends and loved ones: befriend them in Thine own befriending. Remember in Thy mercy those whom we forget. Gather all needy folk within the healing of Thy wings. Teach us to bear one another's burdens, that we may fulfill the law of Christ; for His sake. Amen.   —from The Book of Common Prayer (Episcopal)

Scripture
"Ask, and it will be given you;
seek, and you will find; knock,
and it will be opened to you."
Matthew 7:7

Confession
God gives his grace and Holy
Spirit only to those who pray
continually and groan inwardly,
asking God for these gifts.
Heidelberg Catechism,
Answer 116

25

A petition is a solemn request. Even kids know about petitions. Sometimes they are passed around at school. You are asked to *sign* the petition. Then you wait to see what happens. Adults know about petitions too. Somebody passes around a petition, you sign it, and then the matter is never heard of again.

That is not quite true. Sometimes those whom you petition to act *do* act. But not always.

Believing people have always brought petitions to God. We ask him to do things. Jesus taught his followers to ask. The Heidelberg Catechism thinks of "the chief part of our thankfulness" as asking for more. But sometimes believers ask God to do something wrong: "Rise up and humiliate my enemy, O Lord." Sometimes believers ask God to do what he cannot do without rejecting someone *else's* petition: "Let our side win, O God." Occasionally, believers ask God to give strange gifts: "Let me have the power to become invisible, O Lord, and I shall become a thorn in the side of organized crime."

But most often believers ask God for seemingly innocent—even necessary—things. They ask that a disease be healed, a marriage restored, a daughter protected. Sometimes God grants these requests. But sometimes he does not. And we wonder why. At times our wonder turns into bafflement and fury.

"Ask, and it will be given you." But do I have to stand here every night, yelling like a fool into the darkness?

"Seek and you shall find." But do I have to seek twenty years for some trace of belief in my son?

"Knock and it shall be opened to you." I *am* knocking. I have been knocking till the door is splintered and my knuckles are raw. And no one answers.

What must we say to this? On the one hand, we have such strong, ringing assurances from the lips of our Lord. But, on the other hand, here we are with our strained voices, dashed hopes, and bloody knuckles.

How do these things go together?

A Prayer
Our Father who art in heaven, hallowed be thy name.
Thy kingdom come, thy will be done, on earth as it is in heaven.
Give us this day our daily bread; and forgive us our debts,
    as we also have forgiven our debtors;
and lead us not into temptation, but deliver us from evil.
For thine is the kingdom, and the power, and the glory, forever.
Amen.   —The Lord's Prayer

Postscript

1. Prayer troubles some believers because it seems "unreal" to them. They suspect they are talking to themselves, that the whole enterprise is empty and meaningless. And when God does not seem very real to people, they do not pray. Then the whole force of the Christian faith in their lives diminishes.

   How can a situation like this be helped?

2. How do we dare to give thanks for gifts and food which are withheld from many others?

3. Immanuel Kant, the famous and pompous German philosopher, once found himself revolted by the sight of a person praying on his knees. It looked so compromising! It looked so weak! It looked so unworthy of human dignity!

   When Christians pray in confession of sin, dependence, and inadequacy, are they showing an unseemly weakness?

4. A well-known passage in Mark Twain's *Huckleberry Finn* deals memorably with the problem of petitionary prayer—the problem of understanding the denial of our requests in the face of the lavish promises of the gospel: "Whatever you ask in prayer, believe that you have received it, and you will" (Mark 11:24).

   Miss Watson, she took me in the closet and prayed, but nothing come of it. She told me to pray every day, and whatever I asked for, I would get it. But it warn't so. I tried it. Once I got a fishline, but no hooks. It warn't any good to me without hooks. I tried for the hooks three or four times, but somehow I couldn't make it work. By and by, one day, I asked Miss Watson to try for me, but she said I was a fool. She never told me why, and I couldn't make it out no way. I set down one time back in the woods and had a long think about it. I says to myself, if a body can get anything they pray for, why don't Deacon Winn get back the money he lost on pork? Why can't the widow get back her silver snuffbox that was stole? Why can't Miss Watson fat up? No, says I to myself, there ain't nothing in it.

   Is there anything in it? How do *you* deal with denied petitions?

Week Six

What Has God Called Us to Do?

We have seen that God acts and that we
must respond in prayer. But there is more.
We have to do something besides praying.
We have to go to work. We have to follow
a vocation. Is a vocation only a job? What
has God called us to do?

Scripture

We who first hoped in Christ have been destined and appointed to live for the praise of his glory....For we are his workmanship, created in Christ Jesus for good works.

Ephesians 1:12, 2:10

Confession

We do good because Christ by his Spirit is also renewing us to be like himself, so that in all our living we may show that we are thankful to God for all he has done for us, and so that he may be praised through us.

Heidelberg Catechism, Answer 86

26

Some time after he resigned from office, Richard Nixon revealed that the worst of his personal tortures was a loss of vocational purpose. The ex-president added that in southern California a number of people seem to live purposeless lives. They gather at expensive watering holes where they eat too much, drink too much, talk too much, and think too little. They are without goals. They lack any sense of achievement. These people are overfed but undernourished. Sooner or later they show the strain.

One of our deepest hungers is the hunger for meaning and purpose. God intends that hunger to be fed by our vocation.

Most ideas of a vocation are much too narrow. People who have stumbled aimlessly into tending bar, advertising electric eyebrow tweezers, or selling Twinkies, all talk glibly of their "vocation." Vocation is only a job to them.

But the Bible never talks that way. In the Bible vocation is a vast and broad idea. It means God's calling. First, God calls unbelievers to repent and believe the gospel. When they do, they get a second vocation. The second call, strange to say, is to enlist in the military! The church—the church militant—is God's army for fighting the remaining evil in the world. All Christians are called to take part:

Enemy-occupied territory—that is what this world is. Christianity is the story of how the rightful king has landed, you might say landed in disguise, and is calling us all to take part in a great campaign of sabotage.

(C. S. Lewis, *Mere Christianity*)

The campaign is on. What has God called us to do? We are to *pray*. That is the chief part of our thanksgiving for the king's landing. The other part is *doing good*. In this—and only in this—do we at once find our vocation and our life's purpose. Into this life's vocation of doing good for Christ's sake each of us must fit his or her daily occupation.

A Prayer

Dear Lord, help us to direct all our living—what we think, say, and do—so that your name will never be blasphemed because of us but always honored and praised. In Jesus' name, Amen.

—from Heidelberg Catechism, Answer 122

Scripture
And the shepherds returned, glorifying and praising God for all they had heard and seen.

Luke 2:20

Confession
[God requires] that I do whatever I can for my neighbor's good, that I treat him as I would like others to treat me.

Heidelberg Catechism,
Answer 111

27

Vocation is first a community matter. God calls out a whole church. In fact, the Greek word for church means "the called-out ones." All along, we are called not as individuals, but instead as *members* of the church—the great, quivering body of Christ in the world. There are many members, but one body.

But at some point the question of personal occupation also arises. Though our occupations are only a part of our vocation, they are an important part. We spend a lot of time at them. So each of us has to face not only the question, "What shall *we* do?" but also the question, "What has God called *me* to do?"

One old mistake may be headed off at once. There is a medieval assumption that only ministers, missionaries, and other "religious types" have vocations. Only they are called to "full-time Christian service."

Not at all. *Every* Christian is so called. We are all members of Christ's body, even if we are different members of it. We are all called to serve the King and the King's campaign—each in his or her own way.

How? What is my calling?

Before trying to answer that question, a person has to ask himself a whole series of other questions. How can I best do good and fight evil? Given my own abilities (and liabilities), what little piece of this fallen world can I reclaim for Christ's sake? An advance squadron of shock troops is already moving out to retake enemy territory. Where is a me-shaped place in the line?

Those are the basic questions. More specific ones follow. Can I do more good taking tolls or taking polls? Am I called to work outside the house? Or shall I be a home executive? Suppose I want to spend my life mending elbow joints. Shall I do it as a doctor or as a plumber? Suppose my city is hiring sanitation workers. Certainly sanitation work can do good for Christ's sake. Is the Lord calling *me* to go into garbage? Could it be that Jesus wants me not for a sunbeam but for a truck driver?

All of these, and countless others, are possible occupations in the kingdom of God. As the Heidelberg Catechism says, "I do whatever I can for my neighbor's good." Whatever *I* can. That will be my ministry. I will use my products and services so that I "may be able to give to those in need" (Eph. 4:28).

Remember that the shepherds who visited Jesus Christ, the infant King, did not throw down their staffs and go off to seminary. They went back to their sheep.

A Prayer
O Lord our God, help us carry out the word we are called to, and to do it as willingly and as faithfully as the angels in heaven. Through Jesus Christ, Amen.

—from Heidelberg Catechism, Answer 124

Scripture
Let each of you look not only to his own interests, but also to the interests of others.
Philippians 2:4
Bear one another's burdens.
Galatians 6:2

Confession
Each member [of the communion of saints] should consider it his duty to use his gifts readily and cheerfully for the service and enrichment of the other members.
Heidelberg Catechism, Answer 55

28

There are a number of possible callings in the kingdom of God. A person could be called to be a machinist, or a homemaker, or a zoo keeper. Calls to the ministry are not unknown. God calls some of us to live for him as handicapped residents of nursing homes. Many Christians do so with steadfast faith and good cheer. Some heroic Christians take a handicapped life as an honorable vocation and follow it triumphantly.

There are many possibilities. How do I *know* God's particular will or plan for my life?

Some people expect God's call as a flash in the dark or a voice in the night. After all, there are instances in the Bible of such calls. Such people might expect to graduate from college, come home, and have a helpful family friend look them squarely in the eye and say, "Plastics!" So off they go into plastics.

But often God's call comes less dramatically. You size up your training and experience. You get a sense of your gifts and interests. You face your limitations. (Thus, you may *know* God has not called you to be a concert flutist.) Meanwhile, you inform yourself of needs which may be especially current. Computer programmers, for example, are more in demand than stage-coach builders. And through it all you pray as honestly as you can. You ask God for wisdom and a candid willingness to admit any selfish vocational motives.

You do something else. Recognizing the communal dimension of all Christian vocation, you consult with other Christians. None of us needs to make a vocational decision alone. Others may know where there are gaps and where Christians are needed to fill them. We ought to cultivate a sense of each other's gifts—possibly, in some cases, even of each other's *duties*. Other Christians can see in us the sorts of vocational motives, inclinations, and frustrations to which we ourselves are blind. In the Christian community, we may expect to hear things like this: "Ralph, your heart is not in this work. Have you considered a change?" "Barbara, you have sizable gifts in this area. Why not go on for a degree?" "Jim, your children are over-mothered and under-fathered. I wonder whether you don't need to stay home more."

Other Christians may speak what we later regard as the summons of God himself. Those who find themselves obeying such a summons have the opportunity to live a life instead of merely making a living.

A Prayer
O Lord, thou hast searched me and known me! Thou discernest my thoughts from afar. Search me, O God, and know my heart! Try me and know my thoughts! And see if there be any wicked way in me, and lead me in the way everlasting! Amen.
—from Psalm 139

Confession
What do we do that is good?
Only that which arises out of true faith, conforms to God's law, and is done for his glory; and not that which is based on what we think is right or on established human tradition.
Heidelberg Catechism, Q & A 91

29

In one of his books Richard Mouw takes up a vocational problem which vexes many Christians. The problem is that of vocational *witnessing*. On the job, or in my broader calling, how do I bear witness to what God has done and is doing?

Consider a business persons' prayer breakfast. A group of lively Christians gets together in the morning to pray, eat breakfast, and urge each other on to witness on the job through that day. They will discuss contacts, strategy, witnessing failures and successes. They will ask each other: "How can I use my business contacts today to tell someone what Jesus has done for me?"

These are devout brothers and sisters in Christ. Unfortunately the prevailing idea at their breakfast is that each of them is a business person who *also* wants to witness about Christ. The Christian faith is seen as something *extra*; it is something importantly attached to the job, but not really worked deep into the bones and innards of the job itself.

Consider a more excellent way and a better breakfast. A group of lively Christians gets together to pray, eat breakfast, and discuss strategy for demonstrating the lordship of Christ *in* their business practices that day. They ask: "How, today, can we write a policy, sell a house, lobby for a law, advertise a product in a way which honors Christ and makes God's name more respected? How can we do justice, love mercy, and walk humbly with God *as* members of our profession? How can we keep our jobs and still do what is right? How can we avoid being conformed to this world and yet work effectively in it as transformers of culture for Christ's sake?"

From their own vocational situation these Christians are asking our basic question: how can we be useful in advancing the kingdom of God? What can we do that is *good*? Years ago the Heidelberg Catechism laid out a very Reformed answer:

What do we do that is *good*?

Only that which arises out of true faith, conforms to God's law, and is done for his glory; and not that which is based on what we think is right or on established human tradition.

A Prayer
Lord our God, rule us by your Word and Spirit in such a way that more and more we submit to you. Keep your church strong, and add to it. Destroy the devil's work; destroy every force which revolts against you and every conspiracy against your Word. Do this until your kingdom is so complete and perfect that in it you are all in all. Through Jesus Christ our Lord, Amen.   —from Heidelberg Catechism, Answer 123

Scripture
We know that our old self was crucified with him so that the sinful body might be destroyed, and we might no longer be en-slaved to sin . . . . So you also must consider yourselves dead to sin and alive to God in Christ Jesus.   **Romans 6:6,11**

Confession
What is involved in genuine repentance or conversion?
Two things: the dying-away of the old self, and the coming-to-life of the new.
                     Heidelberg Catechism,
                                Q & A 88

30

Suppose I join with other Christians in doing the work of the Lord—as a homemaker, as a computer salesperson, as a deacon, as a shut-in, as a volunteer fire fighter, as a congresswoman. What sort of life-style will mark my months and years? What may I *expect* in my vocation?

"Two things: the dying-away of the old self, and the coming-to-life of the new." All Christians, on or off the job, are called to this dying and rising. It is a pattern we inherit from our Lord himself.

Christians must experience a *vocational* mortification. A mother, for instance, takes pains to give birth. Later, she will again and again kill off old selfishness to meet her child's newest needs. Other examples abound. A businesswoman loses an account because she will not shade the law to get it. A worker patiently puts up with a neurotic boss. In fact, every Christian who rejects vocational sloppiness, dishonesty, and aimlessness will suffer and die a little. Almost nothing really worth doing can be done without some struggle, sweat, and emotional pain.

But there is also a vocational coming-to-life for Christians. All of us want to be happy. Our happiness is directly tied to our feelings of self-worth. But the old trap is always set: do well in your vocation and you are worthwhile. Fail and you are worthless. It is the devil's denial of the grace of God.

The coming-to-life of the new self has at its core that steadfast trust in God which *keeps us from measuring our self-worth by how well we are doing*—on the job, at our hobbies, in our homes, as parents. Of course we should do as well as we can. But in freedom! In the centered, unshakable confidence that we are deeply treasured by God even when we have blundered into some outstanding failure!

We are called to take delight, to rejoice, in every bit of good God gives us to do. We are to indulge that hearty Christian freedom which lets us fail with regret, but also with a sense of humor, and which lets us succeed with joy, but also with quiet humility.

A Prayer
O God our Father, in all our living help us to be genuinely sorry for sin, to hate it more and more, and to run away from it. Then give us wholehearted joy and delight in doing every kind of good you give us the chance to do. Through Jesus Christ, our Lord, Amen.   —from Heidelberg Catechism, Q & A 89, 90

Postscript

1. Meditation 26 takes a very broad view of vocation. A certain British writer who also takes this view declares that God will be praised today by millions of acts—and blasphemed by millions of others. In fact, he says, in every voluntary act we either praise or blaspheme God.

   Is that true? Suppose I have two quarters in my pocket and I hand *this* quarter to the bus driver rather than *that* one. Does it matter? Is God at all concerned? Would the other quarter have praised him more?

   Here is the general question: must we consciously seek to be obedient to God in every act of our lives? Or are some acts trivial and neutral?

2. According to a number of observers, the hardest step each day for many people is the first one on the way to work. A large number of people are reportedly bored to the marrow with their jobs. A number of these people keep changing jobs.

   Some Calvinists have traditionally assumed that just as there is one "right" spouse for every person contemplating marriage, so there is one specific work to which God calls each of us. Moreover, some Calvinists have interpreted I Corinthians 7:17-24 and some statements of John Calvin ("Therefore each individual has his own kind of living assigned to him by the Lord as a sort of sentry post...") to say that we may not change occupations.

   How about these questions: is there one right occupation for each of us? May a Christian switch occupations? Explain.

3. In Ephesians 4:28 Paul says: "Let the thief no longer steal, but rather let him labor, doing honest work with his hands, so that he may be able to give to those in need."

   What sorts of principles for work do we find here?

4. Optional questions for group discussion:
   - From the biblical point of view is work a blessing or a curse? Explain.
   - What occupational relevance can one discern in the three criteria for doing good listed by Answer 91 of the Heidelberg Catechism?

Week Seven

What Are We Like as Fallen?

Perhaps John Calvin's most famous observation is that there is an unbreakable link between the knowledge of God and of ourselves. We have just spent six weeks on the knowledge of God. We turn now to look at ourselves and to ask our "questions about humanity."

A Reformed theologian would ask at once about our origin as perfect creatures of God. But our *experience* of ourselves has to start where we do—as creatures conceived and born in sin. So we begin by asking, What are we like as fallen? Of course we have to deal here with "the world," with that secular society and culture which is saturated with all the sin and sadness which has come down to us from the fall. But we know the question deals with us too, with who we are *except for the grace of God.*

For those who are yet outside that grace we may harbor no scorn or hatred, but only hope, love, and prayer. So we pray each day for God's fallen creatures, for those in whom there is no proper rootage, no humility, no hope, no shame, no real communion. And, with a view to our own fallenness, we pray also for ourselves, that a gracious God may increasingly have his way with us.

Scripture

Formerly, when you did not know God, you were in bondage to beings that by nature are no gods.
Galatians 4:8

Confession

What is idolatry?

Idolatry is having or inventing something in which one trusts in place of or alongside of the only true God.   Heidelberg Catechism, Q & A 95

31

In 1976 Alex Haley published a powerful book which deeply influenced American culture. In this book Haley traces his ancestry from an eighteenth century African village, through American slavery, to the present. *Roots* is a moving and extraordinary search for human *identity*. All of us, says Haley, are dependent on ancestral tradition to know "who we are."

Well, who are we? For millions of people caught up in the "roots phenomenon" that question has turned almost into a passion. Who am I? Who or what *defines* me? How do I most basically *identify* myself? What turns up when I unearth my deepest roots?

In a secular culture, the answers are legion. You can take a fair sample of them, as someone has wryly noted, simply by watching the almost weekly parades along New York's Fifth Avenue. Each parade features the same bands and the same politicians wearing determined smiles. Only the banners change: One week they say, "I am a feminist!" The next week, "I am an Italian-American." Or black, or Norwegian, or gay, or Republican, or a Knight of Columbus. People define themselves by sex, race, class,

religion, ethnic group, family, occupation, education—even by club membership or astrological sign. "I am a union man." "I am a Mormon." "I am a seventh-generation descendant of Kunte Kinte." "I am a fourteenth-generation descendent of a seasick *Mayflower* passenger." "I am a Princetonian." "I am a Hell's Angel." "I am a Capricorn."

Outside the gospel, these are ways in which we are tempted to see ourselves, place ourselves, define ourselves. We grope among the roots of what St. Paul calls "human tradition" (Col. 2:8) for some final way to bring a name and a significance to otherwise anonymous and empty lives. But when we pin our ultimate loyalties to these traditions, when our hearts cling to these merely human identities, we commit the sin of idolatry. "Idolatry is having or inventing something in which one trusts in place of or alongside of the only true God."

For *all* human beings, the root answer to the question, Who am I? is this: I am a fallen creature of God. But only some people know what that really means. They are the ones who can go on to say: But now I am a Christian. I am a follower of Jesus the Christ.

A Prayer

O Lord our God, we cannot claim to be pure in our loyalty to you and to your Christ. We are too much the products of our culture and too little the products of your Holy Spirit. For those who still look to human tradition, we pray; and for ourselves, that you may have your way with us. Through Jesus Christ our Lord, Amen.

What Are We Like as Fallen?

Scripture
He said to the woman, "Did God say, 'You shall not eat of any tree of the garden'?...You will not die. For God knows that when you eat of it your eyes will be opened, and you will be like God." Genesis 3:1, 4, 5

Confession
For who may presume to boast that he of himself can do any good...? Who will glory in his own will, who understands that *the mind of the flesh is enmity against God*? Who can speak of his knowledge, since *the natural man receiveth not the things of the Spirit of God*?
Belgic Confession, Article XIV

32

At least two generations of young Americans were raised on Horatio Alger novels. Under various titles (*Do and Dare, Sink or Swim, Try and Trust*), Alger wrote the same novel repeatedly. In it a poor but virtuous lad ("our hero") would struggle by luck and pluck to rise from rags to riches. Usually he had a widowed mother. Typically a rich man (perhaps a wicked "squire") and his snobbish son would try to ruin the widow and humiliate our rising hero. Nearly always the virtuous lad would appear on his first date with a girl whom the snobbish boy also liked—but didn't dare approach. Whenever this happened, the rich boy would accuse our hero of "putting on airs." Then he would rest his case by saying haughtily, "You don't know your *place*!"

"You don't know your place!" There isn't much room for an accusation like that in a popular democracy. That's good. For centuries certain people have blocked, frustrated, humiliated, and oppressed other people to "keep them in their place." Whites have done this wickedness to blacks, rich to poor, men to women. Victims of this oppression have rightly sought to be free.

But a great spiritual danger always accompanies the democratic spirit. The danger is that we may seek to rid our lives not only of human but also of divine dominion. The danger is that we human beings forget who made us and whose we are. The danger is that some self-realization fanatic might burble to us about "owning our own power" or some demonic voice whisper to us that if only our eyes were opened we could see God as close as ourselves—in fact, *identical* with ourselves.

Outside the gospel we are tempted to see ourselves as young giants, possible demigods, eventual lords of our lives. We are forever tempted to answer the question, Who is the lord of your life? with the breathless voice and shining eyes of titanic fools: Is it *I*?

Outside of Christ we do not know our place.

A Prayer
God our Father, you are the one who puts down the mighty from their thrones and scatters the proud in the imagination of their hearts. For the proud, we pray. And for ourselves, that you may have your way with us. Through Jesus Christ our Lord, Amen.

Scripture
And when the crowds saw what Paul had done, they [shouted]... "The gods have come down to us in the likeness of men!"...But Jews came there...and having persuaded the people, they stoned Paul and dragged him out of the city, supposing that he was dead.   Acts 14:11,19

Confession
In sin men claim mastery of their own lives, turn against God and their fellowmen, and become exploiters and despoilers of the world. They lose their humanity in futile striving and are left in rebellion, despair, and isolation.
Confession of 1967 I, A, 2

33

In one of his sermons Wallace Alston tells of the difficulty some young people have in "facing life's incredible demands." He mentions a high school teacher who gave his students the chance to ask him anything they wanted—and to do it anonymously. The students asked, of course, about sex, about drugs, and even about life on other planets. But, says Alston, "believe it or not, the question most frequently raised was that of *suicide*."

Teenage suicide, which was almost unheard of a generation ago, has now become a problem and a horror great enough to alarm parents and to prompt national TV reports. Even some nine-year-old children fall into depressions so deep that they are tempted by life's ultimately lonely act.

Why? Experts talk about a broad sense of hopelessness in young lives: some young persons are convinced that they and their lives matter to nobody.

The tragedy is that some of them may be right—at least so far as other human beings are concerned. It is a tragic fact that in a secular society we make some young persons into popular idols and others into throwaways. Sometimes we even do it by turns to the same person.

In fact, that very thing happened to Paul and Barnabas at Lystra. One moment the people of Lystra kissed the dirt at Paul's feet. The next moment they tried to kill him. First they wanted to worship Paul as a god. Then they wanted their god dead.

Before we are saved, this same fickle streak colors our view of *ourselves*. One day we may see ourselves as precious; the next day as worthless. Looking at ourselves outside of Christ we want either to worship or to destroy; either to bow down or to bow *out*. We see ourselves in an unfocused image which is always shifting between pride and despair.

As fallen, we do not know our place.

A Prayer
O Lord our God, raise up Christ in those who have fallen into the deepest darkness. And with Christ in them, raise up hope. For the hopeless, we pray. And for ourselves, that you may have your way with us. Through Jesus Christ our Lord, Amen.

What Are We Like as Fallen?

Scripture
The man said, "The woman whom thou gavest to be with me, she gave me fruit of the tree and I ate."...The woman said, "The serpent beguiled me, and I ate."
Genesis 3:12,13

Confession
From...dignity and perfection man and woman both fell; the woman being deceived by the serpent and man obeying the voice of the woman, both conspiring against the sovereign majesty of God....
Scots Confession, Chapter II

34

At three I had a feeling of
Ambivalence toward my brothers.
And so it follows naturally
I poisoned all my lovers.
But now I'm happy; I have learned
The lesson this has taught;
That everything I do that's wrong
Is someone else's fault.

In this psychiatric folk song, Anna Russell jabs at the no-fault ethics of some psychiatrists. There is a certain kind of secular mind which has developed an allergy to personal guilt.

The allergy has spread. People accused of graft in public office defend themselves by pointing to a *tradition* of graft in that office. Divorce is routinely seen as a kind of happening which everybody is powerless to prevent. The same goes for adultery. These things "happen."

Deep in our fallenness is the urge to shrug off personal blame and shame. We see it early on in the lineup of figures in the garden—each pointing a finger at someone else. And we keep on seeing it in the familiar attempt to fix blame on heredity or environment:

"I can't help it if I have a rotten temper! It runs in my mother's family."

"It's not *my* fault I can't hold a job! My second grade teacher called my safety-first poster rubbish. That cut me down as an artist. Else I might have become another Andrew Wyeth."

Outside the gospel of Christ, we are tempted to say we have no sin. We are tempted to see ourselves not as sinners, but as *victims*; not as fallen, but as frustrated. Not as wrong, but as misunderstood! Unappreciated! Underestimated!

We deceive ourselves, and the truth is not in us.

A Prayer
God our Father, without a sense of your holiness human creatures cannot see their sin. Let that sense of holiness come upon your fallen creatures. We pray for the shameless. And we pray for ourselves, that you may have your way with us. Through Jesus Christ our Lord, Amen.

Scripture
Cain said to the Lord, "My punishment is greater than I can bear. Behold...I shall be a fugitive and a wanderer on the earth, and whoever finds me will slay me.   Genesis 4:13,14

Confession
[I must know] first, how great my sin and misery are.
Heidelberg Catechism,
Answer 2

35

All of us feel a touch of loneliness at some time in our lives. While we are away at school, in the military, off on business, or otherwise separated from people we love, we discover loneliness. There may be people all around us, but they are not *our* people. So we feel alone.

Many of us have experienced the loneliness of sickness, of feeling forgotten and useless. Others of us know the special loneliness of guilt, of not being able to *tell* anyone what we have done. Some of us have known the grip of loneliness which bereavement brings. A spouse dies and, perhaps for the first time, you learn from this painful ripping apart how much you had grown together into one flesh.

Many of these kinds of loneliness may, by God's grace, be temporary. But outside of Christ, all human beings are permanently lonesome. Contemporary literature has played the theme of human alienation and estrangement over and over. We are alienated from the works of our hands, estranged from each other, members of a lonely crowd.

Of course, people make escape attempts. They try to overcome loneliness. Some slip into ill-considered couplings. Some cruise the singles' bars. Others try encounter groups which contrive sharings, touchings, and other artificial intimacies for strangers. Some people sample communal living. Quite a few give it all up and die—perhaps by their own hand. A fashionable writer of the seventies said it for all secularity: "No one is with me....There is no one who won't ever leave me alone."

Outside of Christ's gospel and Christ's church, we come to see that we are *alone*. Fallen brotherhoods dissolve in the lonely crowd or end in rancor—even in murder. Like Cain, we become in some sense fugitives and wanderers on the earth. Our loneliness is in fact a masked homesickness for God and the place with him which we have forfeited. As fallen creatures, we are *displaced* persons.

So the Heidelberg Catechism sums up all human misery with the German word *Elend*. It means "exile." And the last exile from God is hell.

A Prayer
Dear Lord, unless you embrace us, we are unloved. Unless you gather us in, we are scattered on the earth. We pray for those of your children who are still aliens; and for ourselves, that more and more you may have your way with us. Through Jesus Christ our Lord, Amen.

Postscript

1. Meditation 31 lists a number of ways in which human beings attempt to define or identify themselves. Look at the list. What contemporary examples can you think of? Why do people do this sort of thing? What is the danger in it?

2. Meditations 32 and 33 speak of our temptation, outside of Christ, to see ourselves either as godlike or as worthless—or even as each in turn. Our self-image shifts back and forth between pride and despair. Where in personal relationships do you see signs of this? Where in pop culture? How about in the secular view of humanity's future?

3. In the biblical account of Aaron and the golden calf (Ex. 32:1-24), the fallen human tendency to shrug off personal blame is neatly illustrated. How so?

4. In what particular respect is human loneliness a foretaste of hell? Consider some of the following texts—all of them from the lips of our Lord: Matthew 13:49,50; Matthew 25:41; Matthew 25:46; Matthew 8:12; Mark 9:47, 48; Luke 16:22, 23.
    What would be a corresponding foretaste of heaven?

Week Eight

What Are We Like as Redeemed?

There are two mistakes people tend to make when they estimate the redeemed life. The first is to underestimate the sin which remains in us. It is still there and it can still hurt us. The second is to underestimate the strength of God's grace. It is utterly determined to make us new. Perhaps in our own Reformed tradition we are more inclined to make the latter mistake than the former.

So this week we say two things. We admit that we are redeemed *sinners.* But we also say boldly and joyously that we are *redeemed* sinners. And of these two statements, the latter gets the accent.

What Are We Like as Redeemed?

36

Anyone who has ever tried to stick to a diet knows some of the exasperation with which Paul explodes in this chapter. You *know* what is right. It is right to abstain from glazed doughnuts. It is right to become slimmer and trimmer. And yet, as you pass the bakery in your supermarket, or as your hostess springs a sudden chocolate mousse on you, or as you try to slip by the Nut Shoppe just as they are roasting some truly scandalous cashews, you are called into battle once again. Something in you is perversely, outrageously at war with what is right. Something in you wants the evil *you* do not want! And occasionally this enemy succeeds in melting your firmest resolution as a hot apple danish melts a lonesome and defenseless pat of butter.

Later, the guilty deed done, you sit down for an earnest talk with yourself. "Look, self," you say, "you were supposed to be done with all that. I don't get it. Why did you *do* that again? That's not what you want!" And so on.

"I can will what is right, but I cannot do it. For I do not do the good I want, but the evil I do not want is what I do."

Fallenness is complete slavery to sin. In that slavery and blindness we do not even want what is right and good. On the other side, the perfection for which God intends His saints means complete and powerful freedom from sin. Perfect people want and invariably do only what is right.

We are meanwhile in between. Because of the profound work of Jesus Christ, we are no longer slaves to sin. We are now slaves to God. But we are still learning the ropes, still learning obedience. We are no longer dwellers in the land of great darkness. But neither have we arrived at the city of God. We are on the way.

We all live in the tension of being redeemed, but not yet perfected. We know the sin in us has met its Conqueror. We also know the conquering is a process that will not be complete till *for us*, as for himself, our Lord says, "It is finished."

A Prayer
O Lord God, loosen the hold on us of everything but your Holy Spirit. We are divided persons; unify our lives. We are double-minded; build in us the single mind of Christ. So break the fascination of this world for us that even when we fall back into its embrace, it cannot hold us. In Jesus' name, Amen.

Scripture
You are not your own; you were bought with a price.
I Corinthians 6:19,20

Confession
Because I belong to him, Christ, by his Holy Spirit...makes me whole-heartedly willing and ready from now on to live for him.
Heidelberg Catechism, Answer 1

37

Let us face the truth. We are not always "whole-heartedly willing and ready to live for him." We have our mental reservations, our provisos, our escape clauses and contingency plans. Even when we are willing, we are not always *ready*.

But, of course, these words do strike some sparks of recognition in us. They do not leave us cold. There are times when we are flushed with enthusiasm and purposely set ourselves again to seek and do the Lord's will instead of our own. Anyone who has been moved by conversion or delivered from shame, fear, or disease—anyone like that knows the innocence and strength of the pledge never again to look to oneself for aid and comfort.

After all, we are redeemed people. We *know* we are not our own but have been bought with a price. We know that the very Christ who redeemed us is now mysteriously in us and being formed in us. We know that the demonic suggestion "you will be like God" is the first whispering from which has come all the thunder and horror of the fall. We know we are first *creatures* who belong to God our Maker and, more recently, redeemed creatures who belong to Christ our Redeemer. We know that. We hate self-idolatry and the titanic sin of pride—especially in others.

And yet, every day we fall a little again. We progress two steps ahead—and one step back. Every day, as C. S. Lewis said:

We try, when we wake, to lay the new day at God's feet; before we have finished shaving, it becomes *our* day and God's share in it is felt as a tribute which we must pay out of "our own" pocket.   (*The Problem of Pain*)

We are complex persons. In some measure, though we have been transplanted and re-rooted, we still bend backwards toward the alien soil from which we were taken. We are not *of* the world, thanks to the gracious work of Christ. But we are *in* it still. And it is in us.

Who will deliver us from this body of death? Who will cut off our foreign affairs? Who will finally discover our self-interest?

A Recitation
I delight in the law of God, in my inmost self, but I see in my members another law at war with the law of my mind.... Wretched man that I am! Who will deliver me from this body of death? Thanks be to God through Jesus Christ our Lord!
—Romans 7:22-25

Scripture

God so loved the world that he gave his only Son. John 3:16

So you also must consider yourselves dead to sin and alive to God in Christ Jesus.
Romans 6:11

Confession

In Christ I am right with God and heir to life everlasting.
Heidelberg Catechism,
Answer 59

38

Evelyn Newman tells a story about a minister who came upon two boys and a dog. In a friendly, patronizing way, the minister asked the boys what they were doing. "Well," said one of them, "we found this dog. And we're going to have a contest for him. Whichever of us can tell the biggest lie gets to keep the dog."

The minister was shocked. "Boys," he said. "That's no business! You must not *lie*. Why, when I was your age, I never told any lies!"

There was a moment of silence. Then one boy shrugged and said, "Well, I guess *he* gets the dog."

It is a great mistake to underestimate the sin that remains even in a redeemed life. Ministers who act as if they never so much as say "shucks"; people who talk as if they no longer struggle; evangelists who promise converts a hilarious life; people who say they have no sin—all these deceive themselves and others. We are redeemed *sinners*.

But much more remarkably, we are *redeemed* sinners. And somehow we have missed the force of that. Our hymns describe us as "worthless" or as "worms." Our church for-

mularies advise us to "loathe ourselves." Sermons tell us how rotten we are. Soon we begin to believe this sort of thing. Anthony Hoekema has rightly protested the fact that

many of us tend to look only at our depravity and not at our renewal. We have been writing our continuing sinfulness in capital letters, and our newness in Christ in small letters. We believe in our depravity so strongly we think we have to practice it, while we hardly dare to believe in our newness.

(*The Christian Looks at Himself*)

Thus, what should be a life expanding into greater joy, freedom, and heartiness in our relation to God and others turns back to become just as sour, pinched, and fearful as any miserably unredeemed life.

God helping us, we have to break out of this pattern! Lewis Smedes reminds us that the gospel not only tells us how bad pride is; it also tells us how bad, and how unnecessary, is our *despair*. True, we needed to be died for. But in God's judgment we were also worth dying for. We are now accepted—even treasured—by a God who has loved us to the point of death.

A Recitation

Even though my conscience accuses me of having grievously sinned against all God's commandments and of never having kept any of them . . . *nevertheless* . . . *out of sheer grace,* **God grants and credits to me the perfect satisfaction, righteousness, and holiness of Christ,** *as if I had never sinned nor been a sinner, as if I had been as perfectly obedient as Christ was obedient for me.*
**—from Heidelberg Catechism,
Answer 60**

Scripture
Put off your old nature which belongs to your former manner of life...and put on the new nature, created after the likeness of God in true righteousness and holiness.   Ephesians 4:22, 24

Confession
We believe that God created man...after His own image and likeness, good, righteous, and holy, capable in all things to will agreeably to the will of God.
Belgic Confession,
Article XIV

39

Most of us have a rough idea what an *image* is. Look in a mirror. That thing which grins back foolishly at you is not you, nor even your face, but your face's image. You cannot touch the image, but you can see it. It is very real.

We see images in other places. We see them in the viewfinders of our cameras. We see them chiseled into marble and painted onto canvas. We see them even in our own minds. If a light is flashed in your eye a certain way, you will "see" an after-image even after the light is off and your eyes are shut.

We also have a small library of mental images of other people. You can call to mind the face of a loved person, even one who has been dead for years. You can picture that face—the shape of the nose, the set of the eyes, the characteristic half-smile.

So an image is a kind of counterpart, a duplicate, a likeness. And a most striking and mysterious thing the Bible says about us is that we are made, and are now being remade, in the *image of God.*

What does that mean? It is hard to say.

Theologians have been arguing about it for years. Part of the reason for the argument is that the Bible does not give a precise explanation. Perhaps goodness is included in the image (Gen. 1:31). Also righteousness and holiness (Eph. 4:24). We may add knowledge (Col. 3:10) and dominion (Gen. 1:28; Ps. 8:4-8). No doubt *every* created and recreated perfection is part of the image of God.

There is one immediate implication. The perfections that are part of our "new nature" must be reflected in our *self-image.* Of course we must honestly and daily put off the sin that clings to us. But that sin ought to be increasingly on the border of our picture of ourselves. We may no longer see ourselves as essentially rotten, worthless, and entirely to be regretted. Not at all. The living of these days, and the self-image that is so sensitively connected with that living, must reflect both the humility and the strength of those *for whom Jesus Christ died.*

Did we really think he was only salvaging junk?

A Prayer
O Lord our God, let us move away from the old things, the old self, the old manner of life. Putting on what is new, fresh, and full of hope, let us move across our days daring to remember that you have made us into sons and daughters of infinite worth. Through Jesus Christ our Lord, Amen.

Scripture
Then God said, "Let us make man in our image, after our likeness." ...So God created man in his own image...male and female he created them.
Genesis 1:26, 27

Confession
As we believe in one God, Father, Son, and Holy Ghost, so we firmly believe...one Kirk, that is to say, one company and multitude...the communion, not of profane persons, but of saints.
Scots Confession, Chapter XVI

40

Certain people have "charm" or "presence." As a modern novelist notes, it is not that such people have been to charm school. They have probably not endured all the "Be Likable and Make Friends" courses. (You can tell the trained charmers by their memorized phrases, sickly smiles, and instant chumminess.) No, a genuinely charming person will have her own dignity and personal reserve. But the center of her interest is outside herself. She has a highly developed awareness of *you*. Her attention stays fastened to what you say. Her focus centers itself on what is worthy and interesting in you. She has the ability to make you feel special.

All of us are deeply responsive to such treatment. We are charmed. The reason for our response is that this other-regard together with our response is a striking image of God.

From yesterday's meditation we might have concluded that the image of God is some in-

dividual quality which each of us must trap and feed in himself. But in fact the image shows up also in our dealing with *others*. A wonderful reflection of the nature of God is that communion, fellowship, mutuality which results when we love one another.

Think it over. At the beginning, as now, it was not good for the man to be *alone*. So God designed a fitting partner. Communion was set up on earth as it is in heaven. The very God who loves—who begets a Son and, with the Son, a Holy Spirit—says, "Let us make man in *our* image." From the beginning we were meant to be together.

We have been estranged from each other, afraid of each other, lonesome for each other. Sin has adulterated our community. But now a triune God—a *social* God—is breaking down the dividing walls of hostility and building his church.

A Prayer
O Lord, for too long we have been absorbed with ourselves. We have not taken an interest in others. But now you are leading us out of ourselves to see and love and reach out to your other children. Make our bonds with them thick and strong. Through Jesus Christ our Lord, Amen.

Postscript

1. Meditation 36 describes some of the frustration we all experience as we attempt to please God by obeying his rule for our lives. But we might wonder: if we still have to battle and struggle like this, what real improvement has the redemption in Christ brought into our lives? Isn't the exasperation of St. Paul in Romans 7 more characteristic of a secularist than a Christian?

2. Meditation 37 speaks of our dividedness in terms of "mental reservations, provisos, escape clauses, and contingency plans."
   What are some of these?

3. Meditation 38 quotes Anthony Hoekema's charge: "We have been writing our continuing sinfulness in capital letters, and our newness in Christ in small letters."
   Is that true in your experience? What is the danger of the dark and unrelenting emphasis on our continuing sinfulness? What is the opposite danger?

4. Meditations 39 and 40 have to do with the image of God. This includes all human perfections, even the relation of community, or fellowship, which love builds.
   In what way might our self-image include such fellowship?

Week Nine

How, Then, Should We See Ourselves?

Last week we concluded that the Bible's
message about us is positive and hopeful.
Though we are still divided persons—
tugged at both by the world and God—
God's tug is stronger. We are *redeemed*
sinners.

Our question this week follows: How, then,
should we see ourselves? It is a question
of self-image. It is a question of how we
are to assess or estimate ourselves. Is it
an unseemly and self-interested task? Is it
dangerous?

Let us see.

How, Then, Should We See Ourselves?

Scripture
In Antioch the disciples were for the first time called Christians.
Acts 11:26

Confession
But why are you called a Christian?
Because by faith I am a member of Christ.
Heidelberg Catechism,
Q & A 32

41

Two weeks ago we saw that people *identify* themselves in a host of ways. Some do so proudly: "I am a Canadian." "I am rich." "I am a *mean* hombre!" Some do so in despair: "I am a failure." "I am a loser." "My brother is president and I am only a buffoon."

Very often we begin to see ourselves as others see us. We take over their descriptions of us and make them self-descriptions. Thus, a child might never think of himself as "poor" till somebody else describes him that way. A teenager might never think of herself as "attractive" till some wonderful person makes that pleasant observation. An athlete might never think of himself particularly as an animal till his basketball coach says to him, "Klankenfelder, you are a real *horse* on the boards."

"In Antioch the disciples were for the first time called Christians." For the first time they were nicknamed. "Christ"-ians.

The disciples probably did not like it very well. It was not their own name for themselves. They thought of themselves as disciples, brothers, believers, followers of the way. As is sometimes pointed out, "Christian"—probably said with a sneer—was a nickname chosen by *outsiders.*

Yet the name has stuck. We have taken it over. We now see ourselves as Christians. We are not first reds or yellows, blacks or whites; not first "haves" or "have-nots"; not first senior citizens or adolescents, women or men, halfbacks or drawbacks. Those are all secondary distinctions. We are first Christians. That is what *identifies* us.

But is it enough? Does the term still tell enough?

Ernest Campbell has observed that in the United States if you are neither Jewish nor agnostic you are *Christian.* In a standard dictionary, when you get down to the second or third definition, you read things like this— *Christian*: a decent human being. In some circles you are Christian if you are kind to granny and the cat.

Being decent is not enough. Perhaps that is why the Catechism gets very pointed: *But why are you called a Christian?* Because by faith I am a member of Christ.

What do you suppose *that* means?

A Prayer
O Lord God, we have often made mental images and have bowed down and served them. We have seen ourselves as others see us; we have seen ourselves as we would like to be. Too often we have seen ourselves in strange and perilous ways. Now change, correct, and refocus our vision through Jesus Christ our Lord. Amen.

Scripture

So you also must consider yourselves dead to sin and alive to
God in Christ Jesus.

Romans 6:11

Confession

Believers one and all, as members of [the communion of saints],
share in Christ and in all
his treasures and gifts.

Heidelberg Catechism,
Answer 55

42

People who hear sermons and read Christian literature may come upon a number of familiar phrases they do not really understand. Several of these phrases contain the word "in." We used to be "in the flesh." Now we are "in the Spirit." We used to be "in Adam," or "in sin." Now we are "in Christ."

"In Christ" is, in fact, a central phrase in Paul's writings. He uses it over one hundred fifty times. Christians are elect in Christ, die in him, are raised, sanctified, and blessed in him. They are enriched in Christ, wise in Christ, safe in Christ. The whole church is one body in Christ. Paul himself claims to be bold, be established, have power; to speak truth, exhort, labor, rejoice, and hope—all "in Christ."

What could this mean? How could one get "in" a person such as Jesus Christ? Does Paul mean that each of us actually merges into the inner life of Jesus Christ in some way? That mysteriously each is absorbed into Christ's personality? Are we somehow already made *divine*?

Apparently not. When St. Paul talks about being in Christ, he is talking *historically*. We are in Christ in a broad, cosmic sense because of the cosmic work of Christ. The main idea is that by Christ's death and resurrection—that is, *in Christ*—God was "reconciling the world to himself" (II Cor. 5:19). God was renewing an old, ruined creation. In a stunning victory over the powers of sin, death, and despair, he was establishing righteousness and raising up life and hope.

Now for us to be in Christ is for us to be part of that new situation in history. And for us to be part of that new situation in history is for us, first of all, to be living members of Christ's renewed community.

How must we see ourselves? As "members of the 'communion of saints' " says the Catechism. What does that mean? It means we are members of Christ. We "share in Christ and in all his treasures and gifts."

One of the choicest treasures which come to us from the work of Christ is that as a community we are to think of ourselves in a new way. "So you [plural] also must consider yourselves dead to sin and alive to God *in Christ Jesus.*"

A Hymn

The Church's one foundation
    Is Jesus Christ, her Lord;
She is His new creation
    By water and the Word;
From heaven He came and sought her
    To be His holy bride;
With His own blood He bought her,
    And for her life He died.

—"The Church's One Foundation"

Scripture
When we cry, "Abba! Father!" it
is the Spirit himself bearing
witness with our spirit that we
are children of God, and if
children, then heirs.
Romans 8:15-17

Confession
Christ alone is the eternal,
natural Son of God. We, however,
are adopted children of God—
adopted by grace through Christ.
Heidelberg Catechism,
Answer 33

43

Hardcore secularism extends little care to the borders of life—to those who are old and about to die or to those who are young and about to live. Secular people try to pull in their lines, tie off their responsibilities, and hunker down into the pleasures of middle-aged adolescence.

This situation means trouble for children. In some places abortions outnumber live births. A fair number of children who are allowed to emerge from the womb alive are steadfastly ignored in the hope that they will not bother anyone or require anyone's attention. A depressing 70 percent of parents who responded to a columnist's inquiry stated that if they had it to do over again, they would not have had any children. It was not worth it.

But some children who escape the designs of abortionists and the slower death by neglect at the hands of their natural parents are "let out" for adoption. Many of them are almost immediately placed. Others wait. Some of those who wait are handicapped. Some are members of more than one race. Nearly all, as they grow older, are excruciatingly aware that in some way they have been shut out. They keep on waiting for someone to open a door and invite them into their homes and lives.

One of the truly gracious moments in an often ungracious world is that moment when Christian parents undertake to adopt a child. From human carelessness, sadness, and brokenness a child has been conceived and born. From that same carelessness, sadness, and brokenness the child is now delivered. Of course, there are the inevitable adjustments. You cannot take in an image of God without enlarging your life. But for the child there is a new name, a new place, a whole new way of life. There is nourishment for today and bright hope for tomorrow. There may be a whole circle of welcoming brothers, sisters, or friends. Determined parents—even those who are delighted and fulfilled by their adopted children—have, in their own way, attempted the work of *redemption*.

Christians are members of Christ and of his community, family members of the household of faith. Perhaps today, with all the clarity and warmth God gives us, we can see that we ourselves are his *adopted children*.

A Prayer
O Lord, we are all your adopted children. From our loneliness and fear you have graciously redeemed us. Now let us turn with that same grace and redemption to those among us who are still alone and unnourished by love. Through Jesus Christ our Lord, Amen.

Scripture
Vindicate me, O Lord, for I have walked in my integrity, and I have trusted in the Lord without wavering.... I do not sit with false men, nor do I consort with dissemblers.... I wash my hands in innocence, and go about thy altar, O Lord, singing aloud a song of thanksgiving.
Psalm 26:1, 4, 6

Confession
In this life even the holiest have only a small beginning of... obedience.
Heidelberg Catechism,
Answer 114

44

A Princeton preacher retells an old story about a minister who looked out over his congregation one Sunday and asked, "Is there anyone here who has achieved perfection?" No one answered, of course, for if anyone *had* achieved perfection he or she would have been far too modest to mention it. So the minister tried again, asking if anyone had known, or even heard of, someone who was perfect. Immediately a man got to his feet and shouted, "My wife's first husband!"

One sometimes gets the impression that the psalmists are much like this first husband. C. S. Lewis and others have wondered about the degree of self-approval one finds in such psalms, for example, as Psalm 26. Isn't this psalmist too good to be true? Isn't he ready for heaven right now? Parents of small children notice that when they punish one child the others reach up to adjust their halos and begin to speak with a sudden piety: "God doesn't like what Nathan did, *does* he mommy! I *never* do that, *do* I!"

Doesn't that sound disturbingly like a children's version of Psalm 26?

Well, as Lewis says, "we must not be Pharisaical even to the Pharisees." We must not fall into that self-righteousness which says, "I thank thee, Lord, that I am not like other men. I thank thee that I am not self-righteous." Nor may we fall into the modern error of thinking that *any* attempt to do what is right makes a person self-righteous and that any attempt to do good makes one a contemptible "do-gooder." Is it so much better to be a scoundrel than a prude?

Self-righteousness is, however, a real and present danger to the Christian life. As soon as we see ourselves as redeemed, there is the danger that we may see ourselves as better than those not yet redeemed. As soon as we see ourselves being made holy, we may start to see ourselves holier-than-thou.

Would it help if we sternly reminded ourselves that we are only beggars telling other beggars where to find food?

A Prayer
O Lord God, we have set strict standards for others and made plenty of allowances for ourselves. We have shown more interest in orthodoxy than in compassion. Forgive the damage we have done. Yet preserve in us a firm and unflinching stand against what is unholy even as we preach compassion to the unholy person. Through Jesus Christ our Lord, Amen.

How, Then, Should We See Ourselves?

Scripture

But all of us who are Christians have no veils on our faces, but reflect like mirrors the glory of the Lord.   II Corinthians 4:18 (Phillips)

Confession

What is the chief end of man?

Man's chief end is to glorify God, and to enjoy him for ever.
    Westminster Shorter Catechism, Q & A 1

45

Some things can be done well only if we are not watching ourselves do them. You cannot watch yourself swing if you hope to hit a baseball. You cannot watch yourself go to sleep. You cannot watch yourself pray. You cannot even watch yourself *play*.

Itzhak Perlman, the violinist, was once asked about public playing. "You are the center of attention of four thousand people," said the interviewer. "Some are violinists themselves. In front of all these people you have to do terribly intricate work and do it all from memory. How do you keep from freezing up with fright?"

Perlman's answer was definite: "You cannot think about being the center of attention. You cannot think about all those people. You cannot think about how secure your memory is. You have to lose yourself in the music, or else you'll never play well in public."

One of the deadliest traps of our whole line of questioning this week must now be admitted. We have been asking, How, then, should we see ourselves? We have been asking about the Christian's self-image. We have been looking inside.

But there has to be an end to that. A violinist will carefully study both the flaws and the strengths of his technique in his private practice. But he has to forget all that self-analysis when he actually begins to play music.

So with us and our Christian life. We must not get very self-conscious. We must not let our right hand know what our left hand is doing. We must not constantly ask ourselves, like some sinking Peter on the Sea of Galilee, "Hey! Look at me! How am I doing?" We cannot *keep on* looking inside. We have X-rays taken only at occasional checkups and when we suspect we are sick. It is neurotic people who want them every week.

Paul makes the astonishing claim that we are mirrors of the glory of the Lord. His glory. Not ours. Our job is to reflect *away* from ourselves an image and a glory which do not really belong to us. So we must not keep on asking, "How do I look? How am I doing? How glorious am I getting?" Not at all. We cannot spend all our time looking *in* the mirror and reflecting on *ourselves*. We are to do the work of mirroring him.

Isn't it interesting that "when Moses came down from Mount Sinai...he did not know that the skin of his face shone" (Ex. 34:29)?

A Prayer

Lord our God, let us lose ourselves in seeking your will and find ourselves by way of tracing your pattern for our lives. If by the way you make us shine—if your glory should make us luminous—O Lord, let us be the last to know. Through Christ we pray, Amen.

Postscript

1. Meditation 41 states that we are very sensitive to the way others see us; what others see affects the way we see *ourselves*.

   Do you think that's true? Insofar as it might be at least partly true, can you think of examples? Are self-image and behavior related? If others tend to form their own self-image from the picture of themselves they see in *our* eyes, what sort of moral responsibility does this lay upon us?

2. Meditation 42 says we must see ourselves "in Christ." The idea of being "in Christ" is an extremely broad idea in the Bible. As Lewis Smedes put it: "The phrase 'in Christ' is an epigram for the total reality of the new community under Christ's lordship, a community...forming the embryo of a total new race and a whole new creation united and renewed by Him" (*All Things Made New*).

   What is the danger of ignoring this broad context of history and community when we look at ourselves?

3. Read Psalm 26. Meditation 44 suggests that the psalmist sounds to our ears a trifle too self-approving. But what is the deeper issue in this psalm and in, say, II Corinthians 6:14, 15? How can Christians avoid self-righteousness without "going along with the world"?

4. Meditation 45 suggests that we do some things well only if we are not watching ourselves do them. That is true of our own Christian life. We may introspect from time to time, but not constantly.

   Do you think a similar point could be made with respect to the church? Are we too concerned with self-evaluation and self-analysis?

Week Ten

World and Covenant Community: How Do We Fit?

Christians are citizens of two cities and inhabitants of two worlds. We are human beings and citizens of the city of humankind. But, remarkably, we are also redeemed human beings and citizens of the city of God. We are in the world, but not of the world. We belong to the community of human beings; more especially, we belong to the covenant community of God. What is our relation to each? Where in the world do we fit? And how in the world do we fit into a covenant community? That is what we will think about this week. World and covenant community: how do we fit?

Scripture

She caught him by his garment, saying, "Lie with me." But he left his garment in her hand, and fled and got out of the house.

Genesis 39:12

Confession

[Christians have] a perpetual reason to humiliate themselves before God and to flee for refuge to Christ crucified.

Canons of Dort V, Article 2

46

It is very hard to flee and look dignified at the same time. Slapstick comedians count on this. So do kids. That is why kids love to scare people, especially grown-up people. People look funny when they flee.

Except, of course, if the danger is real. It is not funny to see someone move quickly away from a rattlesnake. But if you flee from a rubber snake, all the kids in the neighborhood will clutch their bellies, giggle, and shine. You are a joke.

To a certain sort of worldling, *Christians* are a joke. Especially Christians who flee from evil. In certain films and plays a Christian who makes a wide detour around a saloon, or who backs away from a grinning prostitute, is ridiculous. He's afraid of something harmless! There's the joke.

Well, nobody likes to be a joke. No Christian likes to beat a hasty retreat while people stand around and snicker. That is why Christians sometimes go along with what is wrong. They cannot bear ridicule.

With a glint in her eye, Potiphar's wife said to Joseph, "Lie with me." What if Joseph, wishing to keep his options open, had said, "Look, let's have a drink and see if this is something we both can handle"?

"But he left his garment in her hand, and fled and got out of the house." A ridiculous figure? Twinkling out of the house minus his bathrobe! What is he *afraid* of?

He is afraid of sinning against God. And he is willing to lose both his garment and his dignity if he can keep faith with God.

God calls us out of the land of Egypt, out of the house of Potiphar's wife, out of the world. Covenant people from Abraham to the disciples of Christ are chosen, separated, *called-out* people. The calling is continuous. Every day we are recalled.

Thus a Christian in the world is like a Christian at a party which has taken an ugly turn. There is a time when you feel called upon to get up and walk out. You do not *belong* here. You do not fit very well in this world.

Will people laugh? Perhaps. They may think the danger is imaginary. But Christians are not so naive. They have a healthy fear of sin. They know the danger is real. And they will flee even if they cannot look dignified at the same time.

A Prayer

When we flee, O Lord, remind us that it is not because we are too good for this world, but because we are not yet good enough to stand against it alone. Then, armored and strengthened, send us back to minister help and to speak the strong word of deliverance in the name of Christ. Amen.

Scripture
God is faithful, by whom you were called into the fellowship of his Son, Jesus Christ our Lord.
I Corinthians 1:9

Confession
The Son of God, through his Spirit and Word, out of the entire human race, from the beginning of the world to its end, gathers, protects, and preserves for himself a community.
Heidelberg Catechism,
Answer 54

47

Certain people are what we call *individualists.* They think the individual is more important than the group. In religion, they are afraid of the "social gospel." In politics, they are more afraid of communism than of anything else. They believe that sovereign individuals may band together by a "social contract" to form a corporation, a state, or even a church, but in any case the individual is primary and the group secondary. The group is there only for the sake of the individual. A French political scientist once said: "Individualists owe nothing to any man; they expect nothing from any man. They acquire the habit of always considering themselves as standing alone, and they are apt to imagine that their whole destiny is in their own hands."

Christianity is against individualism. God makes his covenant with a *people.* We baptize our infants not because they are individual believers, nor even because they belong to a family of believers, but because they belong to the *extended* family of believers—the church. We are all baptized into this prior community, into a body which existed long before we did. We do not join this body. We are *called* into it.

When God's people are called out of the world, they are called into fellowship, into what the New Testament calls *koinonia. Common* words are associated with *koinonia:* "common," "commune," "commonwealth," "community," "communion," even, oddly enough, "communism." We were called into *koinonia.* We have something in common.

Rather, we have some*one* in common. Many pictures are used in the New Testament. We drink from a common cup of blessing, we break a common bread, we are connected as branches to a common vine, we are fingers and toes of a common body. But always it is Jesus Christ, our Lord, who is the fount of blessing, the broken bread, the life-giving vine, the head of the body. We *belong* to him—and thus to each other.

As a noted Canadian thinker has said, "Only fallen people are individualists."

A Recitation
The grace of the Lord Jesus Christ and the love of God and the fellowship of the Holy Spirit be with you all.
—II Corinthians 13:14

Scripture
Why should my liberty be determined by another man's
scruples?   I Corinthians 10:29

Confession
God alone is lord of the conscience, and hath left it free from
the doctrines and commandments of men which are in
anything contrary to his Word, or
beside it.
                Westminster Confession,
                            Chapter XX

48

Certain people are what we call *collectivists.* They think the collective, or the group, is more important than the individual. In religion they are afraid of individual Christian liberty and distinctive expressions of Christian faith. Every-one must do and believe the same thing. In politics, they are more afraid of right-wing republicanism than of anything else. They believe that the company, or the state, or the church, may wish to grant the individual cer-tain freedoms, but in any case the group is primary and the individual secondary. The in-dividual is there only for the sake of the group.

Some collectivists in the church cannot stand to see anyone alone. "Togetherness" is their password and solitude their enemy. They are al-ways trying to organize groups. Even when their groups break up, it is always into smaller groups. There you "share." In some groups you hold hands and tell secrets. You are hemmed in, crowded together, pressured into intimacy. You begin to yearn and grope for some breath-ing room. You recall gratefully that St. Paul says something about *individual* Christian liberty.

Christianity is against collectivism. None of us may separate ourselves from the covenant community. But neither may the community erase our individual differences, rip away our secrets, or mash us all into the same mold. The "melting pot" image of people together is not found in the Bible.

Each of us needs to respect the liberty and personhood of others. Christians come in many shapes, colors, ages, and sizes. They come in two sexes. They come married and single. They exist at different levels of maturity. Some of us have an emotional coloring to our faith; some rational; some moral. Some of us drink wine; some do not. Some of us are teenagers. We get uneasy when parents say, "Wouldn't it be nice if all the young people wanted to be with us in-stead of with their friends?"

Certainly the dividing walls of hostility have been broken down. Certainly we are one in Jesus Christ. But we are not one *glob*. We are one body. And that is a very different thing.

A Prayer
Keep us, O Lord God, from trying to make over our brothers and sisters in our own image. Give us a delight in the vast variety of ways and persons by which you reflect your glory. In Jesus' name, Amen.

Scripture
Now you are the body of Christ
and individually members of it.
I Corinthians 12:27

Confession
Of [Christ's] community I am and
always will be a living member.
Heidelberg Catechism,
Answer 54

49

How do we fit into the covenant community? We are not sovereign individuals who contract to get together for convenience. Nor are we a lump or blob of Christian togetherness. We are "the body of Christ and individually members of it."

In one of his matchless speeches, C. S. Lewis reminds us how specially Paul meant this term "member." Sometimes we talk about, say, the "members" of the Democratic party. That is almost the opposite of what St. Paul means. Members of a political party are nearly indistinguishable. Each is simply a voter, or worse, "a vote." One person—one vote.

But members of the body of Christ are at once very dependent on each other and very different from each other. They are like bodily organs or parts, as different from each other as an eye is from a hand—and just as coordinated. Our unity is a "unity of unlikes," an organic unity, a complementary unity. And the body of Christ moves into action only when each member is doing his or her part.

This idea is first a disturbance to us and then a source of great security. It is first a disturbance because it puts us at odds with our culture. Our culture exalts either the individual or the group. Perhaps just lately it has tended especially to blur individual differences. Thus the trend toward making parents playmates whom children call by their first names. Thus the unisex movement. As Lewis says, "The worldlings are so monotonously alike by comparison with the almost fantastic variety of the saints."

But membership in the body is also a source of great security for us. It allows us to be ourselves, to do what *we* can do, to play *our* role. Each of us is created to fill a place shaped just for us.

A famous Jewish rabbi named Zusya used to wish that he was other than he was. Then he reflected, and said wisely: "In the world to come they will not ask me, 'Why were you not Moses?' They will ask, 'Why were you not Zusya?' "

A Prayer
O Lord our God, we pray for the body of Christ, for the church and all her members. Let us work together well. Let us care for those members who are weak. Let us rejoice with those who have found strength and hope. Let us build your kingdom, through Jesus Christ our Lord. Amen.

Scripture
Come to me, all who labor and
are heavy laden, and I will give
you rest. Take my yoke upon you,
and learn from me.
Matthew 11:28, 29
"This is rest; give rest to the
weary."
Isaiah 28:12

Confession
Wherever the church exists, its
members are both gathered in
corporate life and dispersed in
society for the sake of mission in
the world.
Confession of 1967 II, A, 2

50

There is a scene early in *David Copperfield* which warms your heart when the November nights turn frosty and the wind takes on an edge. Davy is put to bed, "a little bed which there was just enough room to get into." He describes a feeling of security in the nest which makes even adults wriggle more deeply into their chairs:

...when the door was shut and all was made snug (the nights being cold and misty now), it seemed to me the most delicious retreat that the imagination of man could conceive. To hear the wind getting up out at sea, to know that the fog was creeping over the desolate bar outside, and to look at the fire...was like enchantment.

Is that a picture of the covenant community for Christians? A "delicious retreat" from the world? An ark to ride out the storm? A private Christian snuggery where we can pull the covers over our heads while the heathen rage outside? Does God offer us that kind of blanket protection against the cold? When Jesus said he would send a *Comforter*, did he mean a kind of quilt?

No. Surely God is our refuge as well as our strength, but never for hiding permanently away. In the rhythm of his dealings with us, God calls us out of the world only to equip us with his armor and send us back.

So there is no staying in bed "till the storm of life be past." We have to be ready to step out onto the cold floor, pull on some clothes, and go out into the night. Someone's hunger needs food. Someone's courage has snapped. Somebody is finally ready to hear a word from the Lord.

"Come to me, all who labor and are heavy laden, and I will give you rest." It is a beautiful invitation and rightly loved. But let us not forget that the same Christ who calls also warns us to count the cost. The same shepherd who loves his sheep sends them out among the wolves. The same Lord to whom we go for rest fits us with his yoke to go out and bear the burdens which would otherwise break our hearts.

A Prayer
We come to you, O Lord, with our burdens to lay down. And you offer us a cross to take up. What an odd kind of rest you give! But what a relief for us to know that at last we are in your company to do what is right. Because we belong to you, we take comfort. And now, in your company, we move out to minister to those who are comfortless. Amen.

Postscript

1. Meditations 46 and 50 describe the Christian's relation to the world. He is first called out of it and then sent back into it. You might call these the "flight" and the "return flight" of the Christian in the world.

   What dangers are associated with these "flights"? And how does a Reformed Christian seek not only to *fight* against the world but also to attempt something more positive in his return to the world?

2. Meditations 47 and 48 describe the errors of *individualism* and *collectivism* where the covenant community is concerned. From a biblical point of view which error, if either, is worse?

   The two questions above reflect the main issues in this week's work. But following are three additional questions you may wish to consider:

3. Suppose that we retreat from the world only to be equipped to go back into the world as transformers of culture. Are you satisfied that the educational system you are using for your children does indeed equip them in this way?

4. Do we dare talk about "our covenant God"?

5. If, as meditation 50 suggests, we are to take advantage of all the resources of the covenant community for our work in the world, what does this say about preaching? Can we rest content with twenty-one minutes of exposition and only two minutes of practical application?

Week Eleven

Male and Female: How Are We Related?

We move this week to our last question about humanity. It is a sensitive one—closely related to who we are, how we see ourselves, and how we fit in the world and the covenant community. There are some particularly blood-warming issues attached to this question which format and brevity prohibit us from raising: women in ecclesiastical office, for instance. But other controversial issues are introduced either in the meditations or in the postscript questions.

Much of this lesson—even where not explicitly acknowledged—was written under the influence of Lewis Smedes's *Sex for Christians,* a book heartily recommended.

Scripture
And the man and his wife were both naked and were not ashamed....Then the eyes of both were opened, and they knew that they were naked.
Genesis 2:25, 3:7

Confession
Anarchy in sexual relationships is a symptom of man's alienation from God, his neighbor and himself.
Confession of 1967 II, A, 4

51

People are interested in sex. Everybody knows that. Ministers know that if they preach on sex, people's attention will not wander and their eyeballs will no longer glaze over. Booksellers know many people are in the market for maps of their erogenous zones and diagrams of the way of a man with a woman. Television advertisers know that sex will sell even chain saws and auto batteries.

Meanwhile, Christians have recently been asking about traditional sexual roles, attitudes, and attributes. Must men give all the orders? Is a woman's place in the home? There are many differences between male and female today. Did God intend all of them? Or did *we* invent some? What *is* the main difference?

Anyone can tell there is at least a physical difference. God made it. For Adam God made a match, a fitting partner, a human person like Adam himself—but with the fascinating difference. For a time that difference between male and female or (Hebrew) *'ish* and *'ishshah* was innocently enjoyed in all its ripe, sensual fullness. God had knowingly designed his human beings to come together, cling together, *cleave* together. They were not ashamed of their difference. There was nothing between them—nothing to fear, nothing to hide, nothing to cover up. They had decent exposure.

But then it happened. In the fall they lost their innocence and they knew it. On perfect human beings nakedness had looked good. But with sin came shame and cover-up. With sin and shame came man's ruling over woman (Gen. 3:16) and the long, troubled history of our attempt to deal with the sexual difference.

Sometimes the attempt is young and awkward. You are a teenager attempting your first kiss. But you and your date accidentally turn your head to the same side and get a poor contact. Or you get your braces hooked. About ten years later you see the humor in it.

But relations between the sexes can go seriously wrong. They can yield a special humiliation and frustration. A woman resents the fact that people do not recognize her and cannot remember her name apart from her husband. A teenage romance which had been fresh and honest is soured, and then painfully abandoned, because of sex. A single adult is haunted by the need to love and be loved. A man humiliates a woman on film while paying customers watch.

Is there a word from the Lord even for such things?

A Prayer
O Lord our God, we confess to you the sin and fallenness which has so often and so long spoiled our relations together as male and female. We have been not only awkward, but also arrogant; not only shy, but also deceitful. We have been deeply confused. Correct and help us by your Word. Through Christ, Amen.

Scripture
There is neither Jew nor
Greek, there is neither slave
nor free, there is neither male
nor female; for you are all one
in Christ Jesus.
Galatians 3:28

Confession
Our Lord Jesus Christ...was
given us to set us completely
free and to make us right with
God.   Heidelberg Catechism,
Answer 18

52

Arthur Schopenhauer, the nineteenth century German philosopher, wrote an essay "On Women" in which he said: "As nurses and educators of our children, women are suited precisely in that they are themselves childish, simple, and shortsighted; in a word, grown-up children, a kind of middle step between the child and the man—who is the true human being."

Sad to say, statements only a little less sexist may be found among the Christian fathers and theologians. There we find that a woman is weak, slow-witted, mentally unstable, childish, a "necessary evil," a "domestic peril," and the "devil's gateway" to man. "How easily you destroyed man, the image of God!" shouts Tertullian at all women. "Because of the death which you brought upon us even the Son of God had to die."

In our own Christian communities, women have often suffered the indignity of not being taken *seriously*. A female college student is referred to by one of her professors as a "cute little number." Someone's grown-up wife is introduced as "the little woman." People gather to discuss "the women's issue," and the men do all the talking. Dorothy Sayers once addressed a troubling remark to men: suppose a man at a dinner party were asked, "And why should *you* trouble your handsome little head about politics?"

However we understand what St. Paul says about male headship in marriage, the radically new covenant teaching about our general relations as male and female is that in Christ we are *one*. From secondary status to Jews, Gentiles have been liberated! From secondary status to masters, slaves have been liberated! And from being the property of male fathers and the mere incubators for male children, women in the New Testament are free at last! Jesus Christ came to "set at liberty those who are oppressed." He came so that as male *and female* we may have life, and have it in its fullness.

Could it be that we have just lately begun to see how revolutionary this is?

A Prayer
O Lord God, we confess our uneasiness with the deepest implications of your Word. We confess our puzzlement with your Word itself, which seems in our deafness and confusion to speak with more than one voice. Guide us by your Holy Spirit to hear what you are saying to us. Then give us the courage to do it, through Jesus Christ our Lord. Amen.

Scripture
So God created man in his own image...male and female he created them....And God saw everything that he had made, and behold, it was very good.
Genesis 1:27, 31

Confession
We are temples of the Holy Spirit, body and soul, and God wants both to be kept clean and holy.   **Heidelberg Catechism, Answer 109**

53

As male and female we are one in Christ. But we were also equipped by God to become one *flesh*. We are related as *sexual* creatures. God has made a way for us to know each other with the deepest intimacy. There is a way to know something of each other's mystery. Do we dare say, "This is the way the Lord has made! Let us rejoice and be glad in it"?

The Christian fathers did not dare say it. Some thought husbands and wives ought to abstain from sex if possible, or else blush in the morning. Many Christians still find it hard to rejoice in their sexuality. They underestimate sex. They think it is not nice. Or else it is a duty one may perform, provided it is no fun: "I have fathered six covenant children and never enjoyed it a bit!" It is as if someone told you to eat, but not to savor your food. Go to bed when you are tired, but do *not* nestle in!

All this is a mistake. We may not despise what God has made and what he calls good. We must not forget that our maleness and femaleness allow us to reflect the image of God himself. It is not, of course, that God is male or female. It is rather that sexual union allows us to *commune* in human imitation of the profound communion among the persons of the Holy Trinity. Sex is the gift which drives us toward the *other*:

> We want to experience the other, to trust the other...to enter the other's life....Personal communion is what the image of God is about.   (Smedes, *Sex for Christians*)

But sex, like fire, is a powerful gift which can not only draw us to its warmth, but also burn us painfully. There is delight in sex. Surely there is humor in it. There are times when it is a romp. But sex for Christians, even when it is a joy, is not a toy. You do not play with fire. Sex needs a context. It needs a *fireplace*. Because it has power to uncover our inadequacies and to explore our tenderest places, sex needs to be guarded by the security of that life-union we call marriage.

We are sexual creatures. We must not underestimate either the joy—or the power—of sex. This great gift can light up two lives, or it can turn them, for a time, to grayness and ashes.

A Prayer
Let us, O Lord, receive your gifts with thanksgiving. And let us respect not only their beauty, but also their power. Give us a sense of the place of sex in our lives. In that place let us commune with joy and tender regard for each other. Through Christ our Lord, Amen.

Scripture
Train yourself in godliness; for while bodily training is of some value, godliness is of value in every way.   I Timothy 4:7, 8

Confession
By the Spirit's power we make the goal of our lives, not earthly things, but the things above where Christ is, sitting at God's right hand.
Heidelberg Catechism, Answer 49

54

Errors come like shoes—in pairs. Take jogging. Not long ago any adult who tried to swell his lungs and reduce his paunch by running around outdoors would have been thought peculiar. *Kids* run around. Grown-ups are supposed to sit around, growing large and soft.

Now all is changed. For some people jogging is nearly a religion. Such people write books with titles like *Running and Being*. They promise that bodily training will raise up every valley and lay low every mountain in your life. They speak of jogging in the same breath with the crusades and the start of dental hygiene.

Against both errors Paul writes to Timothy: "Train yourself in godliness, for while bodily training is of some value, godliness is of value in every way."

Paul might just as well have been speaking of bodily sex. It is of some value—some *real* value. And we have sometimes underestimated it in the Christian tradition. But it is not the most important thing in our lives! As Smedes says,

there are other rooms in the house besides the master bedroom. We must not make the error of a modern culture which pities virgins and grimly seeks the "atomic orgasm." This is a society where sex does not know its place, a society which imagines that bodily sex can by itself *create* communion—only to find that when it does not express a prior commitment to life-union, it only plunges one deeper into emptiness.

We must not overestimate bodily sexuality. We do not have an unlimited right to fulfillment in it. Nor are sexual sins the worst imaginable sins. Nor do single Christians necessarily lack "wholeness" as persons. It is entirely possible to live a fulfilled and godly life without *bodily* sex. One of the ripest fruits of mature Christianity is the discovery that, married or single, we can enjoy each other *as male and female* without intending any movement toward a bed.

Even Adam and Eve had more to do in the garden than just cling to each other in the grass!

A Prayer
Help us once again, Lord God, to put first things first. Remove from us every nearsighted obsession with some single part of a gift you give. Turn us back to you, the giver, and to the widest possible vision of the richness we have as male and female. Through Jesus Christ our Lord, Amen.

Scripture
God has so composed the body...that the members may have the same care for one another. If one member suffers, all suffer together; if one member is honored, all rejoice together.
I Corinthians 12:24-26

Confession
While praying to God for the grace of the Holy Spirit, we may never stop striving to be renewed more and more after God's image, until after this life we reach our goal: perfection.
Heidelberg Catechism, Answer 115

55

He was a young fellow, only fifteen, when he was told he had cancer. The radiation therapy helped for a time, but it was nauseating. And it had another effect. It caused his hair to fall out. On top of the uncertainty and agony of his disease, this young man had to bear the humiliation of returning to school with a head of patches and stubble.

But the first day back, he discovered an astonishing thing. A large number of his friends were walking the halls completely bald! They had all shaved their heads. With a wise and ingenious grace, these teenagers had thought of a way to ease their friend's pain and to fit him in.

"If one member suffers, all suffer together; if one member is honored, all rejoice together."

Empathy—the ability to "feel in" another—is a blessed mark of Christians in community. In a day of great sexual change, a day of sexual lashes and backlashes, of sexist fears and resentments, of liberation fought for inch by inch, perhaps empathy is the main atmosphere in which we as males and females must move. Surely to be "renewed more and more after God's image" means, at least in the first place,

that we attempt to *understand* each other.

Let a woman try to feel the traditional pressure on a man to keep up a "macho" image. Let a man attempt to feel the humiliation of a woman who is utterly ignored when important things are decided. Let a teenaged couple, fumbling toward a dangerous area in their relationship, try to feel the fear and see the darkness in the *other*. Let all of us who attempt to live godly and creative sexual lives show ready compassion for those brothers and sisters who are yet struggling and unhappy. We are related as males and females in many ways. In *every* way we are members of one body of Christ, designed by God to reach in care for one another.

So St. Paul moves across these membership verses toward what is possibly the most glorious chapter he ever wrote. The name of the care we extend to each other is *love*. And love never insists on its own way. Even between males and females love keeps on striving to understand the other person fully, as each of us has *been* fully understood by God."

A Prayer
Dear Lord, only as you love us keenly and thoroughly can we turn in care toward one another. From all our tendencies to belittle and resent the other, deliver us. Fill us with clean, powerful, inventive love so that some part of your beauty may come through us to those with whom, in your providence, we have to do. Through Jesus Christ our Lord, Amen.

Postscript

1. Is sex anything to be ashamed of? Explain.

2. In the long movement from Adam's rib to women's lib there have been two main positions. One is the traditional position of the Christian fathers that in creation man was the main event and woman, taken from man's rib, only a sideshow. The other position, represented by the contemporary women's liberation movement, was expressed by a little Christian girl who described creation thus: "First the Lord made a man. Then he looked at him and said, 'I think I can do a little better.' And that's when he made woman."

   Which of these positions is nearer the truth? And, if the truth lies in between (i.e., in the *equality* of the sexes before God), what do you make of the fact that in Ephesians 5:22 the husband is head of the wife? Does he get to give all the orders?

Short Possibilities for Further Discussion

3. Are we souls or bodies? Is sex a soul or body function? What difference does it make?

4. Will there be sex in heaven? Explain.

Week Twelve

How Do People See Jesus?

In contemporary Western society, nearly every thinking adult has at least some opinion about Jesus Christ. Millions of people faithfully believe Jesus to be the divine Son of God and the living Lord of their lives. Probably as many believe only the first half of that confession: an astonishing number of people claim that Jesus is the divine Son of God but also that he is without significance for their lives. And then there are those who "proclaim another Jesus," those with peculiar, or even blasphemous, opinions. They write books with titles like *Jesus the Magician, The Human Face of God, Jesus the Citizen, Jesus the Pagan, The Man Nobody Knows, Christ the Great Deceiver,* and *Jesus: A Psychobiography and Medical Evaluation.*

So far in our course we have considered some questions about God and some about humanity. Now we turn to ask about the God-man, the divine person who, in the miracle of the incarnation, condescended to become a human being for us and for our salvation.

We begin by asking a very biblical sort of question: What shall we do with Jesus who is called Christ? Who is this that teaches with such authority? What do you think about the Christ? "Who do the people say that I *am*?"

Scripture

They went out and got into the boat; but that night they caught nothing. Just as day was breaking, Jesus stood on the beach; yet the disciples did not know that it was Jesus.

John 21:3, 4

Confession

For there is no creature . . . who loves us more than Jesus Christ; who, though *existing in the form of God*, yet *emptied himself, being made in the likeness of men and of a servant* for us.

Belgic Confession, Article XXVI

56

To many people Jesus Christ is a *remote* figure. Secularists shake their heads in disbelief when they hear Christians say they "love Jesus," "talk to Jesus," or have Jesus as their "friend." To these secularists it is as if you said you loved a person from the planet Pluto, regularly spoke with him, and counted him among your closer friends. You cannot *do* such things! Pluto is so remote that it can be seen only through the most powerful telescopes. And Jesus Christ died nearly two thousand years ago.

Even for some Christians, at least at times, Jesus is a distant person. Liberals who take a highly critical view of the Gospels say the early church made up most of Jesus' words and deeds. Jesus did not really do the things the Gospels say he did. He did not really say the things the Gospels say he said. Those things were said and done only by the "Christ of faith," an imaginary figure drawn into the Bible by the church's piety. The "real" Jesus, the "Jesus of history," is so remote as to be unrecognizable, irrecoverable, unknowable, lost in the mists of time.

Some conservative Christians also think of Jesus as removed from us and all our smallness, dirt, and panic. These Christians think Jesus Christ is alive. But they think he is not, and has never been, really human. He is lofty, misty, high and lifted up. He never laughed. He rarely sneezed. He never dropped a tool or bent a nail. Even as a boy, his knuckles were always clean. "The little Lord Jesus, no crying he makes." He is *unreal!* He is remote.

But the real Jesus Christ is in fact as profoundly and mysteriously near to us as our own thoughts and feelings. And he meets us not only in churches, upper rooms, and the sacred places of our lives. He meets us when we are grimy and mean. He meets us when we have gone fishing and caught nothing. The risen Lord elects to be with us where we live and work and sweat. He is with us "on the beach":

Just as day was breaking, Jesus stood on the beach; yet the disciples did not know that it was Jesus.

A Prayer

God our Father, we have pushed away him whom you meant to be with us. We have held at arm's length your Son who came to embrace and lift us up. Now let Jesus the Christ once more stand on our beach, in our lives, where we work and play. In his name, Amen.

57

To many people Jesus Christ is a *familiar* figure. His picture hangs in the kitchen. His name is a household word. Songs about him—some of them sweet, intimate, sentimental—are played all day as a broadcast background to household tasks. Jesus is a "dear, familiar friend."

Even for some secularists Jesus has become a familiar figure. They see him on the cover of *Time.* Their own culture has made him a dramatic superstar. In some areas of the country, they are assailed on their car radios by "Jesus-preachers" and confronted on their way to work by those Christian billboards on which things of final magnificence are advertised alongside hotdogs and motor oil.

For many people—some of them teenagers in Christian homes—all this familiarity is not a delight but a burden. These people find it depressing. Their religious circuits are overloaded. They are overexposed. By turns, they are bored and rebellious where Jesus is concerned. For them, familiarity breeds contempt.

As is sometimes pointed out, we are here up against one of the most dangerous and stubborn enemies of the faith. Familiarity has blocked commitment one generation after another. Jesus' own townspeople—those who knew him "back when"—could not honestly get very enthusiastic about him. Who does he think *he* is? "Where does he get all this? Is not this the carpenter?"

And is not this all too familiar? What chance does Jesus Christ have among us and our children when his gospel has to make its way through thick layers of religious familiarity? We have heard it all before. We have heard that name till it irritates us and the good news till it seems no longer either new or good. There some of us sit, on the fringes of the church! "Go ahead!" we say. "Preach away! We know all the words. You aren't telling *us* anything new!"

One of the most stunning displays of the power of Jesus Christ is that he can sometimes get himself heard even where people are numbed by years of sermons, hymns, and bumper sticker piety. In some moment of unexpected need, the word begins to speak. In a crisis sharper than we had thought possible, God's Son for the first time becomes real to us. It may happen when Peter's short prayer becomes ours: "Help, Lord!"

The familiar Jesus becomes a new and sudden Savior. The resurrected carpenter becomes the Lord of life.

A Prayer

O Lord God, in some hopeless, human way, we have managed
to make even the splendor of your Son seem dull. Forgive us.
Startle us by your grace, surprise us by joy, and make all things
new among us for Jesus' sake. Amen.

Scripture
"Who do men say that I am?" And they told him, "John the Baptist; and others say, Elijah; and others one of the prophets."
Mark 8:27, 28

Confession
We confess that He is *very God* and *very man*.
Belgic Confession, Article XIX

58

Some people see Jesus as a remote figure; some as a familiar one. But, to tell the truth, there is practically no view of Jesus so outrageous that it has not occurred to *somebody*.

During his lifetime, Jesus was confused with John the Baptist, Elijah, and Jeremiah. He was seen by the scribes as a lunatic, by the Roman soldiers as a fool, by the priestly crowd as a robber, by his own disciples as a political messiah.

Since then there has always been a temptation to twist Jesus into a shape fit for our own cause. We do not support *his* program; he supports ours. The plastic Jesus, the silly-putty Jesus, is the convertible idol of modern culture. He can be hitched to any chassis, packaged for any market, elected charter member of any group. We have all seen this sort of thing done with dismal regularity in our own day.

He can be arranged as a businessman (did he not say, "I must be about my Father's *business*"?). He was a Jesus for capitalists (did he not say, "To everyone who has will more be given"?).

But he can also be set up as a labor unionist (remember, he was a carpenter). Indeed, he was the first real socialist (recall his warnings to the rich and his love for the poor). He can be packaged as a revolutionary, as a women's libber, and as the first pop psychologist and success preacher. He can be seen, and sung to, as a football player ("Drop-kick me, Jesus, through the goalposts of life!"). A contemporary publisher of children's vacation Bible school materials has a Hollywood-handsome Jesus peering out at us with his matineé-idol eyes.

People who have something to sell, something to hide, or something which needs to be propped up have this perverse tendency to present Jesus Christ as the patron saint of their cause. It is, of course, the rankest idolatry. And from faithful Christians it will wrench the ageless cry of Mary: "They have taken away my Lord, and I do not know where they have laid him."

A Prayer
Dear Lord Christ, master of our lives, we have shamelessly tried to enlist you in our projects. We have wanted you not to judge, but to endorse our schemes. In some perverse way, we have tried to convert you instead of waiting for you to convert us. Forgive and correct us, O Lord. Amen.

Scripture
The soldiers plaited a crown of thorns, and put it on his head, and arrayed him in a purple robe; they came up to him, saying, "Hail, the King of the Jews!" and struck him with their hands.
John 19:2, 3

Confession
[Christ] has been anointed with the Holy Spirit to be...our eternal king who governs us by his Word and Spirit.
Heidelberg Catechism, Answer 31

59

A contemporary preacher tells of coming upon one of those pieces of pious graffiti you sometimes see on walls and abutments. Someone had clambered up on a railroad bridge, far above the highway, to swab on in whitewash the words, "Jesus saves!" But someone else had risked life and limb too—someone who scrambled up there to add behind the motto the words "green stamps."

Certain people have always seen Jesus Christ as a *fool*. It is a wickedness which we seldom call to mind. We think of the suffering Christ as looking grieved, hurt, determined. We think of him not as a comic but as a tragic figure. Yet, as Douglas Nelson describes this scene from John, here is the Christ draped with somebody's faded army blanket and crowned with the thorn's nest jammed down on his head. Bored soldiers try to get him into a game of blindman's bluff. A good slap across the mouth: "Take it and like it, your Majesty!" A fist to the nose: "Guess who gave you *that* one, O King!" "Hail, King of the Jews!" And when this part of his humiliation is finished, the Christ is pinned to a crosspiece under Pontius Pilate's trilingual joke: "Jesus of Nazareth, the King of the Jews."

Can the very Son of God be made to look *absurd*?

Mockery is one of the most painful abuses we visit on each other. Youngsters with shaky egos try a fair amount of it. Let another kid be fat, unintelligent, or socially awkward, and she is in for some merciless mockery. It hurts. It hurts a lot. And if you are the parent of a child who is mocked, and you see it just once, you will never forget.

"They came up to him, saying, 'Hail, King of the Jews!' and struck him with their hands." Perhaps we can see, even in this vile irony, that Jesus Christ has borne our griefs and carried our sorrows.

A Prayer
O Christ our Lord, for the grief and shame which weighed you down we look to the weight of our own sin and the folly of our own hearts. Yet give us the wisdom to be fools for your sake. Amen.

Scripture
And Jesus said to them, "Have you come out as against a rob-ber, with swords and clubs to capture me?"   Mark 14:48

Confession
Why is the Son of God called "Jesus" meaning "Savior"?
Because he saves us from our sins.   Heidelberg Catechism, Q & A 29

60

As Ernest Campbell observes, this scene from the gospel has a kind of grim humor. The crowd which snakes its way by torchlight through the garden to capture Jesus is ludicrously overarmed! You do not send out the FBI to trap someone who owes a library fine. You do not dispatch six screaming squad cars to the hideout of a suspected litterbug. Nor do you approach the Prince of Peace, the preacher of nonresistance, with blades, bludgeons, and a show of muscle:

Have you come out as against a robber, with swords and clubs to capture me?

Every day he had been available to them. Every day he had freely preached in the temple. He was no fugitive. Why all this sudden and cowardly force?

Jesus, whose name means "Savior," has often been seen as a *robber*. People think he is out to steal our privacy, our riches, our freedom to do what we want. The poet Swinburne said it famously:

Thou hast conquered, O pale Galilean; the world has grown gray from Thy breath.
                    ("Hymn to Proserpine")

To Swinburne, paganism is a rich and lush green world; Christianity is a tight and narrow little gray world. And the Swinburnes of the world have always wanted to set Barabbas free and eliminate the Christ.

A main obstacle to conversion is the fear that Christian faith dries up our pleasures and leeches all the color out of our lives. No more bright lights and good friends! No more lipstick! No more Miller's High Life! Francis Thompson has it exactly:

For, though I knew His love
    who followed,
    Yet was I sore adread

Lest, having Him, I must have
    naught beside.   ("The Hound of Heaven")

Is Jesus Christ our robber or our Savior? He is both. He means to break and enter our defenses and to carry off every false friend, every hope-less crutch, every deadly comfort. He means to rob us of life itself.

But only of that old, misdirected, dangerous life which leads to death. He wants to give us life as it was meant to be—strong, purposeful, rich with love and joy. Perhaps it takes a veter-an Christian to understand what Jesus means:

The thief comes only to steal and kill and destroy; I came that they may have life, and have it abundantly.   (John 10:10)

A Prayer or Hymn
O Jesus, joy of loving hearts,
Thou fount of life, Thou light of men,
From fullest bliss that earth imparts
We turn unfilled to Thee again,
We turn unfilled to Thee again. Amen.
—"Oh Jesus, Joy of Loving Hearts"

Postscript

1. This week's meditations have presented some answers to the question, "Who do men say that I am?" (See Mark 8:27; cf. Matt. 16:13.) Are all the answers *entirely* mistaken identifications of Jesus? Explain.

2. Look at Matthew 16:13-20. How does Simon Peter answer Jesus' question? Is there more than one question here? What difference does it make?

3. Meditations 56 and 57 are divided according to the perception of Jesus Christ as "remote" or "familiar." You will note that these ways of seeing him are not exactly parallel to emphasizing his divinity, on the one hand, or his humanity, on the other. Thus, some who see Christ as a remote figure are liberals who emphasize his humanity and some are conservatives who emphasize his divinity. The same goes for familiarity.

   But, as an orthodox reminder, ask yourself this: does the Bible picture Jesus as a man who became divine or as a divine being who became a man?

4. Meditation 58 points the finger at certain Christians who have made Jesus over in their own image. Some of these new faces of Jesus are more believable and less blasphemous than others.

   But let us look at ourselves and our own perception of him. How do we sometimes emphasize those parts of the gospel portrayal which support our own life-styles and attitudes—while ignoring those which call them into question?

5. It is not only Christ but also Christians who will be seen by some as fools. What might it mean to be a "fool for Christ's sake" (I Cor. 4:10)?

Week Thirteen

What Did Jesus Do?

Christianity, like Judaism, is a thoroughly
historical religion. Old and New Testaments are testaments to great acts of God
in history. Over and over, the pattern of
relationship between God and his human
creation is one of God's act and our
response.

The New Testament tells us of the acts of
God's Son, of the events of Christ. These
are the events from incarnation through
ministry, suffering, and death to resurrection, ascension, and present rule. They
form the heart of the Apostles' Creed and
the historical foundation of our faith. So
this week we ask five times, What did
Jesus *do*?

Scripture
[He] emptied himself, taking the form of a servant, being born in the likeness of men.
Philippians 2:7

For, behold, darkness shall cover the earth, and gross darkness the people; but the Lord shall arise upon thee, and his glory shall be seen upon thee.
Isaiah 60:2 (KJV)

Confession
The only-begotten Son of God ...for us men and for our salvation came down from heaven, and was incarnate by the Holy Spirit of the virgin Mary, and was made man.
Nicene Creed

61

This year at Advent we will sing and tell of "good news," of the "first noel," of "a great joy which shall come to all the people." We shall do so in a season of the year in which depression deepens across the land and the traffic in suicide thickens.

For, behold, darkness shall cover the earth,
and gross darkness the people....

Even for many Christians there is a leaden familiarity to the old, old story and a glum deafness to the good news. Together, they make Christmas uphill work. Where is the excitement we used to feel? What happened to the freshness of our childhood celebrations?

Well, thank God faith does not depend on any level of joy that *we* manufacture. But with humility let us also thank God that here and there he lets us feel again some of the wonder of his grace which descends to lift up a weary and desolate people. It is wonder, as Paul Scherer put it, at a God who "came one night down the stairs of heaven with a baby in His arms."

For many of us there is a place in Handel's masterwork, *Messiah*, where a good bass can bring back the wonder and make one's eyes smart. "For behold," he sings:

Darkness shall cover the earth,
and gross darkness the people;
But the Lord shall arise upon thee,
and his glory shall be seen upon thee.

It is said that Handel was deeply depressed when he set out to write *Messiah*. He wrote out of the depths. But it is also said that he found himself profoundly moved by the texts for which he reached so deeply into his soul to find music. In fact, there is a famous story of a servant finding Handel in tears after he had just finished the "Hallelujah" chorus. He heard the composer whisper, "I thought I saw all heaven before me, and the great God himself!"

For behold, darkness shall cover the earth,
But the kingdom of this world is become the
kingdom of our Lord and of his Christ;
and he shall reign for ever and ever!

What did his Christ do? Did he *arise* upon us? He did, and he still does. But in the mystery of his way with us, the Christ arises only after he descends upon us. The wonder of Advent is wonder at the humility of the only-begotten Son of God who lowered himself into our darkness to bring every lost one of us to light.

A Prayer or Hymn
O Holy Child of Bethlehem,
Descend to us we pray.
Cast out our sin and enter in;
Be born in us today. Amen.

—"O Little Town of Bethlehem"

62

Scripture
And John, calling to him two of his disciples, sent them to the Lord, saying, "Are you the one who is to come, or shall we look for another?"...And he answered..."Go and tell John what you have seen and heard: the blind receive their sight, the lame walk, lepers are cleansed, and the deaf hear, the dead are raised up, the poor have good news preached to them.
Luke 7:19, 22

Confession
Why is he called "Christ" meaning "anointed"?
Because he has been ordained by God the Father and has been anointed with the Holy Spirit to be our chief prophet and teacher who perfectly reveals to us the secret counsel and will of God for our deliverance.
**Heidelberg Catechism,
Q & A 31**

Some of our creeds and confessions are strangely silent about the life and ministry of Jesus. The Apostles' Creed, as E. A. Dowey remarks, locates the career of Jesus in the comma between "born of the virgin Mary" and "suffered under Pontius Pilate." The Nicene Creed does a similar thing. John Calvin's *Geneva Catechism* claims to find nothing of redemptive substance in the history of our Lord's life:

Minister: *Why do you go immediately from His birth to His death, passing over the whole history of His life?*

Child: Because nothing is said here about what belongs properly to the substance of our redemption.

Calvin must have been dozing at his desk! Our Lord's career has a great deal to do with the substance of our redemption.

What did the Son of God come to do? He came to leave us "an example" that we should "follow in his steps" (I Pet. 2:21). But more: "Christ Jesus came into the world to save sinners" (I Tim. 1:15). But more yet: he came to destroy the devil (Heb. 2:14) and to "disarm the principalities and powers" (Col. 2:15). But most

of all, most broadly and cosmically of all, God sent his Son to unite or reconcile all things to him (Eph. 1:10; Col. 1:20). That is, he sent Christ to restore a broken and rebellious universal *kingdom*.

In his earthly life Jesus announced and demonstrated God's rule over individual human lives, over whole nations, and even over all of *nature*. And in so doing God's Son did not drop onto an empty landscape or into a traditionless people. He was born as a particular Jew among Jews who had for centuries been looking for "the anointed one," the "expected one," the one whose coming would be accompanied by marvelous deeds in nature and human nature.

So John the Baptist sends out his earnest question from "a depth not of years but of centuries." Has the long, arid, troubled history of God's people come to that day when mercy and judgment would shake the world? "Are you the one who is to come?"

And the answer comes back, heavy with the evidence that the anointed one, the *Christ*, has come at last.

What did Jesus do? By proclamation, miracle, prayer, and parable, he ushered in the kingdom of God. And thus he began our redemption.

A Hymn
**Hark! the herald angels sing, "Glory to the newborn King;
Peace on earth, and mercy mild, God and sinners reconciled!"
Joyful, all ye nations, rise, join the triumph of the skies;
With th'angelic host proclaim, "Christ is born in Bethlehem!"
Hark! the herald angels sing, "Glory to the newborn King."
—"Hark! the Herald Angels Sing"**

Scripture
When the days drew near for him to be received up, he set his face to go to Jerusalem.   Luke 9:51

Confession
He has been ordained by God the Father and has been anointed with the Holy Spirit to be...our only high priest who has set us free by the one sacrifice of his body.   Heidelberg Catechism, Answer 31

63

Parents watch the faces of their children. Infants wear those counterfeit smiles which really indicate only indigestion. Later on the real ones appear, the ones which light up a tiny face and much of the room around it. Study an older child's face when she is sleeping. A contented, peaceful face, oblivious to your presence. A face which frowns as a cloud passes through the dreaming mind. The face of your child.

"There's no art to find the mind's construction in the face," said Shakespeare. Martin Luther is said to have claimed that a person's whole attitude toward God and humanity is written on his *face* and that, once past thirty, a person is therefore accountable for the way his face looks.

No doubt Luther exaggerated. But you *can* tell something about a person by looking at his face. Is the person sick? Look at that peaked face. Is she worried? Look at the frown and the tight set of the jaw. Is he old? African? Caucasian? Oriental? Ashamed? Delighted? A face tells so much that a skillful actress can produce the impact of a whole scene just by moving a few small muscles in her face.

Now look at the face of our Lord, set like flint to go to Jerusalem. Every line on that determined face tells us that he is on his way to die and that he knows it. Nobody will take his life from him. He will lay it down. But there is a coming pain and horror against which even the Son of God must grit his teeth. He will make some detours, chat with the disciples, and reach out with divine love to nameless rascals, but always that steadfast look will be on his face. All the vast, demonic forces are gathered and waiting up ahead. But all God's creation is waiting too—waiting for its redemption.

And so, when the days drew near for him to be received up, he set his face and he went to Jerusalem.

A Prayer
O Lord, we do not have enough depth in us to take in the meaning of your dark journey to the cross. Yet when we are humble, we feel some measure of your wondrous love which moved along the way of sorrows for a whole world's redemption. Amen.

Scripture
Pilate said to [the chief priests and the Pharisees], "You have a guard of soldiers; go, make it as secure as you can." So they went and made the sepulchre secure by sealing the stone and setting a guard.   Matthew 27:65, 66

Confession
By his resurrection he has overcome death, so that he might make us share in the righteousness he won for us by his death.
Heidelberg Catechism,
Answer 45

64

It is Saturday, the day between Good Friday and Easter, and the chief priests and Pharisees have not slept well. A particular thought has been nagging at them. What if Jesus' disciples take to grave robbing? What if they stage a "resurrection"? What if they recall the impostor's prediction that he would rise—and conspire to fulfill the prediction themselves? Off to Pilate they go to get a security order:

Order the sepulchre to be made secure until the third day, lest his disciples go and steal him away, and tell the people, "He has risen from the dead."   (Matt. 27:64)

Pilate's answer is rich with a half-humorous, half-hopeless irony. "Go," he says, "make it as secure as you can."

"As secure as you *can!*" In one of his vivid sermons, Frederick Buechner pictures the helpless, bewildered look on the faces of these religious leaders. "As secure as you can. *But how secure is that?*" Are they, perhaps, secretly afraid not of a grave robbery, but of something else? Are they afraid the limp body might start to breathe again, might stand up and begin to move toward them unspeakably?

"As secure as you can." So many schemes and forces of unbelief have tried to secure that tomb against any outbreak of the Son of God. It is a shameful thing to admit that even some theologians have tried, in their own academic way, to tighten security in the area of the resurrection. It is not Jesus' body, they say, but his teachings which have been raised up to become immortal—like the art of Rembrandt and the music of Mozart. Or perhaps his historical impact lives on. Or, maybe, his Spirit still broods over our world as Lincoln's spirit still broods over Gettysburg. Or perhaps some of us can use our seminary training to wax eloquent at Easter about the return of spring to a winter's earth, or the rebirth of hope in a despairing soul.

What the New Testament says is that Jesus arose. For all early Christian preaching and for all the centuries this *is* the gospel, the very core of the good news. On this bedrock fact, all Christian faith, hope, and love are founded. The Son of God has gotten loose in the world and no Pharisee and no theologian is safe.

Go ahead! Make that tomb as secure as you can!

See what happens.

A Hymn or Recitation
'Tis the spring of souls today;
Christ hath burst His prison,
And from three days' sleep in death
As a sun hath risen;
All the winter of our sins,
Long and dark, is flying
From His light, to whom we give
Laud and praise undying.
—"Come, Ye Faithful, Raise the Strain"

Scripture
"For as the rain and snow come down from heaven...so shall my word be that goes forth from my mouth; it shall not return to me empty, but it shall accomplish that which I purpose, and prosper in the thing for which I sent it." Isaiah 55:10,11

Confession
Christ, while his disciples watched, was lifted up from the earth into heaven and will be there for our good until he comes again to judge the living and the dead. Heidelberg Catechism, Answer 46

65

Preachers do not ordinarily welcome the approach of Ascension Day. What had been an overflow congregation on Easter will forty days later dwindle to a faithful few. People are not excited about the ascension. They find it anticlimactic. They regard it as a sort of afterthought.

A disturbing afterthought. People who are not indifferent to the ascension are uneasy with it. They have heard sermons which stretched pretty far for comparisons:

"Perhaps some of you have seen a news helicopter taking off from the top of a building...."

"A number of you kids know about Superman and the way he can fly."

"I want all of us to imagine a *reverse* parachute jump."

People visualize such things and mentally shrink back from the ascension. Is it not intolerable to think of our Lord ascending like, say, the rockets at Cape Kennedy, hurtling upwards through banks of clouds and finally becoming a speck in the sky?

And yet, however crude our imagery for what Luke quite simply attests (Acts 1:9), the event itself is of great significance. It ties us and the future of all creation to very tangible, visible reality.

Our Lord does not evaporate. He is resurrected and ascends with a *body*—a real body which casts shadows, makes sounds in the gravel, and eats fish, but which is also marvelously powerful and free. What we must see is that this is the body of the future, the firstfruits of a whole new nature, the first body of the new heavens and the new earth. Our Lord goes to "prepare a place" for us to inhabit one day with bodies like *his*.

Moreover the ascension tells us that Jesus' earthly work was rounded off in a definite conclusion. It is finished, his mission accomplished. The Word of God who had emptied himself to do his servant work now returns to the Father. He is no longer empty. He returns the possessor of a body and of a redeemed humanity.

"For as the rain and snow come down from heaven...so shall my word be that goes forth from my mouth; it shall not return to me empty, but it shall accomplish that which I purpose, and prosper in the thing for which I sent it."

A Hymn or Recitation
Rejoice, the Lord is King;
Your Lord and King adore;
Rejoice, give thanks, and sing,
And triumph evermore.
Lift up your heart, lift up your voice;
Rejoice! again I say, Rejoice! —"Rejoice, the Lord Is King"

Postscript

1. The four Gospels are versions of the good news according to four apostolic witnesses. Look at the beginnings of all four. What *category* are we in? Philosophy? Fantasy? History? Preaching? Psychology?

   Now look at articles II through VII of the Apostles' Creed. What category do we have here?

   In either case, how much does it matter?

2. The coming of Jesus Christ is accompanied by poetry and song. Luke 1 and 2 contain at least three of these songs—Mary's, Zechariah's, and Simeon's. Note the rich historical references in them.

   But now take a particular look at Mary's song—the Magnificat. Does Jesus the Christ come to comfort or to judge?

3. The quotations from the Heidelberg Catechism at the head of meditations 62, 63, and 65 reveal a famous Reformed way of describing the work of Jesus Christ. What is that way? Is it still helpful?

4. What is more important—who Christ is or what he did? Why?

Week Fourteen

What Is Jesus Doing?

Some Christians who "read that sweet story of old" about Jesus imagine what bliss it would be to "have been with him then." But was it always bliss to have been with him then? Certainly the Pharisees did not think so. Nor the rich young ruler. Nor even Peter. In any case, we are not with him then, but now.

How? How *now*? How in this "in-between time"—in between the coming of the kingdom and its final consummation—is Jesus Christ alive and active in the world? What is Jesus *doing*?

Scripture
"These men who have turned the world upside down have come here also...and they are all acting against the decrees of Caesar, saying that there is another king, Jesus." And the people and the city authorities were disturbed when they heard this.   Acts 17:6-8

Confession
In his human nature Christ is not now on earth; but in his divinity, majesty, grace, and Spirit he is not absent from us for a moment.
                Heidelberg Catechism,
                            Answer 47

66

The Christian church is boring even to some Christians. They hear lifeless, cliché-ridden, entirely predictable sermons. Their preachers are trained in safe, sleepy seminaries. Their congregations undertake only the most timid and socially conservative ministries. Their church councils argue endlessly over small matters. Their worship services are endurance contests. Their children have never witnessed an adult baptism. Nothing is going on! There is no life here! No action! No movement! Somehow their church has lost the distinction between being founded on the rock of ages and being stuck in the mud.

To go from this modern boredom to the first century church is to be culture shocked. Our ascended Lord continues his work by two means: his Spirit sent into the church and his church sent into the world. The disciples had been told to gather and "stay in the city" until they were "clothed with power." They did. And one day the place was shaken. On Pentecost Christ's body arose by the power of the Holy Spirit. The church began its movement through the world and across the centuries.

And look at it! The formerly timid disciples now speak with *boldness*. They are regularly beaten up and thrown into jail. Their mission has power, *dunamis*, dynamite! Modern Christians who yawn through their worship, who gird on their weapons to fight crabgrass on the church lawn—modern Christians who live at a tiddlywinks level of the faith can hardly understand why Christians should be seen as a threat! But the early Christians were. They were regarded quite literally as revolutionaries, as people who had "turned the world upside down."

Wherever we bow before "another king" than Caesar, wherever we are radically obedient to Jesus Christ—there he is at work. It is not safe work. If we oppose the nuclear arms race, smuggle Bibles, fight those who enslave the poor, challenge secularists on campus, practice civil disobedience rather than sin against God, picket porno theaters, insist both on a day's *work* for a day's pay and also a day's *pay* for a day's work, send brave and vital people out on unpopular missions—if we do these things we will face danger, risk, embarrassment, and trouble.

Incidentally, some Christians today *are* doing these things. They are not bored.

A Prayer or Hymn
Creator Spirit, by whose aid
The world's foundations first were laid,
Come, visit every pious mind;
Come, pour Thy joys on humankind;
From sin and sorrow set us free,
And make Thy temples worthy thee. Amen.
                —"Creator Spirit, By Whose Aid"

Scripture

So we are ambassadors for Christ, God making his appeal through us. We beseech you on behalf of Christ, be reconciled to God.   II Corinthians 5:20

Confession

To be reconciled to God is to be sent into the world as his reconciling community. This community, the church universal, is entrusted with God's message of reconciliation and shares his labor of healing the enmities which separate [people] from God and from each other....Wherever the church exists, its members are both gathered in corporate life and dispersed in society for the sake of mission in the world.

The Confession of 1967 II, A

67

One of the greatest of contemporary Christians was Martin Luther King. He was human. His theology left something to be desired. No doubt he had his sins. Perhaps in these respects he resembled us. But who can hear his "I Have a Dream!" speech without being powerfully stirred? There was *greatness* in Washington that day! Of course, as a practicing Christian, King spent some of his time in jail. But who can read his "Letter from a Birmingham Jail" without being permanently *convinced* of the simple, elemental justice of his cause?

Martin Luther King was a prophet of the kingdom of God. He was an ambassador of the good news that the dividing walls of hostility have been broken down in Jesus Christ and that, in him, we are one. To white racists he said, "We beseech you on behalf of Christ, be reconciled to God." To black brothers and sisters bowed down by ignorance and crippled

by poverty, he said, "In the name of Jesus Christ of Nazareth, stand up and *walk!*" King was a powerful man and, in word and deed, a great apostle of the kingdom.

Jesus Christ first gathers his church and then disperses it across the world. From his own day, through the time of the apostles to the present, his rhythm remains. So we gather to hear the good news proclaimed. Then we fan out to proclaim it *prophetically* for every area of human brokenness, oppression, and sin. Christ the prophet is seeking to make his appeal through us. The New Testament verbs are all so insistent: "Go! Tell! Witness! Declare! Proclaim!"

And we, like some arctic river, are so often frozen at the mouth. "I fear the silence of the churches," said King, "more than the shouts of the angry multitudes."

Could it be that we shall one day have to face those who were ruined by our silence?

A Prayer

O Lord our God, we confess the cowardice which has so often let us stand quiet in the face of evil. Fill us with your Holy Spirit so that we may be bold in declaring your justice, your righteousness, and your peace in all the reaches and dimensions of our lives on earth. Through Jesus Christ, who is still the Lord, Amen.

Scripture
You are a...royal priesthood....
For to this you have been called,
because Christ also suffered for
you, leaving you an example, that
you should follow in his steps.
I Peter 2:9, 21

Confession
[Christ] continually pleads our
cause with the Father....God
tells us to love our neighbor as
ourselves...to protect him from
harm as much as we can, and to
do good even to our enemies.
Heidelberg Catechism,
Answers 31,107

68

Søren Kierkegaard, the Danish theologian, once published a work called *Attack Upon Christendom*, a stinging rebuke of the state church of Denmark for its lack of seriousness, for its degeneration into a smug social club. Kierkegaard complained particularly about the fact that Christianity in Denmark was smooth, bland, and effortless, while the Christianity of the Bible faced poverty, peril, and sword. When one sees a Christian's life in Denmark, said Kierkegaard, how could one ever think that Jesus Christ had said, "If anyone wants to come after me, let him deny himself, take up his cross, and follow me"? The ultimate outrage, he concluded, is to see fleshy, comfortable clergymen rising through the ranks to softer and more luxurious positions, finally to stand beaming as they are decorated with the cross. The *cross!*

Jesus Christ the priest carried his own altar through the streets of Jerusalem and on toward the hill. Finally he mounted that altar-cross and offered himself as a terrible sacrifice for all our sin.

He still serves the gathered church. The Christ who interceded with a high-priestly prayer for his disciples prays for us still, representing us before God in the manner of a priest. And every time we gather at his table, he nourishes and serves us with his broken body and shed blood.

But the prayer and nourishment he offers are meant to make *us* searching, active, compassionate priests. The church dispersed is "a royal priesthood" to represent all Christians before God and to pray deeply and keenly for unbelievers that God may have his way with them, that God may forgive them "for they know not what they do."

The church is to bear the cross the world deserves, sharing in Christ's sufferings. We are to move as self-sacrificing *priests* among those who are poor, hurt, diminished, and afraid. We are to identify with them, cast our lot with them, get involved with them, suffer with them.

Only so can we hold up their needs to God.

A Prayer
O Lord God, we confess that we have tried to lighten the cross of its awful freight. We have sought to place our crosses in comfortable places. Now teach us to be priests to one another as your Son is to us still. And make us priests to those whom no one cares to represent. Through Jesus Christ our Lord, Amen.

Scripture
He said, "I have been very jealous for the Lord . . . for the people of Israel have forsaken the covenant, thrown down thy altars, and slain thy prophets with the sword; and I, even I only, am left."   I Kings 19:14

Confession
[The] holy Church is preserved or supported by God against the rage of the whole world; though it sometimes for a while appears very small.   Belgic Confession, Article XXVII

69

Even kids know what an *epitaph* is. It's the bit of writing you find on tombstones. Some epitaphs are sad. Many are thoughtful. A few are disgruntled. Consider this one: "I *told* you I was sick!" Or this one: "Here lies John Alfred Crane. My surgeon was Dr. Anthony Wendell."

For centuries unbelievers have been ready to write the *church's* epitaph. On some monument, perhaps at Rome, the world would write: "Outdated!" "Irrelevant!" "Outclassed!" "Finished."

Oddly enough, even some believers have been ready at times to write the church's death sentence. Here is Elijah, in our text, feeling lonesome and sorry for himself. He is whining about the decline of the church. He wishes to point out that he has worked himself to the bone for the Lord, but everybody else has been tearing down what he has built. He tried to lead, but nobody would follow. All the old breed is gone: "I, even I only, am left." Everybody in the parade is out of step but me.

It is worth noting, as one modern preacher has it, that God gives Elijah not a pat on the head but a vigorous nudge. There is no soothing word from the management. There is a work order: go, anoint two kings and one prophet to serve in your place.

In your place. The torch is handed on. Every generation our Lord renews his church with fresh prophets, priests, and kings. And every Sunday Jesus Christ arises in his body and moves out into the world.

So often the resurrection of the church comes by way of the command to get busy. Don't sit there feeling sorry for yourself and hankering for the good old days. Get to work! Preach the gospel! Give your money away! Raise up a nursing home and two mental hospitals! Start a mission! Apply some pressure against political tyranny! Teach some children the truth!

In so many ways a renewed church can renew the world around it. Meanwhile, perhaps we shall uncover at least seven thousand who never *did* bow the knee to Baal.

A Hymn or Recitation
The Church's one foundation is Jesus Christ, her Lord;
She is His new creation by water and the Word;
From heaven He came and sought her to be His holy bride;
With His own blood He bought her, and for her life He died.
          —"The Church's One Foundation"

Scripture
He is before all things, and in him all things hold together. He is the head of the body, the church; he is the beginning, the firstborn from the dead, that in everything he might be pre-eminent.   Colossians 1:17,18

Confession
Christ ascended to heaven, there to show that he is head of his church, and that the Father rules all things through him.
Heidelberg Catechism,
Answer 50

70

Reformed churches regard church discipline as one of the "marks of the true church." Time was when discipline was both regularly practiced and considerably feared. That time seems to have passed. In many cases nowadays, as Robert Hudnut says, "the standards of a boy scout troup are higher than those of the Christian church." But it is also true that some churches have recently *tightened* their discipline in certain areas. For example, some churches which used to be lax about the sin of racism now regard it as an offense which should start the engines of discipline.

Jesus Christ the King is Lord of his gathered church. He governs us by his Word and Spirit. And he disciplines us further by having us hold each other *accountable*. Then he sends the dispersed church out to discipline the society in which it lives—to guide it, to teach it, to apply pressure to it, to hold it accountable.

"Fundamentalists" favor some social disciplines over others: tougher liquor laws, for instance, and Sunday closing legislation. "Liberals" have another agenda: an Equal Rights Amendment, for example, and handgun control. In any event, the church is attempting to take what it regards as the will of God, or the mind of Christ, and reach with it into the world around.

But isn't Jesus Christ the Lord even beyond the reach of the church? Aren't there times when he "sets at liberty those who are oppressed"—even when the church is nowhere in the vicinity?

Yes. Christians sometimes think that any movement which begins "in the world" must therefore be "of the devil." But that is not so. Christ's lordship is mysteriously at work even where his church is not. "The Father rules *all things* through him." Wherever justice is done, wherever age-old enemies beat their swords into plowshares and their spears into pruning hooks, wherever the hungry are "filled with good things"—wherever genuine good, however modest, is done in this sinful world—it is done because of the common grace of God and the secret work of Christ.

So the church needs the gift of *discernment*. Some worldly movements, judged by God's Word, are clearly immoral. We fight those. But in other movements we will discern a strangely familiar quality of rightness. Then we must not fight the movement but get with it and claim it for Christ the Lord.

A Prayer
God our Father, give us the ability to test the spirits and to tell where your Christ is at work and where he is not. Always govern us by your Word and Spirit so that we may honor Christ as Lord in every dimension of our lives. In his name, Amen.

Postscript

1. Meditation 66 suggests the possibility that the Christian church is boring even to some believers, that we weekly perform a miracle of turning wine into water. Is that so? If so, is there any *general* solution? Explain.

2. The meditations this week talk about "the church" performing prophetic, priestly, and kingly work. What do we mean by "the church"? Does the *institutional* church do all this?

3. This week we have seen that the church is both gathered and dispersed for its mission in the world. Is this a biblical rhythm? Where should the accent fall—on gathering or on dispersing?

4. Several of the meditations this week mention a number of exciting and varied missions of the church. How can any of us *do* all these things?

5. Jesus Christ gathers and disperses his people. In dispersion we do at least three kinds of mission: prophetic ("getting the message out"), priestly (sacrificing ourselves for the needy and identifying with them so as to hold up their needs to God), and kingly (disciplining or influencing the society to which we minister). Which of these three callings is most important?

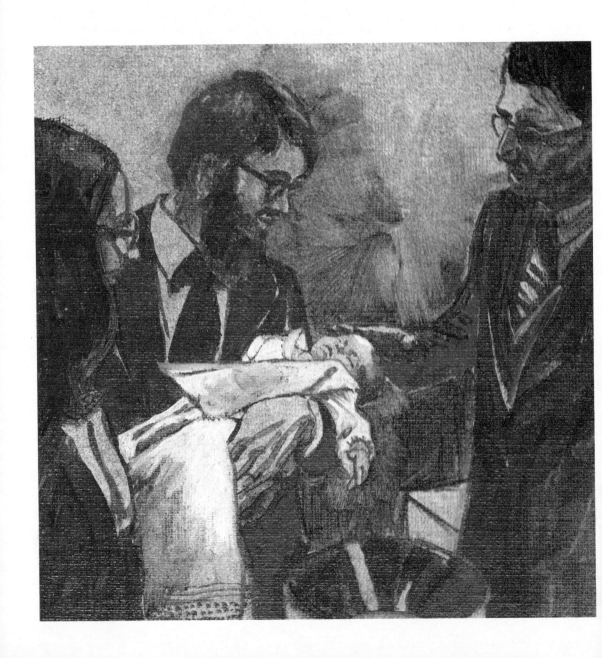

Week Fifteen

But Why Are You Called a Christian?

One of the striking features of the Heidelberg Catechism is the way it keeps relentlessly applying the gospel to our lives. In dealing with the Son of God—as we, too, have been doing in this unit—the Catechism asks why the Son of God is called *Savior* and why he is called *Christ*. Then, turning to look us square in the face, it asks famously, But why are *you* called a Christian?

That is what we are asking this week. In several cases the meditations will try to raise that question as sharply as possible—but without answering it. This course is meant to be a *discussion* course, and if the daily readings should whet one's appetite for a lively discussion session, we will have reached a significant part of our goal.

Scripture

He anointed us, set his seal
of ownership on us, and put
his Spirit in our hearts as a
deposit, guaranteeing what is
to come.

II Corinthians 1:21, 22 (NIV)

Confession

But why are you called a Christian?

Because by faith I am a member
of Christ and so I share in his
anointing.

Heidelberg Catechism,
Q & A 32

71

If modern Reformed Christians had to list the four or five most exciting biblical ideas—the ones most relevant to living as Christ's followers in today's world—they would probably overlook the idea of *anointing*. Somehow anointing has lost much of its zest and appeal.

Ancient people did a good deal of anointing. Much of it was highly religious and ceremonial. But some of it was very practical. For instance, a person who lived in a hot and dusty area would anoint himself with olive oil to keep his skin from drying out. Thus, the psalmist who thanks God for bread to strengthen his heart, and wine to gladden it, does not forget to add his gratitude for "oil to make [one's] face shine" (Ps. 104:15).

Nowadays we do not go in for shiny faces so much. Nor oily hair. With us the wet look is out and the dry look is in. The only anointing of our head with oil still current is perhaps the kind which happens by accident—as when a garage mechanic stands absent-mindedly under an auto crankcase while removing the drain plug.

And yet we *can* recover some of the force of our Scripture and Confession for today. Prophets, priests, and kings in the Old Testament were *anointed*; that is, they had oil poured over them as a sign that God had distinguished, or consecrated, them to do a certain work. In the fullness of time, the Messiah—the anointed one—was sent to perfect and finish the work of all three officers. Jesus Christ was anointed not with oil, but with water and the Holy Spirit. He was baptized.

And so are we. In baptism God claims us, marks us, "sets his seal of ownership upon us." When children are baptized, they are marked quite literally as little Christs, little "anointed ones." In the church the grace of God flows so freely as to anoint not only the head, but also the whole body—not only *the* Christ, but also the little Christs, the Christians.

A Prayer

O Lord our heavenly Father, we confess that we are not our own, but belong to you and to your Christ. Empower us to bear Christ's name, live his sort of life, do that part of his work which you assign to the members of his body. Let us do credit to our name as Christians. Amen.

But Why Are You Called a Christian?

Scripture
There our captors required of us songs, and our tormentors, mirth, saying, "Sing us one of the songs of Zion!" How shall we sing the Lord's song in a foreign land?   **Psalm 137:3, 4**

Confession
But why are you called a Christian?
Because...I am anointed to confess his name.
                    Heidelberg Catechism,
                    Q & A 32

72

Someone has found a haunting modern parallel to the heartbroken question which comes at us from this famous Psalm. The story originally comes from a novel about the years which brought us into World War II.

In this story Nazi storm troopers bring an elderly Jewish rabbi to their headquarters and begin to amuse themselves with him. While two of the troopers over in the far end of the room slowly beat another Jew to death, the rabbi is stripped and ordered to preach the sermon he *would* have preached the next day if the Nazis had not destroyed his synagogue. He asks permission to wear his skullcap. His captors consent. After all, it adds another comic touch. So there he stands naked, delivering his sermon on doing justice, loving kindness, and walking humbly with our God—while the troopers grin and curse and hoot. Through it all, across the room the sound of clubs smashing into flesh and snapping bones goes on and on until it muffles itself in the silence of death.

"How shall we sing the Lord's song in a foreign land?" Apparently, for the exhausted people of God camped in Babylon, the answer to that question was silence. They did not sing.

The question arises among us still. And we may not answer with silence. The New Testament is insistent and uncompromising about our obligation to confess Christ's name and to tell the good news. We are from our roots a prophetic people. We may not keep the bread of life in a cupboard. Any song we have heard must be sung for others. The gospel gift must be regiven by stewards of the giver. Let us say it straight out: if we do not confess Christ's name, we are not Christians.

But how do we do it? How do we do it in a land where secularism is the opiate of the people? How in a society where "puritan" is the magic curse word for all that is not greedy, crude, and lewd? "Jesus Christ" is the only name given under heaven by which we—and others—must be saved. Over the years we learn how to sing or say that name to each other.

But how do we sing the Lord's song in a *foreign* land?

A Hymn or Prayer
Lord, speak to me, that I may speak
In living echoes of Thy tone;
As Thou hast sought, so let me seek
Thine erring children lost and lone. Amen.
                    —"Lord, Speak to Me, That I May Speak"

Scripture
"If any man would come after me, let him deny himself and take up his cross and follow me. For whoever would save his life will lose it, and whoever loses his life for my sake will find it."
Matthew 16:24, 25

Confession
But why are you called a Christian?
Because...I am anointed...to present myself to him as a living sacrifice of thanks.
Heidelberg Catechism,
Q & A 32

73

Self-sacrifice has recently lost ground. A bored and affluent culture has been producing books with such titles as *Winning Through Intimidation* and *Looking Out For #1*. The books sell. The author of these particular delights, one Robert Ringer, preaches a gospel of one-upmanship and of "getting yours." Ringer admits he was a "total turkey" till he discovered shaft-thy-neighbor ethics. Now he claims to have discovered the wave of the future. No more concern for neighbor! No more altruism! No more looking out for others! Why not? Because then "you'll be hurting your chances for getting your share of life's goodies."

Selfishness is as old as the fall. But it has not always been admired. People used to be ashamed of it. But recently selfishness has been packaged, promoted, and *sold* to consciousness junkies who like to sit by themselves and stew in their own juices. In the last days, "men will be lovers of self...rather than lovers of God" (II Tim. 3:2, 4). Even in religion in these last days, the most popular churches seem to be the ones which talk least about self-denial, self-sacrifice, and the cost of discipleship, and which talk most about the religious payoff. If the Christian faith cannot make us healthy, wealthy, and wise, what good is it?

Jesus talks a different language and preaches another gospel. He talks about "counting the cost," about taking on his yoke, about self-denial, about losing our lives for his sake.

What does that mean? Shall we forfeit all our human rights and ignore all our own interests? Shall we become dumb sheep, waiting to be fleeced? Shall we cultivate a shabby self-image and learn to loathe ourselves? Shall we present ourselves to others as living doormats?

Not necessarily. Humility and great strength can go together. Insistence on one's own rights and love for one's neighbor can coexist. Self-sacrifice and self-assertion can dwell together. Self-denial and self-acceptance can join hands. Even losing one's life can be the road to finding it again.

How? "Whoever loses his life *for my sake* shall find it." "For my sake." There is the key. How does it fit into our lives?

A Prayer
Make us your priests, O Lord, seeking and praying for others, offering ourselves to you as a living sacrifice of thanks. Through Jesus Christ, our priest, Amen.

Scripture
You were called to freedom, brethren; only do not use your freedom as an opportunity for the flesh. Galatians 5:13

Confession
But why are you called a Christian?
Because...I am anointed...to strive with a good conscience against sin and the devil in this life. Heidelberg Catechism, Q & A 32

74

Religious cultures change. A generation ago conservative Reformed people ruled *in* certain practices and ruled *out* certain others. All three meals began with prayer and concluded with Bible reading and prayer. Long prayers. Long Bible readings. Also ruled in was attendance at two Sunday church services. Like it or not, you were there twice.

Smoking was not prohibited. Church council rooms were blue with smoke. But many other amusements were ruled out. There was no dancing; no card playing (except "Old Maid"); no movies; in some houses, no TV. On Sunday, work was ruled out--except for the woman of the house. For her, what with big dinners and company gatherings, work was definitely ruled in. For kids, nearly everything was ruled out. On Sunday morning the minister would say, "This is the day which the Lord hath made; let us rejoice and be glad in it," and all the kids would groan inwardly. Oh *no! Sunday* again! For kids, no swimming, no bike riding, no ball playing. You could go for a walk, but not break into a jog. You could take a nap. You could read the church paper.

Young people released from this environment to attend college or war sometimes acted as if they had just broken out of jail. They were free! Sometimes they were wild.

The new generation of this same culture has changed the rules. In some homes, Bible reading at meals happens *at most* once a day. Prayers are short and—because children often do them—sweet. Attendance at the second church service is given up in favor of popcorn and "The Wonderful World of Disney" at home. In some families, a bright spring or summer weekend might include no church attendance at all. Smoking is on the way out, but cocktail parties are on the way in. Movies—even raunchy ones—are in; bridge-playing is in; television is so far in that children sing TV advertising jingles before they learn any hymns.

"I am anointed to strive with a free conscience against sin and the devil in this life." It sometimes seems that one generation does most of the striving and the next generation inherits the free conscience.

Is there any way of getting these things together?

A Prayer
O Lord our God, you have called us in your mercy to be free people, and we have sometimes used our freedom merely to indulge ourselves. Shape our liberty into glad *obedience.* Mold our lives into strong and flexible tools to be used in your service. Through Jesus Christ, our Lord, Amen.

Scripture
"[Thou] hast made them a kingdom...and they shall reign on
earth."   Revelation 5:10

Confession
*But why are you called a Chris-
tian?*
Because...I am anointed...
afterward to reign with Christ
over all creation for all eternity.
                    Heidelberg Catechism,
                    Q & A 32

75

One of the things which strikes you about a great concert artist is that she is never *completely* satisfied with her performance. You may have heard the artist perform a masterwork with power, grace, and precision. Perfection itself. But the artist is not likely to agree. And she is not merely adopting an "Aw, shucks!" attitude. She really thinks she could have done better. She really thinks her best work only approaches the musical ideal.

You find the same sort of humility in science. The truly distinguished scientists are the humblest ones. They are deeply impressed with what a marvel this world is and how little we actually understand and control it. One scientist recently wrote a book in which he wonders at all the fuss over test-tube babies. After all, we have merely changed incubators. The real marvel, he says, is the joining of sperm and egg itself, and the cell which emerges—a cell which can grow into a human brain.

The mere existence of that cell should be one of the greatest astonishments of the earth. People ought to be walking around all day, all through their waking hours, calling to each other in endless wonderment, talking of nothing except that cell.

(Lewis Thomas, *The Medusa and the Snail*)

They would be talking about *creation*, about a wonder created out of the infinite resources of the mind of God. Creation and our dominion over it have been spoiled and limited by the fall. In many ways we are now powerless against the strength of flood waters, the suddenness of sharp winds, the cancerous multiplying of body cells. With all the skill and intelligence God has given us, there are still many times when all we can do is to wonder—either in awe, or fear, or both. Even in our own acts of creation, even in the cultural creation of arts, commerce, government, and education, our gifts are limited and our plans frustrated by sin. So often we are nature's victims and culture's captives.

But the whole Bible is whispering to us that one day we shall be kings over creation and creation's culture. Paradise lost shall be regained. In the final age we shall reign with Christ.

Not in the clouds. On earth. And not just for a thousand years. Forever.

A Prayer
Give us, O Lord, the steady vision of the coming kingdom
which lets us work with all our might, and then rest, knowing
that none of our labor is in vain. Through Jesus Christ, the
King, Amen.

Postscript

1. Meditation 72 raises an ancient question: "How shall we sing the Lord's song in a foreign land?" What do you think our *personal* strategy should be for witnessing? May we buttonhole strangers and ask them if they are saved? Should we all have Christian bumper stickers? Would it be a good idea to recite the Apostles' Creed at work from time to time? What do you think?

2. Meditation 73 claims that a person can be loving, self-sacrificing, and self-denying, and at the same time assertive and self-accepting. How is this possible? Did you ever meet anyone who was both self-sacrificing and also very firm and assertive?

3. Meditation 74 gives a number of examples of how rules change from one generation to another and suggests that one generation may strive and the next inherit a free conscience. Is that true in your experience? If so, give some examples.

Week Sixteen

How Are We Saved?

We have been asking about Christ our Savior. We move on now to ask our questions about his *salvation.* Salvation, or deliverance, or reconciliation, is a broad and dynamic program of God the Father to reconcile all things to himself in Jesus Christ. We must never lose the height and depth, the length and breadth, of that universal perspective.

But neither may we lose the meaning of salvation as it comes to a focus in our own lives. For the next eight weeks, let us explore some of the dimensions of our salvation, including *continuing* salvation—that is, sanctification. Let us begin by asking how salvation comes to our house. How are we saved?

Scripture

"I have uttered what I did not understand.... I had heard of thee by the hearing of the ear, but now my eye sees thee."

Job 42:3, 5

Confession

I baptize you into the name of the Father and of the Son and of the Holy Spirit.

Form for the Baptism of Children

I now welcome you to all the privileges of full communion.

Form for Public Profession of Faith

76

A prize-winning film deals with the Vietnam War. It is not an easy film for a Christian to see, but it portrays a powerful truth. The film and the truth have to do with *Coming Home*. Vietnam was the first televised war. For people who sat in their family rooms watching thatched villages being blown against the treetops, this war came home like no other. And, with an unspeakable hurt and sense of futility, for those who lost loved ones the war came home in coffins and body bags. Even years later that war and its misery still come home every time we see a cousin, friend, or brother whose life is still deeply disturbed by the experience of Vietnam.

Things which were once remote or abstract have a way of coming home to us. Not only bad things—war, divorce, alcoholism, the energy crisis—but also such good things as a parent's kindness in one's youth, the charm and preciousness of one's children, the serene gracefulness of a strain of music you had heard a hundred times but which just now has come alive for you.

One of God's ingenious ways of saving his children is having them born and raised in a Christian covenant community. From early on, by word and example, a child is exposed to the truth. A child who is embraced in this living body cannot help being marked with the fingerprints of Christ. Over and over the child hears with the hearing of his ears that life *centers* on the Christ, his community, and on the reach of that community to those who may be powerless, faithless, or alone. Even when he does not say so, the child is deeply influenced.

And one day a child who had been carried in for baptism years before walks in and stands up before God's people to make an astonishing confession. To the Lord of whom he has heard so much for so many years, the child now says: "I had heard of thee by the hearing of the ear, but now my eye *sees* thee. O Lord, you have *come home* to me."

And the Lord says, "My child, so have you."

A Prayer

O Lord, for our own children and for children of the Christian community we pray. Help us to receive them in love, to care for their instruction in the faith, to encourage and sustain them in the fellowship of believers. And for all who have not yet come home, we ask your mercy. Now reach for them strongly with an outstretched arm and bring them back for their own sake, and for the sake of Christ who wishes to gather us all in. Amen.

Scripture
Out of the depths I cry to thee, O
Lord! Lord, hear my voice!
Psalm 130:1,2

Confession
This is that regeneration so
highly extolled in Scripture, that
renewal, new creation, resurrection from the dead.
Canons of Dort III-IV,
Article 12

77

There is a Christian hymn which practically everybody knows. It became a popular hit in the seventies when the folksinger Judy Collins recorded it. The hymn is "Amazing Grace," and whenever it is scheduled in church, it is sung with volume and verve.

Except one line. Or, perhaps, except one word. Can you think which one? Preachers sometimes remark that the volume and clarity of the singing suddenly drop on the second line when people get to the word "wretch." People seem to cover the word and flatten it out to something like "wresh."

Amazing grace! How sweet the sound,
That saved a...(wresh) like me!

Even Calvinist people seem to shrink from that word! A *wretch*? Me? With this two-hundred-fifty-dollar suit and Florida tan? *Wretch-ed?* Why, a wretch is one of those pitiful creatures who whines on street corners in the slums or who stares out at you from one of those photos of leper work in Calcutta. Maybe I'm a mite jaded. Worried, maybe. Bored. Hung over from time to time. A wresh, perhaps. But a *wretch?* Come now, we are all being far too modest!

And yet for every saved person there must be a time when we confess that, except for Christ, we are fallen and wretched creatures. The gospel fastens itself to our *guilt* and to our *need*. There is no gospel and no fastening when we are leaning back comfortably with our thumbs hooked in our vests. Rather, our Lord speaks peace to hagridden lives, brings uplift to depressed people, offers mercy for those guilty sinners who have spilled shame all over themselves, fills gray and meaningless lives with the sound of the trumpet, and brings love, fellowship, and laughter when our loneliness is spread out like a desert. In his hand are the depths of the earth.

Out of the depths I cry to thee, O Lord! Lord, hear my voice!...
If thou, O Lord, shouldst mark iniquities, Lord, who could stand?

A Hymn or Recitation
Amazing grace! how sweet the sound,
That saved a wretch like me!
I once was lost, but now am found,
Was blind, but now I see.
—"Amazing Grace! How Sweet the Sound"

Scripture
And he arose and came to his father. But while he was yet at a distance, his father saw him and had compassion, and ran and embraced him and kissed him.
Luke 15:20

Confession
In this the love of God was manifested, that He *sent his only begotten Son into the world, that whosoever be-lieveth on him should not perish, but have eternal life.*
Canons of Dort I, Article 2

78

Our Lord's parable of the prodigal son brings together into one inexpressibly rich story nearly all the themes of the gospel. You can read this parable as the story of smug Pharisees and guilty publicans. You can read it as the story of a lost son who is found, or as the story of hunger and soul-food feasting, of poverty and riches, of los-ing one's life to find it, of sin and repentance. You could even read it with an eye to the *clothing* with which God so often and so grace-fully covers our guilt and nakedness. This tat-tered and shameful son, like a legal defendant who enjoys a "cloak of innocence," is immed-iately covered with his father's goodness: "Bring quickly the best robe and put it on him!"

In its heart, this is a parable of amazing grace—of our Father's free, lavish, uncalculating love for us while we are "yet at a distance." Salvation, as the Reformation shouted down the centuries, is by grace alone.

There is a modern story which, in one ver-sion or another, makes this same point. A cer-tain man was traveling by train through the hill country of West Virginia. He noticed that the man next to him looked tense and ill at ease.

So he asked him if anything was wrong. The second man then explained that he was an ex-convict. He had spent the last ten years in a penitentiary and was now on his way home. Neither he nor his family could write very well and there had been little communication be-tween them. He knew he had brought disgrace on his family. But a week before, he had gotten someone to write a letter to them. In the letter he said he could understand if they did not want him back. But if they *did*, if they *should* have it in their hearts to forgive him, they should tie a white ribbon around a branch of the last apple tree in the orchard, a tree he could see from the train. If he saw no ribbon, he would travel on to the next town, and they would not have to deal with him again.

Now, as the train drew nearer and nearer, the ex-convict became more and more nervous. So the first man volunteered to watch for him. As the train rounded the last curve, the ex-convict asked in a small voice, "Is it there?" And his companion suddenly shouted: "Look! There are *hundreds* of them! That whole tree is *blazing* with ribbons!"

A Prayer
Keep us, O God, for in thee we have found refuge. In thy presence is fullness of joy; in thy right hand pleasures for evermore. Amen.

Note: The story above is paraphrased from William Sloan Coffin's version of it in "On Winning Defeats," a sermon in the Riverside Church, New York, October 1, 1978.

Scripture
Judah said, "The strength of the burden-bearers is failing, and there is much rubbish; we are not able to work on the wall."...And I said... "In the place where you hear the sound of the trumpet, rally to us there. Our God will fight for us."
Nehemiah 4:10,19,20

Confession
Much less cause to be terrified by the doctrine of reprobation have they who, though they seriously desire to be turned to God...cannot yet reach that measure of... faith to which they aspire; since a merciful God has promised that He will not quench the smoking flax, nor break the bruised reed.
Canons of Dort I, Article 16

79

Someone has made up a wonderful story which extends both to heaven and hell. Sometime after Lucifer and his angels were exiled from heaven, the archangel Michael met Lucifer roaming around in outer space. Because of their old comradeship, they fell to talking. Michael asked what was the worst part of living in hell. And Lucifer, with a wistfulness beyond telling, said, "I miss the sound of the trumpets in the morning."

All the gospel sounds its triumphant note that Jesus Christ has come with God's saving grace for sinners, that God loves us in our weakness and wants us to come home. The business of the kingdom begins each day with this trumpet call. *Faith* is the instrument with which we are to answer that call.

And yet there are Christians who for a time cannot hear the call and cannot raise any faith to answer it. Their lives find little to praise and little relief from a daily grayness and hopelessness. Some feel guilty beyond all forgiveness; some live with an anxiety which has them by the throat; some think their lives are slipping into failure. With a growing despair they have come to the conclusion that they are not *making* it! They feel abandoned by God.

"The strength of the burden-bearers is failing...."

Someone needs to speak a stout comfort to these people. Someone with strength, tenderness, and glistening eyes needs to tell these people that God loves them and that Jesus Christ suffered for them. Someone with all the terrible gladness of heaven must point them to that place in their lives where the trumpet is sounding through their predawn blackness and a strong arm is reaching out to lift them up. Someone with a faith *beyond doubt*.

Someone like Nehemiah: "In the place where you hear the sound of the trumpet, rally to us there. Our God will *fight* for us."

A Prayer
Almighty God, in your great mercy embrace any of your children who feel unlovely and unloved. Steady their wobbling faith. Arrest every slippage toward the darkness. In all your goodness, strength, and tenderness make yourself unmistakable to those who are soiled, weak, and bruised. Through Jesus Christ, our Lord, Amen.

Scripture

He also told this parable to some who trusted in themselves that they were righteous...: "Two men went up into the temple to pray...."   Luke 18:9,10

Confession

Could some believers become lazy in their observance of the commands of God or sinfully complacent? This is...likely to happen to those who, though rashly presuming to have the grace of election, or idly and boldly chattering about it, refuse to walk in the ways of the elect.
Canons of Dort I, Article 13

80

In one of his probing sermons Douglas Nelson points to the picture of guilt Shakespeare draws in the last act of *Macbeth*. Lady Macbeth, the icy, viciously effective woman who had nagged her spouse into becoming a wholesale murderer, now walks the corridors of the castle at night, sound asleep but never at rest. Her dreams keep taking her back to the night the two of them slaughtered the saintly old King Duncan. Now, in her sleep, she keeps scrubbing at the red spots on her fingers, the blood that will not go away. Over and over she mutters, "Who would have thought the old man had so much blood in him?"

Lady Macbeth is not suffering from a failure of human relational adjustment dynamics. She is suffering the effects of *sin*. Her problem is not a guilt-neurosis. She is *guilty*.

Lady Macbeth and her guilt, Martin Luther and his agony of conscience, our own ancestors and their religious fear of the Lord's table—all these are almost incomprehensible to a certain sort of modern Christian. For some of us, at least at some times in our lives, our problem with faith is just the opposite of the one we saw in meditation 79. We do not despair of salvation; we presume it. We do not worry too much; we worry too little. We do not say, "I'm not *making* it!" We say, or at least we feel, that we've made it. We're in. God's business is to forgive? Well and good. Let him be about his business. And let the *neurotics* lose sleep over their sins.

For people with power, money, intellect, or health this sort of blasphemous "carnal security" can be a deadly trap. The New Testament has a dark strain in it about those who trust in themselves that they are righteous. The danger is that one day the door of their trap will spring shut with heaven's coldest words: "I never knew you."

Faith is the gift with which we grasp God's grace. His *grace*! Grace is not God's applause for the comfortable. Grace is God's undeserved favor for such sinners as we all are.

A Prayer
O Lord God, comfort the afflicted and afflict the comfortable among us. Teach our hearts to fear—and then our fears relieve, through Jesus Christ our Lord. Amen.

Postscript

1. A deeply devout and highly Reformed mother of four children was telling some of her relatives about her anguish over her children's unbelief. One of the relatives, seeking to comfort her, said: "Yes, but remember that they are in the *covenant!*" The woman replied: "I'm not very fond of that covenant idea anymore. All four of my kids were raised in it, and not one of them believes a thing."

   What do you say to that?

2. Do you have to have a "conversion experience" to be saved?

   Do you have to be able to name the "*hour* I first believed"? Explain.

3. Salvation, according to Ephesians 2:8-10, is "by grace and through faith." *By* the one and *through* the other. What difference is suggested by the choice of those two prepositions? Is it important?

4. Meditations 79 and 80 discuss equal and opposite dangers to faith: the temptations to despair and to presumption.

   Which of the two dangers is greater today? Are people agonizing over assurance of salvation, so that one needs to "speak comfortably to Jerusalem"? Or are they simply presuming it, so that one needs to speak sharply to those who are "at ease in Zion"?

Week Seventeen

What Do We Expect From Salvation?

Some people expect very little from salvation. And they get it. They expect God's salvation to cure a few of their bad habits and to help them live more decently. They expect to be able to believe the right doctrines without raising any question about them. And they expect God to be night watchman over their possessions till they die and go to heaven.

Others seem to expect too much—or, at any rate, too much too early. These are people who expect sinlessness, or the wealth of heaven, or rest from their labors, or unceasing ecstasy. They want glory *now.*

What do we expect from salvation? Hidden in that question is another: What *should* we expect?

Scripture

A man lame from birth...fixed his attention upon them, expecting to receive something from them. But Peter said, "I have no silver and gold, but I give you what I have; in the name of Jesus Christ of Nazareth, walk."
Acts 3:2, 5, 6

Confession

In his grace God grants me the righteousness of Christ to free me forever from judgment.
Heidelberg Catechism,
Answer 56

81

Charles Dickens wrote a novel about a young man with *Great Expectations.* He expected money. He ended up with happiness instead.

In our text Peter and John face a similar man at the temple. Like a veteran bellhop or waiter, the man has doubtless become an expert at sizing people up. This one will give a dollar. That one is good for more. This one will be good for nothing.

The lame man "fixed his attention upon them, expecting to receive something from them."

Well, you know the famous response with its wonderful irony. "I have no silver or gold, but I give you what I have." The man's heart must have sunk like a stone. He was going to be handed a tract instead of a meal. He had heard it all before: "I don't want to part with any of my money—but God bless you."

What actually happened is that the man received a gift far greater than he asked. He expected money. He got a miracle.

That miracle is still needed. God's salvation promises divine forgiveness and acceptance. It promises us a new standing, a new *status*, with God. Somehow people keep expecting things like money or power instead. Somehow they keep expecting *worldly* status. In fact some preachers and some Christian advertisements inflame that expectation.

It is a grave mistake. Salvation does not promise us material wealth—at least not for now. And it is a good thing. For when people fix on wealth as their main comfort, their attention wanders away from Jesus Christ. It also seems to wander away from society's cripples.

It is said that the Pope stood one day with Erasmus outside the gates of the Vatican. A long line of horse-drawn carts creaked heavily past them, loaded with the annual income of the church. A regiment of soldiers with drawn swords and cocked crossbows guarded this parade of treasures. The pope turned to Erasmus and said with satisfaction, "No longer can the Holy Church say, 'gold and silver have I none.'" Erasmus answered very quietly, "No. Neither can it now say to a cripple, 'Walk.'"

A Prayer

O Lord our God, we have looked for riches which would corrupt us. We have wanted human approval more than yours. And we have expected you to be night watchman over our goods. Forgive us, we pray, and direct our attention back to Christ and to the least of his brothers and sisters. Amen.

Scripture
Jesus said to them again,
"Peace be with you. As the
Father has sent me, even so I
send you."   John 20:21

Confession
The benefits which in this life do
accompany or flow from justifica-
tion . . . are: assurance of God's
love [and] peace of conscience.
Westminster Shorter Catechism,
Answer 36

82

One of the worst of modern miseries, judging from the drug traffic backed up all across the Northern Hemisphere, is anxiety. People feel tense, constricted, uptight, on edge. The number of people who wish to smooth and mellow out their lives by bottle, needle, or pill has become legion. For all the rootless souls in every city, all the jangling nerves on every job, all the restless teenagers in every high school, there are modern peddlers of peace. They do business in Valium, heroin, and lime vodka. These are the prophets who shout "Peace, peace!" where there is no peace.

Certain people look to the Christian religion for peace. Some of them hope for the sort of pacifier which will let them float:

How sweet it were, hearing the
    downward stream
With half-shut eyes ever to seem
Falling asleep in a half-dream!
                    (Alfred Lord Tennyson,
                    "The Lotos-Eaters")

Is *that* the peace Christ offers? No. Salvation offers us release from our burden of guilt, rest for our terrible restlessness, and wholeness for all the bits and pieces into which our lives crumble. In some deep and wondrous way the Christian faith offers a "peace which passes understanding." But it is no sedative peace, no opium peace, no peace which falls asleep "in a half-dream."

Jesus Christ talks about peace in the same breath with talk about *sending*. "As the Father has sent me, even so I send you." And we recall, somewhat uneasily, that the Father sent his Son not to be served, but to serve. He made peace only "through the blood of the cross."

The disciple is not greater than his master. For us too there is a cross to take up, a race to run, a fight to win. Strange to say, the peace we are given is a peace we take with us into battle, into all the dust and struggle of our lives. The peace of Christ is not for escape, but for survival.

A Recitation or Prayer
The Lord bless you and keep you. The Lord make his face to
shine upon you and be gracious to you. The Lord lift up his
countenance upon you and give you peace. Amen.
—The Aaronic Benediction (Num. 6:24-26)

Scripture
As for man, his days are like grass; he flourishes like a flower of the field; for the wind passes over it, and it is gone, and its place knows it no more.
Psalm 103:15,16

Confession
By the Spirit's power we make the goal of our lives not earthly things, but the things above where Christ is, sitting at God's right hand.
Heidelberg Catechism, Answer 49

83

The words from Psalm 103 quoted above are among the most haunting in all the Bible. Usually they find their way into the readings at a funeral. With good reason. The words say so simply, and yet so movingly, what impresses every reflective human being who pauses at a milestone to consider the brevity of the lives God gives us.

The career which begins in diapers and moves on through the "seven ages of man," through the years of strength and productivity, on into the ripe old years when a person slows, turns, and looks back—that career seen from near its end seems so short. Already, the body which has been a moving temple of the Holy Spirit through the years can move on no further. Finally, the Lord whom we seek suddenly comes to his temple and reaches for us.

"Like grass!" says the psalmist. A trembling blade of grass sprouts and pushes its way up among all the other young blades. And one day a good sharp wind lays it low, and it is gone. Or, "like a flower!" Once, in this place, a person flourished—a person with roots, growth, color, complexity, and a unique sort of beauty. But now its place knows it no more.

People are born; they toil and die. Generations of people. What is the meaning of this passing of the generations? Poets and philosophers have tried to say something of the fleetingness, the pathos, the wonder of human life which is here and then gone. What does it mean? Where have all the flowers *gone*?

There are really only two answers. One of them is found in a famous passage of world literature:

Life's but a walking shadow, a poor player
That struts and frets his hour upon the stage
And then is heard no more: It is a tale
Told by an idiot, full of sound and fury,
Signifying nothing.   (*Macbeth*)

The other answer begins the same way: "As for man, his days are like grass." But then it goes *on*:

...its place knows it no more.
But the steadfast love of the Lord is from everlasting to everlasting upon those who fear him. . . .

The only meaning our lives will ever have is a meaning conferred by that everlasting love. This is the love which has planted the generations, cultivated and delighted in us, worried over us, and which one day comes not as a grim reaper to cut us down, but as a faithful husbandman who wants to transplant his trees to a place where their leaves can be "for the healing of the nations."

A Hymn or Prayer
O God, our help in ages past,
Our hope for years to come,
Be Thou our guard while troubles last,
And our eternal home. Amen.
—"O God, Our Help in Ages Past"

What Do We Expect From Salvation?

Scripture
And the Lord said ... "I will put you in a cleft of the rock, and I will cover you with my hand until I have passed by; then I will take away my hand, and you shall see my back; but my face shall not be seen."   Exodus 33:22, 23

Confession
I already now experience in my heart the beginning of eternal joy.   Heidelberg Catechism, Answer 58

84

Moses is like us. There are times when he is close to God, sure of God, filled to the brim with God. And there are times when he feels uncertain, misled, and spiritually dried up. Moses has been on the mountain with God. But he has also struggled through some valleys.

One day he grows tired of these dips of the spirit. He wants to be done with his questions and uncertainties. He wants God to come out of hiding. He wants the veiled God to unveil. He wants to see all there is of God and to see it now. He wants the full-strength dose.

Moses says, "I pray thee, show me thy glory."

Haven't we heard something like that request among us? The lust for glory can turn a Christian into a glutton. He is never content, never satisfied, always hungry for more. For him a gathering of Christians is empty and frustrating unless the gathered ones get "high" with him. He wants glory *now*. Rapture around the clock!

Colors, voices, prickly flesh, psychedelic visions, heavenly razzle-dazzle! He thinks God wants us all to have fireworks in our faith!

Does he? Perhaps it is wise for us to remember that among the fruits of the Spirit are not only love and joy, but also patience and self-control. Already we are given a quiet, steadfast joy which has the power to persist even when the realities around us turn menacing. But we needn't be frustrated if we are not regularly in ecstasy. Nor may we bring guilt and reproach on those Christian brothers and sisters whose yearning lies along another line.

God knows how much glory we need. He will not flood our engines. He will not fill our teacups with a fire hose. He lets Moses glimpse his "back." It was enough. And, one day, to disciples begging to see the Father, Jesus Christ said, "He that has seen me *has* seen the Father."

For all of us, it is more than enough.

A Prayer
To you, O Spirit of God, we have prayed for gifts we cannot handle. Let us first show your fruits of love, joy, peace, patience, and self-control. Then equip us with your gifts to serve the church of Jesus Christ our Lord. Amen.

Scripture

Watch therefore—for you do not know when the master of the house will come.　　Mark 13:35

Confession

Regeneration...is evidently a supernatural work, most powerful, and at the same time most delightful, astonishing, mysterious, and ineffable.

Canons of Dort III-IV, Article 12

85

One last word must be said about our expectations. This week's meditating should be edging us toward the conclusion that God's salvation is often *surprising*. He comes when we least expect him, from a direction in which we are not looking, and in a way we are not sure we like at first. His ways are not our ways.

It has always been so. Saul hoped to go to Damascus to rescue God's people from the people of "the Way." Along the way, by the Way, he was arrested. Peter wanted to preserve salvation for those with clean hands and kosher habits. He was disturbed by a broader vision. For centuries God's people longed and hoped for a mighty warrior in David's line who would come to sit upon their throne. One night the Son of God slipped into the world in a stable.

It still happens. In places where nobody sings hymns or wears good clothes. In places where most of the words come to about four letters. Even in the power places where humility is forbidden and kindness is a sign of weakness. One of the most improbable of all the things to come out of the Nixon White House was a set of Christian conversions. Charles Colson, the hatchet man, was born again.

Whittaker Chambers started on the road to faith by noticing the divinely creative design of his daughter's tiny ear. But there was another step in his conversion. As Douglas Nelson tells it, Chambers remembered a girl in his grade school. She was ugly, red-faced, raw-boned, foul-tongued, and violent. The boys called her filthy names and loved to badger her into kicking and cursing. One day at lunchtime Chambers looked into a classroom and saw "Stew-Guts" (which was one of the more printable names for her) very patiently drilling her little sister in spelling. The child was retarded and had trouble with even the simplest words. But over and over the ugly big girl took the little one through the words with that praise and encouragement which the teacher reserved for the brighter children. Then, when the bell rang, Stew-Guts very gently kissed her sister on the head and sent her off to her room.

The treasure in earthen vessels, the small flicker of God in unexpected places and in unlikely people—all of it had its part to play in the salvation of Whittaker Chambers.

Watch therefore—for you do not know when, or where, or from what direction God's salvation may come. Not at the end. Not even now.

A Prayer

In our blindness, O Lord, we have missed the signs of your presence. Quietly, unexpectedly, you have been working in places where we were not looking and where we did not want to go. Open our eyes to see, our hearts to receive, and our lives to show forth the great salvation you work through Jesus Christ our Lord. Amen.

Postscript

1. We sometimes hear testimonies like this: "I was out of work and deeply in debt. Then I became a Christian. The next day, just as my mortgage was going to be foreclosed, a check arrived in the mail for the very amount due—and $67.14 extra for the gas company bill I had forgotten about. Isn't it wonderful how God's salvation works?"

    What do you think about this?

2. How do we get the sort of peace our Lord offers? And what makes us think he means us to have it? After all, the Prince of Peace himself said: "Do not think that I have come to bring peace on earth; I have not come to bring peace, but a sword" (Matt. 10:34).

3. May we expect the "gifts of the Holy Spirit"? Or the "fruits of the Spirit"? Or both? What is the difference? See I Corinthians 12 (esp. 1-11 and 27-31) on the gifts and Galatians 5:22, 23 on the fruits.

Week Eighteen

What About Doubt?

Several decades ago a well-known New York
preacher remarked that the word *doubt*
has a bad ring. Preachers do not ordinarily
use it with approval. *Faith* is our word.
Doubt is a word we keep in the doghouse.
With some reason! When it gets deep enough,
doubt is a real affliction, a disturbing loss
of our grip on the things of the faith. Most
of us experience days or weeks when a
darkness seems to settle over our faith
and we lose our way for a time. We lose
our sense of the presence of God. As the
psalmist said, "We do not see our signs."
In fact, a whole era can lose its signs.
Perhaps doubt, in all its forms, is one of
the most obvious sufferings of the contemporary Christian church.
What is it like? What about doubt?

Scripture

[Thomas] said to them, "Unless I see in his hands the print of the nails...and place my hand in his side, I will not believe."

John 20:25

Confession

I believe in God the Father, Almighty, Maker of heaven and earth. And in Jesus Christ, His only begotten Son, our Lord;... I believe in the Holy Spirit.

The Apostles' Creed

86

The most famous doubter in the Bible is Thomas. After all, he skipped church one night when the Lord appeared and later had the audacity to deny what the disciples reported. "When I see it, I'll believe it," Thomas said.

Thomas has taken a lot of abuse for his doubts. Thomas the cynic. Thomas the arch-skeptic. To all the ages, this man is known as "Doubting Thomas"—as if "Doubting" were his first name. Thomas is always contrasted with the others—the women, the disciples, all who believed the resurrection at once. *They* had no trouble believing! They all gladly embraced the resurrected Lord! Nobody else was shaky in the faith—nobody but this one miserable holdout who so stubbornly demanded evidence!

It is a sharply drawn contrast, and an old one, and a memorable one. It has every advantage except that of being a *true* one.

The fact is, practically no one received the resurrected Lord very easily. When the women burst in on the hopeless disciples to report the resurrection, "these words seemed to them an idle tale, and they did not believe them" (Luke 24:11). Later, the Lord himself stood among them and they "still disbelieved for joy, and wondered" (Luke 24:41). In Galilee, "when they saw him they worshiped him; but some doubted" (Matt. 28:17).

Was Thomas an agnostic in a group of fundamentalists? Not a bit. They *all* had trouble taking in the central fact—and the central person—of history. These things seemed to them too good to be true.

The disciples stand in a long line of doubters who grow into heroes of the faith. The whole Bible is full of doubts. The psalmists keep asking, "Hath God forgotten to be gracious?" Job complains that God is silent. Jeremiah asks boldly, "Wilt thou be to me like a deceitful brook?" As someone has said to Christian doubters, "The Bible is your book."

But the strange and wonderful thing is that God so often chooses doubt as his highway to Zion. God can turn even this desert into a fruitful field. *The sturdiest faith often comes out of doubt.*

So "Doubting Thomas" gasps out perhaps the shortest and most beautiful confession of faith in all the Bible: "My Lord and my God."

A Prayer
Dear Father in heaven, raise our drooping arms and stiffen our shaking knees. Keep our steps from wavering. Let us do our wrestling with you at night, but then bring us a new day of joy and reconciliation, through Jesus Christ our Lord. Amen.

Scripture
I wait for the Lord, my soul
    waits, and in his word I hope;
my soul waits for the Lord
    more than watchmen for the
        morning,
    more than watchmen for the
        morning.   Psalm 130:5,6

Confession
Those in whom a living faith in
Christ...is not as yet strongly
felt...ought...diligently to per-
severe in the use of means [of
grace], and with ardent desires
devoutly and humbly to wait for
a season of richer grace.
                    Canons of Dort I,
                    Article 16

87

As these lines are written, people in California are waiting for gasoline in lines thirteen
blocks long. They are not enjoying it. People
usually do not like to wait for things. Kids can't
wait for their birthdays. Teenagers count the
days till they get their driver's license. Young
lovers find it hard to wait until they are married. The waiting rooms of passenger terminals
and hospitals are filled with people who would
rather be doing something else.

There are times when our Christian faith
thins down to a limp and pasty level. Douglas
Nelson tells of a little boy who won a prize by
writing to a breakfast cereal company: "I like
your cereal because it doesn't snap or crackle or
pop. It just lays there and sogs." Perhaps that
will do for the Breakfast of Champions. But if
our faith just "lays there and sogs," we starve.
Sooner or later we need what the Canons call
"a season of richer grace."

Meanwhile, we do what the psalmist does.

We wait for the Lord. But let us be clear. Our
waiting is not for nothing. It is not aimless or
purposeless waiting. We are not *Waiting for
Godot*. Nor are we waiting for some *thing*. This
psalmist is not merely optimistic. He is not saying to himself, "Buck up! Cheer up! Chin up!
Things are bound to get better!"

No. The psalmist is waiting for some*one*. Alert-
ly. On tiptoe. He is waiting and yearning ardently
not only for a season of richer grace, but also for
the giver of that grace.

For all of us who have been hurt by sin, or
shaken by some grief, or who have felt the bottom
drop out of our faith in some other way, there will
be times and seasons of waiting. We will wait for
the Lord. And he will come—by a friend's
gracious act or wise counsel, by some part of the
Holy Word in which we hope, by a quiet return of
confidence and trust.

He *will* come. As surely as tomorrow's dawn
will turn our darkness to light.

A Recitation
I wait for the Lord, my soul waits,
and in his word I hope;
my soul waits for the Lord
more than watchmen for the morning,
more than watchmen for the morning.

—Psalm 130:5, 6

What About Doubt?

Scripture
[After the Last Supper] when they had sung a hymn, they went out to the Mount of Olives...to a place called Gethsemane.
Matthew 26:30, 36

Confession
Faith keeps us in the service we owe to God and to our neighbor and strengthens our patience in adversity.
Second Helvetic Confession, Chapter XVI

88

In the first chapter of his masterful *Screwtape Letters*, C. S. Lewis talks of "the pressure of the ordinary." Most of us will recognize what he means. You are listening to a fine part of *St. Matthew's Passion* on your car radio when a stronger signal suddenly cuts in and stuns you with the raucous shouts of "The Grateful Dead." Or, during an afternoon nap you are lost in a delicious world of lapping waves and gentle sunshine when, more and more, you cannot help noticing a shrill voice at your ear demanding to know what you did with its snow pants. Ah, yes. Back to real life.

But the pressure of the ordinary can also tend to crowd out Christian faith. You are at your prayers and the phone rings; someone you do not know wishes to discuss cemetery plots with you. Or, at church, you are considerably moved by your pastor's sermon and by the closeness of Christian friends who wonderfully sing a great hymn. Then you step into the foyer and somebody wants to know whether the Expos won or lost last night. Or, you are converted at an evangelistic rally. You feel the tugging of the Spirit of God, surrender, and move forward toward a new life. But the next morning you discover your job is still tough and your inter-office memos still as popular as a dead cigar floating in a punch bowl. *This is the real world!* Sad to say, the pressure of the ordinary can make us doubt the reality of "the things that are unseen."

We may thank God that Christian faith is not fueled only by the high octane of those exciting times when we can almost *feel* his presence. For the long walk through dry valleys we will need a disciplined *will* which sets itself stubbornly to please God, even when God himself seems distant. As Lewis says, the devil's cause is most in danger when a Christian, "no longer desiring, but still intending, to do our [Lord's] will, looks round upon a universe from which every trace of Him seems to have vanished, and asks why he has been forsaken, and still obeys" (*Screwtape Letters*).

"Not my will but thine be done." Even for our Lord himself, there is the hymn in the upper room—and then there is Gethsemane.

A Prayer
O Lord, let the faith you give us also keep us in the service we owe to you and our neighbor. Let us move straight on, even through valleys of dry bones and abandoned hopes. O Lord, increase our faith. Through Jesus Christ, we pray. Amen.

What About Doubt?

Scripture
Love...believes all things.
I Corinthians 13:7

Confession
Christian faith is not an opinion or human conviction, but a most firm trust and...a most certain apprehension of...Christ who is the fulfillment of all promises.
Second Helvetic Confession,
Chapter XVI

89

Doubt can be a good thing. It is often God's gift, a sure defense against the flimflam man. When a candidate for parliament tells you he will provide more of everything for everybody while lowering taxes, doubt is needed. When a TV ad solemnly announces that all of life will slide into depressing ruin unless you soak in Burbles' Bubblebath, doubt is indicated. When somebody says "my alarm didn't go off" or "there's no reason why we can't still be good friends," you may be excused for doubting. Doubt often saves us a trip down the garden path. And, as Galileo noticed, doubt is often the father of discovery.

But there are some people who get hardened into a habit of doubting practically everything. We call such people "cynics." To them all kindness is a mask for self-interest; all religious hope is a fraud and a delusion; all politicians are liars. Cynics are hard to talk to.

One of the most tragic features of human fallenness is that sin makes us cynics. Our own sin and others' sin. We have lost our innocence. We have been fooled so many times by empty promises, hoodwinked so often by con artists, that we tend to look at the world through narrowed eyes. The little boy who cried "Wolf!" as a joke could not get the villagers to come when a *real* wolf appeared. The same thing can happen when the shout goes up, "Behold the lamb of God!" People smile knowingly and go about their business.

Let us be honest. Even the devoutest Christian sometimes wonders if we have not been deceived. C. S. Lewis somewhere says that there were times and moods in which the Christian faith seemed to him incredible.

Christian faith is a determined risk. We have our eyes narrowed as much as anyone else's against the frauds and fakes of this world. It is just that we cannot help opening our eyes wide to behold him who has actually borne our griefs and carried our sorrows. Even when our faith is wobbling and our foundations are shaking, something in us cannot help trusting Jesus Christ.

Why? Why, for once, do we dare lower our guard and expose ourselves? Why, for once, are we *convinced* that he fills what are else empty promises? Perhaps Lewis Smedes is right. Perhaps it is because we are convinced—not just in our minds, but in the depths of our hearts—that he *loves* us. Where Christ is concerned, it is love which "believes all things."

Deep answers to deep.

A Prayer
O God, we believe; help our unbelief, through Jesus Christ who loves us. Amen.

Scripture
Immediately the father of the
child cried out and said, "I
believe; help my unbelief!"
                    Mark 9:24

Confession
*What then must a Christian
believe?*
Everything God promises us in
the gospel. That gospel is summarized for us in the articles of
our Christian faith—a creed
beyond doubt, and confessed
throughout the world.
                    Heidelberg Catechism,
                    Q & A 22

90

In a famous sermon on doubt, Harry Emer-
son Fosdick, who had a few doubts of his own,
suggested that believers who doubt must pass
on, by God's grace, eventually to *doubt* their
doubts. He tells of two incidents in which
history has laughed not at the person with
faith, but at the doubter.

When it was first announced that it was possible to build a steamship capable of crossing
the Atlantic Ocean, a fair number of people
doubted it. In fact, one man was so sure he
published a small book in which he tried to
prove it couldn't be done. No steamship, he
believed, could possibly carry enough fuel to
keep its engines running long enough for a
trans-Atlantic passage. Later, the first steamship
to cross the ocean carried a copy of that book!
Here was a skeptic who should have doubted
his own doubts.

Abraham Lincoln made a great speech at
Gettysburg. Generations of students have
learned it. But a newspaper editor from nearby
Harrisburg was not impressed. "We pass over
the silly remarks of the President," he wrote.
"For the credit of the nations we are willing
that the veil of oblivion should be dropped over
them and that they shall be no more repeated
or thought of." Here was a doubter who stood
in the presence of greatness and missed it!

For us who are committed to Jesus Christ, the
great danger is not that we shall believe some
part of popular Christianity which isn't so. Nobody, as C. S. Lewis remarked, ever went to
hell for believing that God sits bodily on a
throne in heaven. Our great danger is rather
that by our foolish skepticism we may miss
God's *greatness* and by our dithering we may
miss the richness of the full life Christ came to
bring.

Certainly all of us will have times when we
are hanging on by our fingernails: "Lord, I
believe; help my unbelief." But growth in grace
and in the knowledge of God should lead us
one day to doubt our doubts and to say simply,
"I believe."

What we believe has been summarized for us
in the articles of the Christian faith—a faith
beyond doubt and confessed throughout the
world.

A Recitation
I believe in God the Father, almighty,
    maker of heaven and earth.
And in Jesus Christ, his only begotten Son, our Lord....
I believe in the Holy Spirit;
    I believe a holy catholic church, the communion of saints;
    the forgiveness of sins;
    the resurrection of the body;
    and the life everlasting. Amen.   —The Apostles' Creed

Postscript

1. Most of us have had periods of doubt and of waiting for God. As you think back, can you tell what caused the doubt? *Why* do we doubt?

2. Is doubt sin? Why or why not?

3. Suppose I never doubt. Am I abnormal? Should I be worried? Explain.

4. What can we do about our doubt?

Week Nineteen

What About Sin?

A *cliché* is an idea or expression which has lost its force and freshness through overuse. There are single clichés ("a grain of salt") and double clichés ("rack and ruin") and mixed clichés ("a bird in the hand gathers no moss"). There are even Christian clichés—some of them originally from good sources.

A cliché often shows verbal deftness or contains some real wisdom. That is why it is used so often. That is why it became a *cliché.* So it is with our Christian clichés about sin. Following the *Book of Common Prayer,* we often ask God's forgiveness for sins of "omission and commission" and for those of "thought, word, and deed."

You will remember that in week eight we touched on the problem of continuing sin in the redeemed life. But much remains to be said. This week let us discuss sins of omission and commission, of thought, word, and deed. What about sin?

Scripture
No one born of God commits sin;
for God's nature abides in him,
and he cannot sin because he is
born of God.   I John 3:9

Confession
Because of Christ's blood, do not
hold against us, poor sinners
that we are, any of the sins we
do or the evil that constantly
clings to us.
Heidelberg Catechism,
Answer 126

91

Here we have a problem. The Scripture text for today seems to say that no born-again Christian commits sin. But the Catechism prayer plainly says we are "poor sinners." It is not merely that evil "clings to us" like a barnacle. We also *do* sins. We *perform* "sins of commission."

The Catechism is right. We are wonderfully redeemed by grace and through faith. We are accepted, delivered, rescued, forgiven. We are born again. We are saved. And we have grown attached to our Savior. We believe he has saved us. And we trust him now to keep us.

But we also sin. Is it always in spite of ourselves? Do we always have good intentions? Are our sins usually accidents? Are we generally *aiming* right when we miss the mark? Are we typically bewildered by our sin—like Aaron who could not *imagine* how that golden calf popped right into existence? Do we "fall into sin" as a blindfolded party guest suddenly falls into a swimming pool?

No. We deceive ourselves. Let us face the truth. There are times when even redeemed people purposely plunge themselves into sin. In fact, we use a diving board. We go in head first, eyes wide open. We *commit* sin. And we often like it. Half-desperate or merely rebellious, we go after the pleasure we think some sin will bring. We *hanker* after our old fleshpots. Sometimes we even take pride in a particular sin and try to defend it. Can any one of us honestly say he or she has never relished a put-down of another human being—and then defended it on the ground that the person "had it coming"?

We sin. We *commit* sin. And sin is no joke. The memory of our sins of commission is not the occasion for a wink or a shrug or a cocktail party reminiscence. Sin needs repentance. That is why every Sunday at church and every day on our knees we confess our sins and beg God's forgiveness.

We sin. We *commit* sin. But, then, whatever could that Scripture text mean?

A Prayer
Dear Lord, because of Christ's blood, do not hold against us, poor sinners that we are, any of the sins we do or the evil that constantly clings to us. In Christ's name, Amen.

Scripture
"Lord, when did we see thee
hungry or thirsty or a stranger or
naked or sick or in prison, and
did not minister to thee?"
Matthew 25:44

Confession
*What does God's law require of
us?*
Christ teaches us this summary
in Matthew 22—You shall love
the Lord your God with all your
heart....You shall love your
neighbor as yourself.
Heidelberg Catechism,
Q & A 4

92

Thomas Muenzer, one of the more colorful figures in the Protestant Reformation, regarded Martin Luther as a half-baked reformer. He criticized Luther not for his beer drinking, but rather for drinking beer while he *should* have been working harder for reform. He called Luther "Professor Easy-Chair" and "Dr. Pussy-Foot."

Sins of omission are easy to see in others. And they are very real in others. More than one mission has failed because no one could be budged out of her easy chair to do it. More than one ministry to the hungry, the old, or the imprisoned has foundered because Christian people were simply indifferent. More than one family of children has grown up starved for a father's love because the father omitted to bother himself with them. We see such omissions in others and wonder why *they* do not see them.

Sins of omission are harder to see in ourselves. And yet they are very real. One of the most disturbing teachings of Jesus Christ is that you and I will be judged not merely for what we have done, but also—maybe particularly—for what we have *not* done. We will be asked about those things we never did—perhaps, as C. S. Lewis remarks, about those things "we never *dreamed* of doing." It is a sobering thought that the heaviest charge against any one of us may be the charge that we were silent, uninvolved, withdrawn, unconcerned.

Someone's need was at our door, and we preferred to watch TV. A call went out to begin a prisoner-visiting program, and we answered the call to start a bowling league. Someone wrote a troubled letter, and we never answered. A cancerous relative was dying, and we were too timid to visit. Another kid at school was unpopular and unhappy, and we tried not to notice. Our whole nation pointed itself toward destruction, and we did not even bother to vote.

Of course, we could always plead ignorance. On the last day we could say, "Lord, *when* did we see thee hungry or thirsty or in prison?"

But how good an excuse is that?

A Prayer
O Lord Christ, we flee to you for mercy. Forgive those things we
ought to have done and did not do. Soften our hearts and ready
our hands to do your work. Amen.

Scripture
Search me, O God, and know my heart! Try me and know my thoughts! And see if there be any wicked way in me.
Psalm 139:23, 24

Confession
What is God's will for us in the tenth commandment?
That not even the slightest thought or desire contrary to any one of God's commandments should ever arise in my heart.
Heidelberg Catechism,
Q & A 113

93

People are sometimes compared to animals. Often the comparisons stretch the truth. Someone is said to be "as strong as an elephant." But he isn't. Or to be able to "run like a deer." But she can't. Or to "swim like a fish" or "see like a hawk." But nobody can swim or see like that. Many animals are bigger, stronger, and faster than we are.

Yet, we can think. We can be not only as sly as a fox, but slyer. We can be not only as wise as an owl, but wiser. We can think better than animals can. Thinking helps us plan cities, write books, span gorges, explore space—and husband animals. Thinking enables us to respond to God intelligently. The gift of thought lets us ponder "whatever is true, whatever is honorable, whatever is just, whatever is pure, whatever is lovely, whatever is gracious, excellent, or worthy of praise." God's gift lets us think about *these* things.

The same gift, when we set it too low, lets us think of other things: whatever is false, whatever is sleazy or foul, whatever is cheap, whatever is vulgar or depressing, whatever is crummy, whatever is mean, low, or sour. We can think about these things too. And, sad to say, sometimes we do. We sin in our thoughts. The greatest saints have admitted to "thoughts that would make hell blush."

Our thinking needs discipline. Not just to think as clearly and cleanly as a trained logician. But to think as highly as we ought to think of God's gifts, excellences, and created wonders. In thought as well as in travel, we have to take the high way. For thought leads to word and deed—either to the good word and the kind deed or to the harsh word and the shameful deed.

A Prayer
Search me, O God, and know my heart!
Try me and know my thoughts!
And see if there be any wicked way in me,
and lead me in the way everlasting! Amen.
—Psalm 139:23, 24

Scripture
From the same mouth come blessing and cursing. My brethren, this ought not to be so.
James 3:10

Confession
We [must] use the holy name of God only with reverence and awe, so that we may properly confess him, pray to him, and praise him in everything we do and say. Heidelberg Catechism, Answer 99

94

G. K. Chesterton once remarked on the fact that some people will try to end an argument by saying, "We're only quarreling over words." Words are *worth* quarreling over, said Chesterton.

Why shouldn't we quarrel about a word? What is the good of words if they aren't important enough to quarrel over? Why do we choose one word more than another if there isn't any difference between them?

(Chesterton, *The Ball and the Cross*)

Chesterton is right. Think of the difference between saying "You're kidding!" and "You're lying!" Think of the difference in shading between "steadfast" and "stubborn," between "good" and "goody-goody," between "wise man" and "wise guy." In one of his sermons, David H. C. Read points to this last distinction. Just ask yourself, he suggests, how you would like to be introduced at a banquet as "one of the true wise guys of our generation"!

Words matter. Sticks and stones may break my bones—but words may break my heart.

We know the power of words. We know from painful experience the power of bad words. There are the curses against God by which we blacken our own souls. There are the words against others which come from a tongue which has been honed into a keen cutting tool. And there are the words of group gossip, that "Protestant confessional," as Charles Fairbanks put it, where people confess their neighbors' sins instead of their own. We can commit sin by our *words.*

But, as we have seen before, our silence can be just as dangerous: the word of encouragement and love never said to a struggling son or daughter; the word of gratitude withheld from an aging parent; the word of protest against injustice smothered by our self-interest; the omitted word of glad thanks to God for his mercies which are new every morning.

James knew the power of the tongue for good and for ill. "From the same mouth come blessing and cursing," he said.

Blessing is better.

A Prayer
Let our words be few and well chosen, O Lord. Give us the grace and humility to praise, to bless, and to give thanks, through Jesus Christ. Amen.

Scripture
The saying is sure and worthy of full acceptance, that Christ Jesus came into the world to save sinners. And I am the foremost of sinners.
I Timothy 1:15

Confession
I am not to belittle, insult, hate, or kill my neighbor—not by my thoughts, my words...and certainly not by actual deeds.
Heidelberg Catechism,
Answer 105

95

Sins of omission and commission, thought, word, and deed, are a continuing presence in the lives of God's people. Partly because of the attitudes in our society, we live with them too easily.

An armored car lost two bags of money near Trenton, New Jersey. Perhaps it had a leaky door. An unemployed worker found the money. It was a great deal of money, hundreds of thousands of dollars. The man did not keep the money. He returned it at once to the office of the armored car company.

The company was grateful to this honest man. It gave him a reward of a thousand dollars.

The man was *not* grateful for the thousand dollars. He told reporters it should have been far more. "Is *that* all honesty is worth?" he demanded. "A lousy thousand bucks? Why that hardly bought my gas to *return* the money!"

No doubt the man underestimated his car's fuel efficiency. And later he apologized for his ingratitude. But his first reaction was interesting because it took crookedness as the rule and honesty as the exception. You used to hear about people refusing a reward—saying they had only done what was right. Nowadays people sometimes think honesty is a foolishness so far beyond the call of duty that it deserves a medal, a speech, and a hefty check!

One of our continuing problems as Christians is that we live in a pocket of history where, as C. S. Lewis has it, "mere decency passes for heroic virtue and utter corruption for pardonable imperfection." These attitudes rub off. And then our moral sense enters that no-man's-land which knows neither the depths of sin nor the heights of grace.

St. Paul called himself the "foremost of sinners." It was not just pious balderdash. He meant it. He had developed *sensitivity* to sin. The saintlier a person is, the more aware that he still sins in thought, word, and deed—and the more aware that Jesus Christ came to save sinners.

A Prayer
O Almighty Father, Lord of heaven and earth, we confess that we have sinned against thee in thought, word, and deed. Have mercy upon us, O God, after thy great goodness; according to the multitude of thy mercies, do away our offenses and cleanse us from our sins, for Jesus Christ's sake. Amen.
—from *The American Book of Common Prayer*

Postscript

1. What do you suppose I John 3:9 *does* mean? (See also I John 5:18.) Can you think of any Christian groups which would have a special interest in these texts?

2. The division of this week's material suggests that our sins fall into neat compartments—thought, word, and deed, for instance. What evidence from our daily lives indicates the division is not quite so neat?

3. Are all sins equally bad? For example, is lust just as bad as adultery (Matt. 5:28)? Explain.

4. Calvinists believe in the "perseverance of the saints." Once saved, you are always saved. None of your sins can remove you from the grace of God.

   But, then, what difference does it make whether we sin or not? We're going to make it anyhow. So why not take advantage of some of the opportunities for mischief here below?

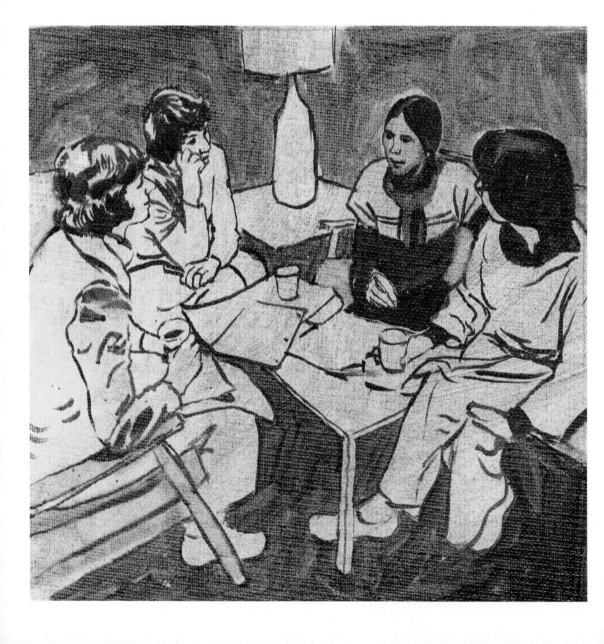

Week Twenty

What About Christian Liberty?

Freedom or *liberty* in the Bible is a synonym for *salvation.* The Old Testament people of God always thought of the exodus as the event in which God saved them "out of the house of bondage." In the New Testament, Paul writes practically his whole letter to the Galatians to make one point: "for freedom Christ has set us free."

We have already noticed this theme in other contexts. We have already seen that we need both communal discipline and individual liberty (weeks ten, fourteen), both "striving" and "a free conscience," both law and liberty (week fifteen).

Let us now consider some remaining liberty questions. What about Christian liberty?

Scripture

"If you continue in my word, you are truly my disciples, and you will know the truth, and the truth will make you free."

John 8:31, 32

Confession

It is therefore essential for us to lay hold on Christ Jesus, in his righteousness and his atonement ...since it is by him that we are set at liberty.

Scots Confession,
Chapter XV

96

"You will know the truth, and the truth will make you free." These words have become a secular motto. Someone once observed that probably no other words have been carved over the gateways of as many colleges or lettered across the facades of as many public libraries as these have been. And few famous words have become so detached from the lips and meaning of the person who uttered them.

"You will know the truth, and the truth will make you free." Here is the modern motto not only for intellectual freedom, but also for free speech, a free press, and free people. The idea is that ignorance weakens and finally enslaves us. Look at the first move dictators always make: they take control of the news media. If "the powers that be" can keep us from knowing the truth, they can have their way with us. Or, if they can at least *contain* the truth with a "modified, limited hang-out," they can frustrate justice.

True enough. We have a need to know and, in a free society, a *right* to know. A loss of this right is an invitation to tyranny.

But that is not what Jesus is talking about. Jesus is not saying that the gathering of intelligence or the assembling of data is the source of our most basic personal freedom. There are, after all, plenty of well-informed scoundrels who are enslaved to their own lust for power. There are plenty of highly educated scientists who are sick with worry over the possibilities for oppression which have come along with the truth about atomic fission.

No, the truth in the fourth Gospel is not so much a set of facts as a Person. It is this Person who so speaks the truth, points to the truth, and exemplifies the truth that he says, "I *am* the truth." The gospel Truth has a cross on his shoulder and the word "Father" on his lips.

And if *he* makes us free, we are free indeed.

A Prayer

O Lord our God, move us out of the house of bondage and into the glorious liberty of the children of God. Through him who is the way, and the truth, and the life, Amen.

Scripture
For those whom he foreknew he also predestined to be conformed to the image of his Son.... Do not be conformed to this world....

Romans 8:29; 12:2

Confession
The liberty which Christ hath purchased for believers under the gospel consists in...their being delivered from this present evil world.

Westminster Confession of Faith, Chapter XX

97

If you page through a popular illustrated history of the United States in the twentieth century, you will see a fascinating parade of the fads and fashions which color our lives here below. Kids in the thirties were offered escape from the Depression by such heroes as Flash Gordon, Jack Armstrong, and Little Orphan Annie. As teenagers in the forties, these same kids clung together in their baggy jeans, sloppy shirts, bobby sox, and loafers. It was a rigid code. In the fifties, as young adults, they moved to the suburbs and bought barbecue grills and power mowers. By the late sixties, these people were worried about their own teenagers' attraction to loving-in, lighting-up, and dropping-out. And so on.

We all conform to our culture, more or less. Some youthful conformity is dangerous, but much is harmless—perhaps even necessary for a sense of social security. Your teenager wants to wear bib overalls? Well, why not? Even for adults, conformity to established patterns of behavior (not telling jokes at funerals, for instance) is mere courtesy. You do not want to go around deliberately unnerving people—like the black hairdresser in Marin County, California, who keeps harassing his white customers by constantly changing the "soul handshake."

Christians are free to live in the world and to conform to many of its ways. These are "indifferent things."

What does Paul mean, then, when he says, "Do not be conformed to this world"? He means we are not to take our orders from this world. We are not to derive our strength, our satisfaction, our *identity* from this world. We are not "of" the world. For when Paul speaks of "the world," he means the whole array of law, sin, and death—the powers of this world. We are not to be *conformed* to this world or "squeezed into its mold."

Christians are called to another conformity. We are to be conformed to the image of God, to that image who has been among us with a face and a name and a power not of this world.

Strange to say, the closer our conformity to him, the greater our freedom.

A Prayer
Give us the gift of discernment, O Lord, so that we may know your will—what is good, and acceptable, and perfect. Through Jesus Christ our Lord, Amen.

What About Christian Liberty?

Scripture
Take care lest this liberty of
yours somehow become a
stumbling block to the weak.
I Corinthians 8:9

Confession
The powers which God hath ordained and the liberty which
Christ hath purchased, are not
intended by God to destroy, but
mutually to uphold and preserve
one another.
Westminster Confession of Faith,
Chapter XX

98

A certain TV ad shows a mighty little car pulling a mobile home. To demonstrate the car's powerful front-wheel drive, the advertisers have removed the car's entire rear wheel and axle assembly. Another ad shows a rugged pickup truck smashing across the countryside, leaping over gullies, clattering through rocky riverbeds, and generally raising quite a shine. In both cases, the advertisers helpfully run a cautionary note across the bottom of your TV screen. It says: *Do not try this yourself!*

Perhaps they should run the same caution across "Three's Company" and "Wide World of Sports."

People are imitators. The results of their imitations are sometimes very bad. In 1974, after Evel Knievel tried to leap Idaho's Snake River Canyon with his rocket motorcycle, there was a rash of accidents across the United States. Young imitators were breaking their legs trying to set jumping records with their bicycles.

The Christian faith gives us great liberty. We may accept with thanksgiving a rich harvest of God's gifts—meat, wine, music, film, books, ballet, painting, sports, and much more. We are free to use these things heartily, openly, and joyously to the glory of God and the building up of others.

But we have to look to those who *imitate*. We may not use our liberty so as to "give offense." We have to take responsibility for the "weaker" brother or sister who cannot yet use some of these gifts with a free conscience. Even though something we do may not be wrong, we shouldn't do it if we know it would tempt some other Christian to do it while *he* still thinks it's wrong.

Of course weaker Christians need to be gradually educated and strengthened. They're missing some of what God wants to give them. But meanwhile we who are "strong" may have to suspend our liberty at times when we might tempt the weaker ones to violate their own conscience.

For deliberate violation of one's conscience is moral suicide.

A Prayer
Give us the maturity, O Lord, to use our Christian liberty wisely and responsibly. Help us to love our neighbor as ourselves. In Jesus' name, Amen.

Scripture
Let not him who eats despise him who abstains, and let not him who abstains pass judgment on him who eats . . . . Who are you to pass judgment on the servant of another?   Romans 14:3, 4

Confession
God alone is lord of the conscience, and hath left it free from the doctrines and commandments of men.
Westminster Confession of Faith, Chapter XX

99

Yesterday we heard Paul's instruction to strong Christians, people who are able to use some gift of God with a free conscience. To them Paul says this: be prepared to give up your liberty on those occasions when you would tempt weaker persons to go against their own conscience.

Today we see that Paul balances his instruction with an equally strong word to the weak. You may be a vegetarian or a teetotaler, says Paul. O.K. But be sure you do not "pass judgment" on those fellow Christians who are not. The stronger ones must not tempt you to violate your conscience. But neither may you judge those who eat or drink. They too are servants of God, just as you are. And *God* is the one who will judge us all.

Here is crucial direction for our living together as Christians in community. The strong must not "give offense." But neither may the weak "*take*" offense." We who are weak must not be quick to put the worst face on what other Christians are doing. If they do something we don't like, we may not just *assume* they have become "worldly." Do they drink a cocktail, see a film, dance waltzes with their spouses, prefer not to get married, smoke cigars, hang around with socialists, hobnob with rich capitalists? Perhaps so. Perhaps they can do some of these things with thanksgiving to God. They must face their Lord every day just as we do. And we must be slow to judge and ready to respect fully the freedom which God gives us all.

Does this mean the death of all discipline in the Christian community? Not at all. There are a number of nonnegotiable items—those in the Ten Commandments, for instance. But there are also the free items which we do not have to declare. The Christian community must be large enough for Christians with different tastes, habits, and ways than our own.

This is a matter not only of fairness to others, but also of our very survival as a community. Suspicion and the rush to judgment will tear us apart as fast as any other sin we commit.

A Prayer
O Lord, you know how much we need firmness, discipline, and mutual accountability in the Christian life. But you also know how much we need a little room to breathe. By your Holy Spirit among us, give us both we pray. In Christ's name, Amen.

Scripture

Let us then pursue what makes for *shalom* and for mutual up-building...let each of us please his neighbor for his good, to edify him.   Romans 14:19; 15:2

Confession

Man is free to seek his life within the purpose of God: to develop and protect the resources of nature for the common welfare, to work for justice and peace in society, and in other ways to use his creative powers for the fulfillment of human life.

Confession of 1967 I, B

100

We are not to offend the weak; nor are we permitted to judge the strong. We must live *together*, respecting each other's freedom.

But more. Not only do we have to respect each other's freedom; we also have to *promote* it. We have to "pursue what makes for *shalom*"; that is, for *wholeness*. We have to try to provide for, to insure, the freedom of fellow Christians. Our goal is to promote this wholeness in others, giving them ample room to live, move, and enjoy the treasures and tasks of the kingdom.

That is why those of us who are parents try more and more to lead our children to a place where they can stand on their own. We want to ease them out into a life in which they are still utterly dependent on God, but no longer so dependent on us. We want them one day to be as free as we are. Similarly, those of us who are husbands and whose wives have not had full opportunity to develop their own interests will not merely respect our wives' freedom to do this; we will positively promote this freedom. Again, a good relief organization does not simply offer charity in the form of handouts to the needy—necessary as that may be in emergencies. Rather, a wise and imaginative relief committee will try to promote independence and self-sufficiency in those whom it serves. We want poor people to become as free as we are. We want to honor the Christ who came to "set at liberty those who are oppressed."

Charity can be a blessed thing on a temporary basis. But it is far more blessed to give respect, extend justice, and mount a determined effort to liberate others for the same wholeness, the same fullness of life, which God has given us.

Let us then actively *pursue* what makes for *shalom*.

A Prayer
Keep us, O Lord, from patronizing the poor in the name of charity and from controlling the weak in the name of love. Let justice roll down like mighty waters and righteousness like an everflowing stream. And let us be as jealous for the freedom and shalom of others as we are for ourselves. In Jesus' name, Amen.

Postscript

1. Contemporary "liberation theology" stresses liberation and freedom as the essence of salvation. In this sort of thinking Jesus Christ is a radical *Liberator*. (See, for example, Luke 1:52, 53; 4:18,19.)

   Is there anything to this? Or is it merely the invention of liberals who have lost all their doctrine?

2. Neckties change in fashion from narrow to wide and then back to narrow again. If you think of narrow ties as "conservative" and wide ones as "liberal," then we are swinging like a pendulum from conservative to liberal and back to conservative again.

   Is that the case in public mores and morality too? Are we oscillating between an emphasis on order—tending toward oppression—and an emphasis on freedom—tending toward anarchy? Or are we now headed in just one direction? What should be our attitude toward these trends in our society?

3. Suppose I drink wine with my meal. My father-in-law thinks wine drinking is wrong. Should I give up wine drinking in deference to my weaker brother? Why or why not?

Week Twenty-One

How Shall We Handle Our Wealth?

One of the most sensitive questions in a capitalist society is the question of money or wealth. You are either a "success" or you are not. Indeed, with little sense of irony, our society uses words like "successful" and "well-to-do" with an almost exclusively financial reference.

There was a time when many Puritans and other Calvinists saw wealth as *worldly*. But we are getting more liberal. We now have wealth ourselves, and it no longer seems so worldly. And yet, we cannot rid ourselves of a troubling and biblical question: what does God want us to do with our wealth? The question has recently come alive in the Reformed churches. Books, agencies, committees, and reports have had that question in mind as they look at a world of hunger and poverty. If we are "saved to serve," how shall we *show* our salvation in this area? By what financial service to the poor? With what biblical sense of justice?

How shall we handle our wealth?

Scripture
The earth is the Lord's and the fulness thereof, the world and those who dwell therein.
Psalm 24:1

Confession
The eternal Father of our Lord Jesus Christ...out of nothing created heaven and earth and everything in them.
Heidelberg Catechism, Answer 26

101

Most of us who read this meditation rank among the world's materially wealthy people. We are the economically privileged. Even those of us with "modest" incomes have vastly more financial power than the bulk of the world's population.

True, we may not *feel* terribly rich. But that is only because we have lost our perspective. When yesterday's luxuries become today's bare necessities, when we keep comparing ourselves with even wealthier people than ourselves, when out of custom and superstition we "talk poor" and restrict our cash flow with immediate reinvestment, then we can fool even ourselves into thinking we are not so very well off. News magazines report that a fair number of people who make $100,000 per year feel uncomfortably pinched—a fact which brings tears to the eyes of the rest of the population.

Let us face the truth. By world standards most of us are prosperous. Let us face another truth. We ourselves are therefore "the rich" whom the Bible addresses so pointedly, and with such fearful warnings, and out of such a disturbing bias in favor of the poor. Let us face a third truth. None of our wealth is ours. The earth is the Lord's. The fullness of our granaries is the Lord's. Whatever part of our gross national product can stand moral scrutiny is the Lord's. Our "personal assets" are not personally ours.

Salvation is a free gift of God. Wealth is not. It comes with strings attached. It is given only in trust. We are all *trustees*. We have been entrusted with varying amounts of the Lord's vast resources. One day there will be an accounting. It is likely to be embarrassing—or worse. Even now, if all bank card statements were open and all checkbook entries known, what consternation there would be in the Third World! What dismay among the poor brothers and sisters of the world church!

The question for Christian stewards, for saved trustees, is never the question which first comes to mind. Our question is not, "All right, how much do I have to give away?" *That* question still assumes we own our wealth. Our question is far more troubling: before God and the poor people of the world, *how much do I dare keep for myself?*

A Prayer
O Lord our God, let us look at ourselves honestly and without evasion. Then let us look at those who have far less than we. Finally, let us realize that you care deeply what we do next. Through Jesus Christ, Amen.

Scripture
But among you there must not be even a hint of sexual immorality . . . or of greed, because these are improper for God's holy people.   Ephesians 5:3 (NIV)

Confession
What is God's will for us in the tenth commandment?
That not even the slightest thought or desire contrary to any one of God's commandments should ever arise in my heart.
Heidelberg Catechism,
Q & A 113

102

Christians have sometimes asked a test question about theater attendance. "Suppose Jesus returned," they said. "Would you want him to find you in a theater?"

Make the question contemporary. "What if he returned while you were in a *porno* theater? Wouldn't you be ashamed?"

But suppose he found us not at a porno show, but at a fashion show. Suppose he found us lusting after $80 designer blue jeans or $550 evening gowns. Suppose he found us in an atmosphere of materialism, greed, and snobbery. Is this a better theater? Are these more godly lusts? Even though the clothes are on instead of off, is the whole show much less obscene?

The Bible is against sexual looseness—what it calls *porneia* (por-NAY-ah). It is also against greed—what it calls *pleonexia* (pleh-oh-NEX-ee-ah). It is against them in the same breath and the same text. Both are unthinkable for Christians. Both show an unseemly itch, an almost unmentionable human weakness.

Pleonexia is the "annexing of more." If I al-

ready have two recordings of Brahms' Violin Concerto but keep hankering for more, insatiably for more and more—and then for more yet—I am a moral clown as a Christian. I display the "more" syndrome. The same is true with land, cash, trinkets, and toys for grown-ups.

The problem is that our society thinks *pleonexia* is just fine. Our whole economy—product design through advertising—is built on the unshakable foundation of competitive greed. This makes financial obedience to the Lord considerably more difficult for all of us.

But we have to keep trying. Teaching our children to laugh at TV commercials, boycotting all planned obsolescence, rejoicing to see how many wonderful goods we can do without, treasuring simple and lasting things, we have to fight back in an acquisitive society.

And one day the Lord who came to set at liberty those who are oppressed may set *us* free—free from the lust for more.

A Prayer
O Lord, liberate us from the need for more. Give us such pleasure in the simple gifts you give that we savor and treasure them with grateful hearts. Through Jesus Christ our Lord, Amen.

How Shall We Handle Our Wealth?

Scripture

If any one has the world's goods and sees his brother in need, yet closes his heart against him, how does God's love abide in him?

I John 3:17

Confession

I [must] do whatever I can for my neighbor's good....And I should do what I can to guard and advance my neighbor's good name.

Heidelberg Catechism,
Answers 111, 112

103

We are the rich. We *do* have "the world's goods." We are trying hard not to want even more of those goods.

But do we see our "brother in need"? We do. TV news programs have shown us the world's dingy, famine-ridden areas. We have seen skinny mothers holding their spindly infants. We have seen the little kids with their sad faces and slow ways—kids with legs you could circle with thumb and forefinger. Even in rich countries like the United States and Canada some household pets eat better than some people. Retirees on fixed incomes, forced to economize in the only flexible part of their budget, do without meat and then without milk. Some of them shop in restaurant garbage cans. We see them.

And yet, in another way, we do not. We do not *really* see them—not with enough compassion and indignation to do something about it. We do not want to see human need that way. It's unpleasant. And perhaps we are secretly afraid that too much indignation over financial inequality might develop into full-fledged economic reform. Reluctantly, but deliberately, we "close our hearts" against the poor. Like Lazarus at the rich man's door, the poor become

once more merely a part of the landscape to us. They may have all the crumbs they like, just so they make themselves scarce.

We "close our hearts." How? Few of us have the heart to say that the poor all *deserve* their misery—that the reason for the awkward difference between them and us is that they are bad and we are good. They are all lazy, stupid, and corrupt while we are diligent, intelligent, and upright. They are the ones who irritate God while we are the ones on whom God smiles. We don't dare say any of that because we know the Bible talks another way. The Bible sternly warns the rich and seeks to protect and promote the interests of the poor.

No, we close our hearts in other ways. We *all* do. We say the problem of poverty is too big, too remote, too complex, too disturbing. Besides, none of our close friends are poor. And so we go on, feeling guilty at times, but essentially unchanged.

We may be in deadly trouble. "For if any one has the world's goods and sees his brother in need, yet closes his heart against him, *how does God's love abide in him?*"

A Prayer

Dear Lord, we have to admit our sins of omission. We have passed by on the other side. We have tried not to see human misery. Forgive us, we pray. Kindle in us a light of compassion and a will to do what we know in our heart of hearts is right and just. Move us out of the grayness of guilt to a new day of excitement and hard work in doing whatever we can for our neighbor's good. Through Jesus Christ our Lord, Amen.

Scripture

He who oppresses a poor man insults his Maker.   Proverbs 14:31

He who is kind to the poor lends to the Lord.   Proverbs 19:17

Confession

Enslaving poverty in a world of abundance is an intolerable violation of God's good creation. Because Jesus identified himself with the needy and exploited, the cause of the world's poor is the cause of his disciples.

Confession of 1967 II, A, 4

104

The Bible, Old Testament and New, tells us that God cares for the poor in a special way. The poor have God's ear, God's concern, God on their side. God's care for the poor is so intense, his "identification" with them so strong, that any of us who oppresses the poor insults not only them, but also God himself! "He who oppresses a poor man insults his *Maker*."

Thus we are called not only to compassionate "seeing" of the poor, but also to frank acceptance of responsibility for them. We may not let them struggle on their own. We must not "provoke" the poor with fancy possessions or tempt any of them to envy. As Isaiah says (32:7), we must not "ruin the poor with lying words"—claiming, for example, that welfare mothers all drive new Cadillacs and use their food stamps to buy steaks. Instead, we ought to defend the poor from attack—even from verbal attack. And, as Ernest Campbell somewhere says, in our politics we ought to fight "the mood that would see more done for those who have

enough already and less for those who lack."

We have to take a stand with those who "have not." For, once again, God watches closely, sensitively, *personally* how we act in this. "God sends us the poor as *His* receivers," says Calvin. "He who is kind to the poor lends to the *Lord*," says the Bible.

But further, the Bible does not talk first about *charity* for the poor. It does not assume that we ought to keep all the power. There is no biblical warrant for *patronizing* poor people.

Rather, the Bible talks first about justice, about the rights of the poor, about the fact that the poor have a moral *claim* on us.

A righteous man knows the rights of the
        poor; A wicked man does not understand
        such knowledge.   (Proverbs 29:7)

Talk about justice, rights, and claims is the hardest talk of all. That is the stuff of godless Marxist revolution—or, if we act before it is too late, of godly economic reformation.

A Prayer

O Lord, give justice to the weak and fatherless;
    maintain the right of the afflicted and the destitute.
Rescue the weak and the needy;
    deliver them from the hand of the wicked.
In Jesus' name, Amen.   —from Psalm 82

Scripture
They gave according to their means, as I can testify, and beyond their means...begging us earnestly for the favor of taking part in the relief of the saints.
II Corinthians 8:3, 4

Confession
[God requires] that I work faithfully so that I may share with those in need.
Heidelberg Catechism, Answer 111

105

Ronald Sider wrote a prophetic book on prosperity in the midst of poverty, *Rich Christians in an Age of Hunger*. Sider suggests that we who are "upwardly mobile" ought to keep on increasing not only the amount but also the *percentage* of our income which we justly and benevolently give away. Thus, if a Christian now gives 10 percent, perhaps later he or she could give 20 percent, or 30, or 50. What Sider opposes is the simple assumption—widespread even in the Christian church—that our standard of living ought to increase automatically and proportionately with our income. Not necessarily, says Sider. If even the government taxes on a graduated scale, can the Christian church be content with a lesser righteousness? Why not a "graduated tithe"?

Certain Christians have already begun. There are heroes of *giving*—people who, though rich, become comparatively poorer so that others, in their poverty, might become richer. Like the Macedonians Paul praises in today's Scripture, these Christians count it a "favor" to give according to their means, and even beyond them. Here are people who, though having the form of prosperity, do not count the keeping up with the Joneses a thing to be grasped, but empty themselves and take on the form of servants.

How do they dare? How do they dare cripple their own position and endanger their own financial security? Where did they ever get this idea of self-sacrifice?

They got it from Jesus Christ. And they dare to do it because they have no fear. We are often *afraid* to give because we are privately banking on financial security as our main comfort in life and in death. Thus, instead of celebrating the opportunity to give strongly, intelligently, justly, cheerfully, we shrink back and build bigger barns for our goods.

But we know it won't work. It's no good. Our wealth won't last. There will come a time when all our earthly goods will be either a reproach to us or else a sheer irrelevance. For what we "take with us" when we die is only so much as we have given away.

It's a question of security, finally. A question of where we put our trust. A man in one of Jesus' parables said to himself, "Self, you have ample goods laid up for many years." To him God says, "You fool." Another man, in another parable, says, "I will arise and go to my Father." And God says, "My son."

A Prayer
O God our Father, we remember our Lord Jesus Christ who, though rich, became poor for our sakes so that we, in our poverty, might become rich. Help us to follow in his steps. Amen.

Postscript

1. At Newport, Rhode Island, one can visit a number of seventy-room mansions (twenty full baths), built between 1895 and 1915. In these mansions whole rooms and fireplaces are Italian imports. There are marble and semi-precious stone everywhere. There is gold leaf in abundance, rare paintings generously on display. These $15 million mansions were called, without humor, "summer cottages" and were used only eight to ten weeks of the year. One, Cornelius Vanderbilt's Renaissance cottage, "The Breakers," has a curious motto over one fireplace: "Little do I care for riches."

   Was Cornelius no materialist, then? Is God interested more in your *attitude* toward your wealth than in how much of it you have and what you do with it? If you do not "care for" your wealth, does it matter what you do with it? Is attitude the main thing? Explain.

2. When the Holy Spirit was poured out at Pentecost, the early believers at once became "communists" (Acts 2:44, 45). Why does this make us uncomfortable? Why do we use "communism" as a term for something shameful or fearful instead of using it for something inspired by the Holy Spirit?

3. Do we have any Christian communism in our churches today? If so, where?

4. Some Christians are offended and provoked by our snazzy cars, houses, and boats. They say all this is an affront to the poor—like dangling your Phi Beta Kappa key in front of a drop-out. They say Christians ought to steer clear of boutiques, country clubs, swanky restaurants, and any other sort of place that trades on class privilege and economic status.

   What do you think?

Week Twenty-Two

How Can the Forgiven Forgive?

The Bible connects our duties as saved people with the acts of God and Christ. The small word "as" often serves as the link. "Love one another *as* I have loved you" (John 15:12). "Whoever would be great among you must be your servant . . . *even as* the Son of man came not to be served but to serve . . . (Matt. 20:26, 28). With forgiveness, the pattern is classic. "*As* the Lord has forgiven you, so you also must forgive" (Col. 3:13). "Be kind to one another, tenderhearted, forgiving one another, *as* God in Christ forgave you" (Eph. 4:32).

To forgive is to let go, let off, release, give up claim to. Forgiveness is hard work. It is almost impossible if you do not yourself feel forgiven by God. But it is the soul of our life together. We are forgiven to forgive.

How do we do it? How *can* the forgiven forgive?

How Can the Forgiven Forgive?

Scripture
I said, "I will confess my transgressions to the Lord"; then thou didst forgive the guilt of my sin.... Be glad in the Lord, and rejoice, O righteous, and shout for joy, all you upright in heart!
Psalms 32:5,11

Confession
We believe that our salvation consists in the remission of our sins for Jesus Christ's sake.
Belgic Confession,
Article XXIII

106

For many contemporary people life has lost all religious *dimension*. These people live a flat life, recognizing neither the depths of sin nor the towering heights of God's grace. Perhaps they do get high on a number of stiff drinks. Perhaps they are indeed laid low the next morning. But for them life mostly stretches out in a plain—shapeless, endless, pointless.

Two main dimensions of created human life since the fall are sin and grace. We cannot live with God, with each other, nor even with ourselves till we see how great is our sin and how much greater is God's grace. When the Christian life goes flat, the first place to look for the reason is in some loss of our sense of the one or the other.

Every Sunday we confess our sin in church. And every Sunday we receive an assurance of grace and pardon. But often neither means very much to us. David H. C. Read remarks that confession and pardon become trivial to us. If you cannot quite catch what a person is saying,

you say, "I beg your pardon." It is merely a way of saying, "Speak up, please!" If you get a wrong telephone number, you say, "I'm sorry." The other person says, "Forget it." And you both do. It's a small thing. Life goes on.

So with sin and forgiveness. It is often just a ritual. "I beg your pardon," we say to God. "Forget it," we think he says. "It's no big deal."

Here is a blasphemously trivial Christianity for bored people—for people who fall asleep in church, drift through prayers, and flatten the Christian faith out to a thin, tasteless, little slice of life.

The Bible, especially some of the Psalms, shows us the heights and depths we ought to have. Prayers "from the depths" whisper guilt and yearn passionately for pardon. Then free, exuberant, exultant prayers ache with wonder at the grace which has pardoned even *this*.

The movement from one prayer to the other has come through forgiveness.

A Prayer
Have mercy on me, O God, according to thy steadfast love; according to thy abundant mercy blot out my transgressions.... Create in me a clean heart, O God, and put a new and right spirit within me.... Restore to me the joy of thy salvation, and uphold me with a willing spirit. Through Jesus Christ, Amen.
—from Psalm 51

Scripture
"You wicked servant! I forgave you all that debt because you besought me; and should not you have had mercy on your fellow servant, as I had mercy on you?"
Matthew 18:32, 33

Confession
I believe...the communion of saints; the forgiveness of sins.
Apostles' Creed

107

Serious Christians take sin seriously. Any of us who has been attacked, ignored, or scorned knows that sin is no joke. We do not say, "It doesn't matter." It does. Sin hurts.

But shouldn't real Christians be more tolerant? No. The Bible never tells us to tolerate sin, to condone each other's sins, to indulge each other. It tells us to *forgive* each other. Tolerance overlooks sin. Forgiveness looks right at it, suffers its full force, and then reaches for the sinner.

The people of God must be a forgiving people. There is little room in the church for the tight-lipped, cold-hearted, compassionless person. There is little room for any of us who shows no mercy. In fact, being right with others is so central to the life of the covenant community that we cannot even worship God till we have taken steps to be reconciled to a person with whom we are at odds (Matt. 5:23, 24). The church must be a society of those who know themselves unbelievably pardoned—and who *therefore* turn toward each other with hearty, kind, lavish, unusually generous forgiveness. The communion of saints is impossible without the forgiveness of sins.

Jesus tells us a parable of an unmerciful servant. Here is a man who has just been forgiven a debt of twenty million dollars. He then goes out to collect forty dollars. One moment he is on his knees begging the landlord, "Lord, have patience with me." The next moment, released and forgiven, he is back on his feet. He has some fellow servant by the throat and is squeezing away and rasping, "Pay up!"

You and I do this sort of thing all the time. God forgives us an accumulated debt so great that it buckled the knees of God's Son. And yet we steam and fret, toss and turn, over even the smallest—over even *imagined*—snubs by a brother or sister.

How is this possible?

A Prayer
Impress us, O Lord, so deeply with the grace that has come to speak our names that we, in turn, relax our hold on brothers and sisters. Let us forgive so that grace may abound. Through Jesus Christ our Lord, Amen.

Scripture
"And now, we pray you, forgive the transgression of the servants of the God of your father." Joseph wept when they spoke to him....[He] said to them, "Fear not, for am I in the place of God?"   Genesis 50:17,19

Confession
The church, in its own life, is called to practice the forgiveness of enemies.
          Confession of 1967 II, A, 4

108

It is hard to repent. And while it is hard enough to repent before a perfect God, it is even harder to repent before an imperfect human being. To realize fully that you have injured another person or neglected her, then to go to her and say, "I'm sorry; I'm ashamed; will you forgive me?"—to do and say such things is *mortifying*. It *kills* you a little. It takes pains. And it takes a pretty strong and courageous person.

It is hard to repent. It is often just as hard to forgive. We have seen how prominent forgiveness must be in the Christian community. But some things are harder to forgive than others. Some things take *time* to forgive. Some things rankle even after they're forgiven.

Suppose someone tells a lie which gets you fired. Suppose someone humiliates a defenseless member of your family. Or suppose other horrors: a greedy landlord evicts your widowed mother. A partner cheats your father. A Nazi shoots your grandfather through both knees. Someone violates your child!

Forgive? You feel like you want to kill somebody instead! Forgive this? As C. S. Lewis says, the call to forgiveness can sound like too *low* a calling. It sounds contemptible at times. Forgive *this*? As if it didn't matter?

Of course it matters. It hurts. We may have to grit our teeth to forgive. For some outrages, we may not be able to forgive at all for a while. Yet we must keep trying. Jesus' orders are unmistakable. Forgive or you will not be forgiven. That is, quite literally, forgive or be damned.

Joseph's brothers come shamefaced into Joseph's presence with the fear that he will "hate us and pay us back for all the evil which we did to him." They repent. Joseph weeps.

Then, to these chastened brothers, these grown-up men so desperately afraid their younger brother will not forgive them, Joseph says a word we have to hear. "Fear not," he says. "For am I in the place of God?"

God, you see, can withhold forgiveness. We cannot.

A Prayer
O Lord, in the sharpness of the pain which sin brings we struggle to forgive. Yet give us the grace to try it and to do it for the sake of Jesus Christ who has first forgiven us. Amen.

Scripture
And forgive us our debts, As we also have forgiven our debtors.
Matthew 6:12

Confession
We pray that God, for Christ's sake, would freely pardon all our sins; which we are the rather encouraged to ask because by his grace we are enabled from the heart to forgive others.
Westminster Shorter Catechism, Answer 105

109

In this famous petition of our Lord's Prayer, we ask forgiveness while simultaneously declaring our debtors forgiven. We pray, "Forgive us, O Father, just as we have right now declared others forgiven." "Cancel our debt as we have *herewith*, at this moment, cancelled our neighbor's debt."

The idea is that we cannot ask forgiveness of God while refusing it for others. Every time we pray this prayer we declare our neighbors forgiven. Of course, we may not *feel* terribly forgiving toward them. We may not even like them. That is not the point. Forgiveness is not a feeling but an act. It is something you *do*.

What do you do, exactly, when you forgive? Jay Adams and other Christian thinkers have suggested several considerations.

First, if I forgive a person, I promise not to let his offense "come between us" anymore. It may no longer ruin our relationship. I no longer hold it against him; I let it drop. I ought to be able to look him in the eye and speak with him. Perhaps this is one person I cannot laugh with,

at least not for a time. And perhaps I cannot forget what was done. But it is just that—it is *done* now. I put the offense in the past and keep it there. It is past its prime, spent, over with.

Secondly, I promise not to use this incident against this person in the future. I will not bring it up in public or explore it with friends. And, if I bury the hatchet with this person, I will not later go back, dig it up, and try to cut him with it again.

Finally, if I cancel someone's sin, I must quit dwelling on it, quit nursing it, quit turning it over in my mind. Lewis Smedes reminds us that a grievance we are nursing provides a delicious pain—like a tongue which keeps going to a sore place in your mouth. But to forgive is to exercise mind control over oneself and to declare an old injury off limits for private thoughts.

Three steps in forgiveness. They are hard steps. But we have our Lord's footprints to follow. And, in any case, they are steps which lead to peace, freedom, and even a good night's sleep.

A Prayer
Our Father who art in heaven, forgive us our debts as we have now forgiven our debtors. For thine is the kingdom, and the power, and the glory forever. Amen.

Scripture
Esau said, "I have enough, my brother...." Jacob said, "No, I pray you, if I have found favor in your sight, then accept my present from my hand; for truly to see your face is like seeing the face of God, with such favor have you received me."
Genesis 33:9,10

Confession
The new life takes shape in a community in which men know that God loves and accepts them in spite of what they are. They therefore accept themselves and love others, knowing that no man has any ground on which to stand except God's grace.
Confession of 1967 I, C, 1

110

In *The Forgiving Community*, William Klaassen reports a question Abigail Van Buren ("Dear Abbie") once asked her readers. Abbie asked, "Is there a reader somewhere who has caught her husband being unfaithful, has forgiven him, and has since had a happy marriage?"

There was a heavy response. Many who answered stated that the knowledge of adultery caused a particularly acute suffering. They had reacted with anger, shame, and a sense of great insecurity. It upset them more than they could say. But, interestingly, a number of the respondents also testified to the power of forgiveness. They knew there would always be scars. But for those who were determined to go on, the forgiveness which they were able to offer, even for this treachery, had helped them and their marriage grow stronger.

Forgiveness has great power. It opens the channels of grace in the Christian community, in a marriage, among friends, between parent and child. While forgiveness must be Christlike in the pain it suffers, it is also Christlike in its steady, unflinching determination to deal again with the offending person. Forgiveness liberates people. It restores community. It *reconciles*.

And one of the strangest and most wonderful discoveries you make when you forgive is that forgiveness can do more than just restore a broken relationship; it can actually strengthen it. People who meet each other halfway, one seeking and the other seeking to grant forgiveness, often find that their love for each other has deepened and thickened.

Jacob goes limping into a sunrise on his way to meet the brother he had so cunningly cheated. Jacob has learned penitence and humility—though only after having wrestled with God. Esau, in turn, is able to call Jacob "my brother." Across all the years they now come together in a reconciliation which speaks some of the very grace of heaven: "Truly to see your face is like seeing the face of God, with such favor have you received me."

A Prayer
O God our Father, form in us such strength and humility, blended together, that we may keep on in the attempt to forgive. Forgive, we pray, and gather to yourself all who have sinned against us. And forgive us again and again till that day when there shall be no more need for this emergency measure in a fallen world. Through Jesus Christ our Lord, Amen.

Postscript

1. Suppose someone cheats you, insults you, or otherwise sins against you. It is all very well to forgive such a person when he comes to you humble and penitent, but suppose he keeps on. Suppose he's not the least bit penitent. Suppose he taunts you with what he's doing.

   Do you still have to forgive? *Can* you forgive even if there is no penitence? Why or why not?

2. We sometimes think of a given rape or murder or infidelity as a sin so heinous that we can never forgive it. And some of these vicious sins do cause the victim lifelong suffering.

   But are they—in God's sight—unforgivable sins? *Are* there any unforgivable sins? Explain.

3. Roman Catholics have a "confessional" in which the penitent hears the priest say to him or her, "Your sins are forgiven. Go in peace."

   Would something like that help us guilt-ridden Protestants? We confess our sins to the Lord, but do we actually *hear* the words of forgiveness?

   How about confessing sins to one another as in James 5:16. Would that help us? Or would such confession create a spiritual nudist colony in which we soon could not bear to look at each other?

4. Do you forgive a *person* or do you forgive her sin?

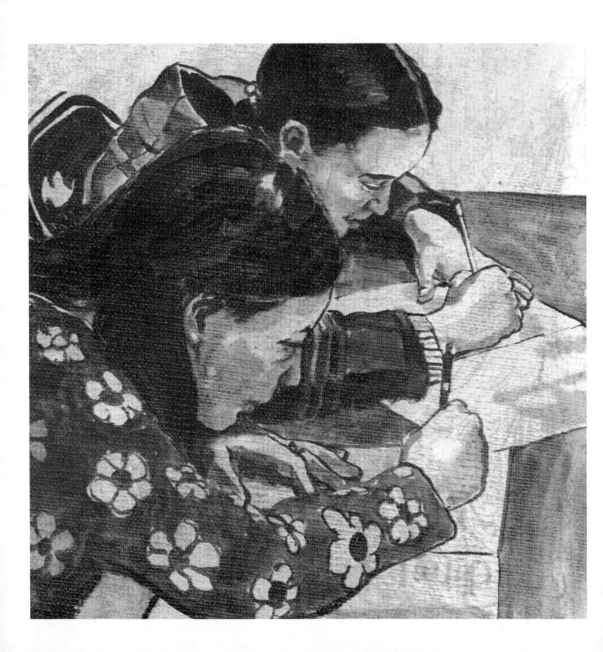

Week Twenty-Three

What Is the Shape of the Godly Life?

People have various recipes for "the good life." Playboys, for example, serve two masters: lust and greed. Right-wing, "macho" salvation promotes a saving trio of three G's: God, guns, and guts. Reformed Christians suggest godliness.

There are many names for this biblical and Reformed style of life. You could call it "life in Christ," or "the new life," or "covenant life," or "the transformed life." Because obedience to the will of God is so central in it you could call it "the obedient life." Or, you could call it simply "the Christian life." Here we shall follow the pastoral Epistles and talk of "the godly life" or "godliness."

A rich young man asked Jesus, "What shall I do to be saved?" We ask, "What shall we do now that we are saved?" What is the shape of the godly—and the goodly—life?

What Is the Shape of the Godly Life?

111

Scripture

Go into your room and shut the door and pray. **Matthew 6:6**
[Be] nourished on the words of the faith. **I Timothy 4:6**
Come, let us worship and bow down. **Psalm 95:6**
Sing to the Lord, bless his name. **Psalm 96:2**
Whatever is pure, whatever is lovely . . . think about these things. **Philippians 4:8**
Let a man examine himself, and so eat of the bread and drink of the cup. **I Corinthians 11:28**

Confession

Confess him, pray to him, and praise him in everything we do and say. **Heidelberg Catechism, Answer 99**

Godliness is the proper manner of life before God. It includes believing right doctrine. Thus, to reject silly myths and believe the truth is a *godly* thing to do. It includes social action. Thus, to liberate the oppressed is a *godly* thing to do. And it includes devotional piety—the whole range of religious acts in the texts above. Thus, praying, reading the Bible, worshiping, praising, meditating, and celebrating sacraments—all these are *godly* things to do.

Some of these devotional acts we perform with others. We worship publically. We sing together. We celebrate the *communion*. But much devotional piety is private. There ought to be times for each of us—regular, daily times—when we go into a room, shut the door, and do our exercises. This is a time for confessing personal sin, giving thanks for a particular mercy, asking for the measure of God's grace we need to go on. This is a time for gauging the drift of our lives and for making a moral resolve. This is a time for reading the Bible, for exploring its deep places and taking to heart its counsel.

Personal devotions often stir in us a powerful sense of the presence of God. There may be a feeling of that mystery and godly beauty which shyness and delicacy forbid one to tell.

But those feelings are special graces, secret reassurances. Often they will be absent. Still we keep on. That is because devotions are not so much something we feel as something we do. We exercise faith. We *train* ourselves in godliness (I Tim. 4:7).

Spiritual exercise is like jogging. You often do it gladly. But you are no hypocrite if you jog even when you don't feel like it.

A Prayer
O God, thou art my God, I seek thee, my soul thirsts for thee; my flesh faints for thee . . . . Because thy steadfast love is better than life, my lips will praise thee. Through Jesus Christ, Amen.
—from Psalm 63

Scripture
Have nothing to do with godless and silly myths. Train yourself in godliness.... For the time is coming when people will not endure sound teaching...and will turn away from listening to the truth.
II Timothy 4:7; II Timothy 4:3, 4

Confession
Especially on the festive day of rest, I [must] regularly attend the assembly of God's people to learn what God's Word teaches.
Heidelberg Catechism, Answer 103

112

Karl Barth was one of the most learned and productive of contemporary theologians. He had a richly furnished mind and a fertile theological imagination. He wrote volumes and volumes of theology, much of it technical, refined, sophisticated.

According to one version of a famous story, Barth was once asked about his vast theological accomplishment. What was its center? "If you had to sum up all your work," someone asked, "what would you say?"

Barth's reply was disarming: "Jesus loves me. This I know—for the Bible tells me so."

Here, as Barth rightly believed, is a place to stand. And a place to start. Perhaps it is even a place to end one's study of the words and truths of the faith. But meanwhile a mature Christian, a godly person, will have explored far and wide in her attempt to love God with all her *mind*. She will want to know as much of the faith as she can. She will want as much as she can get of what the books of Timothy call "sound doctrine."

Certain Christians regard this as a disagree-

able chore. They can't see the point of it. Isn't the Christian life, after all, a personal *relationship* to a living Lord? Then why learn all this dead dogma? Why rattle these old bones? Why bother with dry *skeletons* of the faith?

Why indeed? Unless you want to know *who this Lord is* to whom you are related! Unless your faith needs spine and structure! *Who* loves me—this I know? *How* do I know this? What has this Lord done? What is he doing? How, then, must we live?

Intelligent and mature Christian life is supported by sound doctrine, by right teaching, by knowledge of "the mind of Christ." Perhaps even by an adult education course or two. Else we will have to be forgiven, for we know not what we do. Else we become pushovers for fads, myths, and nonsense.

Let us admit that doctrine, as sometimes taught, is a tinkering with old bones. It is remarkably boring. (Some people could make even a tornado sound boring.) But the truth is that for Christians who want to learn something of the height and depth of the riches of Christ, these old bones can *live*.

A Prayer
Make me to know thy ways, O Lord; teach me thy paths. Lead me in thy truth, and teach me, through Jesus Christ our Lord. Amen.
—from Psalm 25

Scripture
"You shall love the Lord your God with all your heart, and with all your soul, and with all your mind. . . . You shall love your neighbor as yourself."
Matthew 22:37, 39

Confession
[The coming-to-life of the new self] is wholehearted joy in God through Christ and a delight to do every kind of good as God wants us to.
Heidelberg Catechism, Answer 90

113

Parents who let their child visit someone else's house for a day often do it with fear and trembling. What if he hogs all the toys? What if at lunch he prays one of those unusual prayers again? What if he tells lies about our family? Worse, what if he tells the truth?

Before you leave, you plead with your child. "Please," you say, "try to be good."

Try to be good. No doubt it is a high calling. A good man is hard to find. So is a good woman.

But the Bible talks much less about being good than about *doing* good. And though worldly people sometimes snort about "do-gooders," the Heidelberg Catechism regards doing good as the delight of the new life.

What kind of good should we attempt? All kinds: "every kind of good as God wants us to." In as many areas of life as sin has done bad—in that many areas we must do good. The Reformed strategy is to fit oneself into Jesus Christ's great work of reclaiming, restoring, recreating a corrupted creation.

We all know the way human beings have of corrupting a good thing. Someone has observed that for centuries "Bethlehem" has been a favorite name among Christians for hospitals. It seems right to associate these places of mercy with the birth of our Lord. One hospital, in particular, was in London. Over the years, the hospital's name was shortened and slurred from Bethlehem to "Bedlam." People called "lunatics" and "maniacs" were kept there. Eventually the hospital began to charge admittance for those who wanted to come in to gawk and giggle at the inmates.

Sinners turn Bethlehem to Bedlam. Redeemed sinners try to turn it back. A cheerful Christian nursing home attendant cleans up after helpless human beings. A keen businessperson attempts to create jobs for jobless people. A forest manager goes daily about the wonderful task of preserving and restoring a part of God's creation. In thousands of ingenious ways, the followers of Jesus Christ seek to show their love for God and neighbor by turning sickness to health, depression to hope, ignorance to knowledge, Bedlam to Bethlehem.

A Recitation
Therefore, my beloved brethren, be steadfast, immovable, always abounding in the work of the Lord, knowing that in the Lord your labor is not in vain. **—I Corinthians 15:58**

Scripture
While he was at Bethany...a woman came with an alabaster flask of ointment of pure nard, very costly, and she broke the flask and poured it over his head.... And they reproached her.... But Jesus said, "Let her alone.... She has done a beautiful thing to me.... She has done what she could.
Mark 14:3, 5, 6 ,8

Confession
Each member [of the church] is...endowed by the Spirit with some gift of ministry and is responsible for the integrity of his witness in his own particular situation.
Confession of 1967 II, A, 2

114

Our obligation to do good is as high, deep, and wide as life itself. To love God with all that we have and are, to love one's neighbor according to the blueprint of all the commandments—to do these things is to occupy us the rest of our lives. The godly life is shaped by the law of *love*. And love means doing good.

But do we all have to do the same thing? Do we all have to do the *same* good?

Christians used to glare at each other over discussions of whether individual witnessing or social action was the thing most needful. We now know both are required. Do you try for individual conversions or for changed social structures? Both. Do you testify to your next door neighbor or to a government bureaucracy? Both.

But who is equal to all these things? Who has sufficient time and talent for them? Nobody—at least not "personally." We can verbally encourage Christians who are doing other sorts of work than we, and we should. We can pray for other sorts of work, and we should. We can send a check (which *represents* our work) to support still other kinds of do-gooding, and we should. But no one of us can do everything. No one of us can do social work in Appalachia, ghetto ministry in the South Bronx, hospital counseling downtown, neighborhood coffee hour ministry on our own block—all the while preparing a new Chinese translation of the Bible and caring for our own children.

Where we get into trouble in the Christian community is where we start issuing identical marching orders for all Christians, as if each of us must follow Christ in exactly the same way.

Jesus himself cuts through all that. A woman has ministered to him in a lavish and peculiar way. She has drenched him with perfume. With a whiplash in his voice, Jesus says to the disgusted bystanders, "Let her alone. She has done a beautiful thing to me. She has done what she could."

Her contribution in her style. She has done a charming, unique sort of thing. She has done what she could.

A Prayer
Help us, O Lord, to treasure the gifts and the work which you give to others. Inspire us to let each other know of our concern, our benevolence, our sense of making up a powerful, vibrant body together. Through Jesus Christ our Lord, Amen.

Scripture
Let us not grow weary in well-doing, for in due season we shall reap, if we do not lose heart.
Galatians 6:9

Confession
By ourselves we are too weak to hold our own even for a moment.
Heidelberg Catechism,
Answer 127

115

It is the first good day of spring. Someone asks you to wash the car. At first you don't relish the idea, but gradually you get into the spirit of the thing. You not only wash that car thoroughly and dry it with a chamois. You also vacuum it out, take some chrome cleaner to the bumpers, and start in on a bit of waxing and polishing.

It hasn't been so bad, actually. You've rather enjoyed the task. You get into a job and soon see yourself as a sort of crusader on a great adventure, on a mission of industry and lasting significance. You see yourself moving to bigger and better tasks. When the car is done, then you'll clean out the garage and put up the awnings. After that you'll rake, mow, and edge the lawn. Next you'll move over to your neighbor's lawn and then clean his basement—on and on as you demonstrate to yourself, to your family, to the whole neighborhood what a real worker can do.

Then, as you wax and whistle, your back starts to ache and your right arm begins to feel heavy and sore. Your whistling slides down into a slower rhythm and shifts into a minor key.

Drop by drop your enthusiasm begins to dribble away. Perhaps you'd better leave the basement for another day. And the lawn too, you guess. And the garage can wait. Doing this car is a big enough job all by itself. Well, leave the rest of the car for next Saturday too. Now find a place to stretch out and rest!

"Let us not grow weary in well-doing...." At some time or another most of us have felt a sense of adventure in the Christian life; we have also felt a pain in the neck and all the adventure running off in sweat. We have known not only the rush of enthusiasm for doing good in the name of Christ. We have also felt that helpless, sinking sense of futility when others do not notice or do not care.

"In due season we shall reap," says St. Paul, "if we do not lose heart." Here is a word for any of us who have been Christian do-gooders till we cannot move another muscle or think another thought or make one more telephone call. For all spent-out, burned-out, worn-out Christians a heartening word: we shall reap the fruits of the Spirit in a life which never ends.

If we do not lose heart.

A Prayer
Build in us such strength, O Lord, as we need to carry on and to take on the burdens of those who are sagging. Stretch our endurance for the long haul of those who are handicapped, sick, or afraid. And give us security and joy in the knowledge that when we do good for Christ's sake then once more your kingdom comes and your will is done on earth as it is in heaven. Amen.

Postscript

1. In Matthew 21:28-32 we find a parable of two kinds of people. Which kind does Jesus prefer? What does this say to us about the relation between *talking* a godly life and *living* the godly life?

2. Meditation 112 suggests the need for doctrine as at least part of our knowledge of God. But, really, is it so necessary? Can't a little girl "know Jesus" better than a theologian? Explain.

3. The meditations this week suggest that devotional piety, belief in correct doctrine, and "doing all kinds of good" are features of the Christian life.

   Which of these is the most important?

4. The last meditation deals with "weariness in well-doing." If courage is so important to our well-doing, how do we keep it? How do we keep from "losing heart"?

Week Twenty-Four

What Is the Nature of the Church?

None of us are saved alone. We are summoned, redeemed, and then commissioned as part of a *people,* members of a *body,* participants in a *community.*

The church is a community gathered by Christ and empowered to be his witnesses, agents, and models in the world. Yet even among Christians there is a fair amount of impatience, frustration, and misunderstanding where the church is concerned.

For four weeks let us ask some of our questions about the church. And let us begin with a basic one: what do we confess the church to be? When we recite the Apostles' Creed, we claim to believe "a holy catholic church, the communion of saints." What does that mean? What is the nature of the church?

Scripture
Maintain the unity of the Spirit in
the bond of peace. There is one
body and one Spirit...one Lord,
one faith, one baptism, one God
and Father of us all, who is
above all and through all and in
all.   **Ephesians 4:3-6**

Confession
I believe *a* holy catholic Church.
                        Apostles' Creed

116

Variety is often a virtue. An old-fashioned garden boasts a splendid variety of fresh flowers. A well-stocked butcher shop features a good variety of fresh meats. A sizable produce market displays a tempting variety of fresh fruits in a riotous variety of sizes, shapes, and colors. The Creator who made all these things has wondrous *imagination.* He delights us with the sheer difference between a banana and a plum. He delights us with the incredible variety of his creation.

Yet he made only one church. We believe *a* holy catholic church. Here it is we, and not God, who have introduced a foreign variety. By the work of the one Lord Jesus Christ and the one Holy Spirit, the one God and Father has called one people to be one body. It is we who have divided up that body.

The divisions keep on across the centuries, across the world. North America by itself has far more than fifty-seven varieties of churches. A yearbook of churches lists not only usual churches—Roman Catholic, Baptist, Methodist,

Lutheran, Presbyterian, Congregationalist—but also some less usual ones—Kodesh Church of Immanuel, Romanian Orthodox Episcopate Church, Fire Baptized Holiness Church, Church of the Foursquare Gospel of Western Canada, Church of Daniel's Band, Christian Reformed Church.

We are supposed to be one body, *visibly* one body. But we are not. And our divisions are a scandal before the face of heaven and before the eyes of the world. The world sees our dividedness with "a scornful wonder." *Schism,* the breach of union in the church, is a sinful tragedy, like divorce. It is a painful tearing and ripping as of a leg from a body.

But what can we do? Declare our own denomination alone to be right and invite all the others to be converted back to us, the one true church? Or say it really doesn't matter what the various churches believe? Or give up our own distinctive confession?

Or what?

A Hymn or Confession
Though with a scornful wonder men see her sore oppressed,
By schisms rent asunder, by heresies distressed,
Yet saints their watch are keeping, their cry goes up,
    "How long?"
And soon the night of weeping shall be the morn of song.
                        —"The Church's One Foundation"

Scripture
You are . . . a holy nation, God's own people.　　　　I Peter 2:9
Christ loved the church and gave himself up for her, that he might sanctify her . . . that he might present the church to himself in splendor . . . that she might be holy and without blemish.
Ephesians 5:25-27

Confession
I believe a *holy* catholic Church, the communion of *saints*.
Apostles' Creed

117

A saint is a holy person. Usually we use the term for a person of special godliness. We say a man who steadfastly seeks to do God's will under maddening conditions is a *saint*. We say a woman who, though already loaded with responsibilities, seeks to bear the burdens of others as well—we say she is a *saint*. Mother Theresa of Calcutta is a saint. St. Paul is a saint. Perhaps your mother or grandfather is a saint.

Our secular society takes a different view. In our society saints are thought to be either pretentious hypocrites (nobody is *that* good) or else sissies. Saints are impostors who deserve to be unmasked, or else they are fogies—like those silly preachers on airline commercials who have to be guided through airports by knowing flight attendants so they won't miss their plane.

The fact is that all Christians are called to be saints. We are not called to be hypocrites or sissies, but we are separated from the world and then sent back as people being deeply cleaned and reshaped. We are to be *saints* for heaven's sake.

And often we do not like it. Sainthood is far beyond our modest wishes. We are like a man who is told by his physician that the best thing for him would be to quit smoking. "I don't deserve the best, Doc," says the man. "What's second best?"

We, the holy catholic church, are too easily satisfied with second best. We do not want to be so holy. Thus, on our liberal side we learn to cuss a little, to laugh at simple piety, and to sneer at "fundamentalists." We learn religious snobbery. On our Roman Catholic side we engage in bingo, raffles, and candle sales in church. On our conservative side we hustle religion with magicians, miracle prayer cloths, inscribed bricks, "karate for Christ," and assorted TV freebies, gewgaws, and religious schlock. Most of it gets our names inscribed not in the Lamb's book of life, but only on the mailing list of some religious show-biz operation.

How worldly can you get? How worldly can the church get and still be *holy*?

A Prayer
O Lord, we confess that we are often most worldly when we are being most religious. Do not cast us away from your presence, but do cast away from us whatever is not fitting for a holy nation of your people. Through Jesus Christ our Lord, Amen.

Scripture
[God] has put all things under [Christ's] feet and has made him the head over all things for the church, which is his body, the fulness of him who fills all in all.
Ephesians 1:22, 23

Confession
I believe a holy *catholic* Church.
Apostles' Creed

118

In *The Significance of the Church*, Raymond McAfee Brown rightly states that it would be perfectly proper to call oneself a "Reformed Catholic" or a "Protestant Catholic." Anyone, even a Reformed person, who believes in the lordship of Jesus Christ over the whole church across the world is a catholic Christian. He believes a catholic church; that is, a universal church. He may not be a *Roman* Catholic, but he is still a catholic.

It is mightily important for us to keep a sense of the catholicity or universality of the church. Sometimes we let our vision of the church shrink so small that it includes only our own little denomination in our own country—or, worse, only our own local church in our own city. *That* is "the church" to us. And, clinging to such a shrunken idea of the church, we sometimes feel more at home with native secularists than with foreign Christians.

It is a mistake. When we celebrate the sacrament of the Lord's Supper, we should think with awe and warmth of the millions of Christians across the world who say with us: "The body of Christ broken for you"; "The blood of Christ shed for you." When we read of Christians in the Sahel who manage to feed starving people where every government agency has failed, *we* should feel their triumph. When we hear about the hundreds of thousands of Christians being murdered in Uganda, *we* should feel their pain. I believe a catholic church. I am a catholic Christian.

A modern Reformed confession says, "Each member is the church in the world." That is not quite right. You are not the church in the world. Nor am I. We are individually *members* of the universal church in the world—a church so vast, so deep, so multinational, so incredibly catholic that only the Lord of the universe can be its head.

A Hymn or Confession
Elect from every nation, yet one o'er all the earth,
Her charter of salvation, one Lord, one faith, one birth;
One holy Name she blesses, partakes one holy food,
And to one hope she presses, with every grace endued.
—"The Church's One Foundation"

Scripture

Now you are the body of Christ.
I Corinthians 12:27

You are...God's own people.
I Peter 2:9

We are the temple of the living
God.   II Corinthians 6:16

Confession

I believe a holy catholic *Church.*
Apostles' Creed

119

You sometimes hear people discussing a certain local church as if it were someone's private enterprise. Just as they refer to "Duffy's Pre-Owned Garment Outlet" or to "Crazy Eddy's Bank and Trust," so people refer to a church by the name of its minister. Thus a church in which the Right Reverend Allis Chalmers is senior pastor gets to be known as "Chalmers's Church."

There may be good reason for the name. Perhaps Mr. Chalmers thinks of himself less as the congregation's servant than as its boss. Perhaps he "runs" the church, conforming it to his plans, steering it in the direction of his goals, impressing upon it his personality and style. He is the captain. The church is the ship. "Chalmers's Church."

The New Testament talks another way. So many of its descriptions of the church impress upon us the fact that we are not our own. Nor do we belong to any preacher. The church is rather the body of *Christ*, the temple of *God*, the bride of Christ, God's people. Out of the whole human race Christ gathers for *himself* a community. Even the word *church* reflects this fact. The English word *church* (like the German *Kirche* and the Dutch *kerk*) derives from a Greek word which means "belonging to the Lord." The church belongs to the *Lord* of the church.

What follows from this? A great deal. The institutional church is not our club to be rigged and outfitted merely to suit ourselves and to meet our own religious needs. The church is rather a living, pulsing instrument of Jesus Christ, equipped to do his work in the world and set up to serve not only ourselves but also those outside our gathering. It is not as if we form ourselves into a church by our voluntary cooperation. We are rather *called* as a people to praise God, to serve his children, and to sacrifice ourselves for others—even as a church—in the same way as Christ sacrificed himself for us.

A church that is turned in on itself is like a person who shuts herself in a closet and tries to live by breathing her own carbon dioxide. It doesn't work.

A Hymn or Confession
The Church's one foundation is Jesus Christ, her Lord;
She is His new creation by water and the Word;
From heaven He came and sought her to be His holy bride;
With His own blood He bought her, and for her life He died.
—"The Church's One Foundation"

What Is the Nature of the Church?

Scripture
And they devoted themselves to the apostles' teaching and fellowship, to the breaking of bread and the prayers.... And all who believed were together.
Acts 2:42, 44

Confession
I believe a holy catholic Church, the *communion* of saints.
Apostles' Creed

120

It is Sunday morning at the campground. A Christian family gathers around its portable TV. They might have attended a local Presbyterian church, but the kids have persuaded the parents that it is much less hassle simply to watch TV church. And the parents agree that the service on TV is much better—bigger crowds, more dynamic "special music," real celebrities appearing instead of local wonders, and a smoother preacher with a far more fetching smile. So there the family sits, watching worship. They are a part of the wholly electronic catholic church.

Here is the church without the communion of saints. Here, as someone has said, is a "phantom, non-people church" for those who like their public worship private, or who like to "go to church" without bestirring themselves, or who like to change channels on a prayer which lacks pizzazz. Here is church for the convenience of those who like to discharge their weekly church obligation while munching raisin bran.

Originally, of course, the electronic church was intended to serve shut-ins and to evangelize the unchurched. It still does both. But somehow it also tempts able-bodied church members to stay home and try to tune in a blessing. In late 1978, one expert estimated that in an average week 47 percent of the American population tunes in at least one religious program while only 42 percent actually attends a service "personally."

This is a strange and unhappy trend. The church has always thrived on *koinonia*, on fellowship. In the early Christian church there was a remarkable and revolutionary togetherness—Parthians and Medes, Elamites, Judeans, and Cappadocians together. Later on, red and yellow, black and white together. Weak and strong, male and female, wise old women and impatient little boys together. There is no real Christian life and no real Christian faith unless it is faith and life *together*.

The church is not a set of individuals watching TV. It is a communion of living, breathing human beings, of redeemed people who worship, care, share, and serve together.

I believe the *communion* of saints.

A Hymn or Confession
'Mid toil and tribulation and tumult of her war,
She waits the consummation of peace forevermore,
Till with the vision glorious her longing eyes are blest,
And the great Church victorious shall be the Church at rest.
—"The Church's One Foundation"

Postscript

1. Meditation 116 states that the dividedness of the church is a scandal. But doing something about that dividedness is not easy. Look at the series of questions with which this meditation closes. What *can* we do?

2. Meditation 117 discusses the holiness of the church. *Holiness* is the dimension of the church's separateness from the world and its continuing sanctification, its continuing reshaping according to the will of God.

   Does our own church—either locally or as a denomination—show real marks of *holiness*? Have we accommodated ourselves too much to our society or should we be less aloof and accommodate a bit more?

3. Is the "electronic church" a help or a hindrance to the communion of the saints? Why?

4. Why do we say, "I *believe* a holy catholic church"? What's to *believe*?

Week Twenty-Five

What Does the Institutional Church Do?

The one, holy, catholic church is the set of all those people who truly believe in Jesus Christ. It is sometimes called the "invisible" church.

There is also the set of all those people who make a Christian profession. Many of these are members of the invisible church. Some are not. We call the set of all those who profess Christ—whether or not they actually believe in him—the "visible" church.

You can look at the visible church in two ways. You can see it as a vast, pulsing organism—millions of professing Christians doing Christ's work in the world. Or you can see it as an organization with officers, rules, membership requirements, set services, budgets, and buildings. We call people organized in that fashion the *institutional* church.

This week we will be asking about the institutional church. What is it good for? What are its "marks"? What does the institutional church *do*?

What Does the Institutional Church Do?

Scripture
And his gifts were that some should be apostles, some prophets, some evangelists, some pastors and teachers, to equip the saints for the work of ministry.   Ephesians 4:11,12

Confession
We believe that this true Church must be governed by that spiritual polity which our Lord has taught us in His Word; namely, that there must be ministers ...also elders and deacons.... By these means everything will be carried on in the Church with good order and decency.
Belgic Confession,
Article XXX

121

There is a certain sort of secularist who thinks religion bad enough, but *organized* religion even worse. He is afraid of religious people getting together in orderly, disciplined power blocs. What if they get together on abortion? Or on government spending? What if they try to "impose their morality on others"? That is to say, what if they vote? You can't have people doing *that* in a free society! At any rate, not religious people. For organized religion is clearly a threat to secularism and freedom.

Interestingly enough, some professing Christians are a bit uneasy about organized church religion too. They know the institutional church is "the mother of believers." If they are Calvinists, they know they ought to be "nourished at her breast." But, somehow, their own church's arrangement of forms, orders, prescriptions, budgets, committees, offices, building plans, task forces, and "projected five-year plans for ecumenical interfacing and societal impacting" seems less like a mother than like a business. Can you get nourished at the breast of a business?

Richard Mouw divides the people who complain about our institutional mother into two groups. First, there are the "underfed." These Christians are looking for rich, varied, creative, liberating nourishment from the church and they are not getting it. Week after week they come home from church bored, frustrated, and still hungry. But there are also the "overfed." These people spend their lives at work, in their neighborhoods, with their families, and in private study doing explicitly Christian worship and service. When Sunday comes, they do not think they can stomach one more crumb. They are already fed to the point of being almost fed up.

How can the institutional church equip *these* saints? How can it help both the overfed and the underfed? Suppose your church is not feeding you or equipping you. What can you do?

Can you undertake to correct your own *mother?*

A Prayer
O Lord, we know that the church is not some *other* group on the other side of town. We know the church is we, ourselves. Correct us, the church—but in just measure, not in your anger, lest you bring us to nothing. In Jesus' name, Amen.

What Does the Institutional Church Do?

Scripture
Paul spoke to the people and...
kept on talking until midnight.
...Seated in a window was a
young man named Eutychus,
who was sinking into a deep
sleep as Paul talked on and on.
When he was sound asleep, he
fell to the ground from the third
story and was picked up dead.
Acts 20:7, 9 (NIV)

Confession
The marks by which the true
Church is known are these: If the
pure doctrine of the gospel is
preached therein....
Belgic Confession,
Article XXIX

122

Christians "identify with" figures in the Bible: strong people identify with Samson, wise ones with Solomon, tall ones with Saul, and short ones with Bildad the Shuhite. Many of us identify with Eutychus, "who was sinking into a deep sleep as Paul talked on and on." For any of us who has fallen asleep during a sermon, Eutychus is our man. He knew no souls are saved after twenty minutes.

Preaching is proclamation of the Word of God. Preaching is an official task of the institutional church and a mark of the *true* church. By a preacher's interpretation of God's ancient Word, God himself may speak to us again today. There is something old in preaching: a biblical word is read and explained. But there is also something new: that word is particularly directed to us here and now—to *these* people at *this* time and place. A good sermon, as Karl Barth said, is prepared by a preacher who has one eye on the Bible and the other on the newspaper.

A sermon has failed if after it anyone could reasonably ask, "So what?" A proper sermon will lay forceful claim on us, demand clear response from us. It will be preached so deeply into our lives—into our guilt and our longings, our moral puzzlement and frustration, our fresh fears and fragile hopes—that we will leave church with two ideas running powerfully through our minds: "What a great God!" and "What a great obligation we now have!"

Let us admit it doesn't always work out that way. Those of us who are preachers sometimes manage no better than to thrash around helplessly among several heads of doctrine. Or we get fascinated with matters which are truly uninteresting to the rest of the congregation. Or we belabor what is painfully obvious. Some of us preach at great length, supposing we may never see these people again. How right we are. Meanwhile, we who listen set up the Eutychian defense: we begin to nod as if in agreement and gradually fall dead asleep.

The church today needs not less preaching, but better preaching. It also needs better listening. The two go together.

Could it be that Paul and Eutychus owed *each other* an apology?

A Prayer
Inspire among us, O Lord, strong, fearless, nourishing preaching. And stimulate in us open, receptive listening. Through Jesus Christ our Lord, Amen.

Scripture

As often as you eat this bread and drink the cup, you proclaim the Lord's death until he comes.
I Corinthians 11:26

You were buried with him in baptism, in which you were also raised with him.   Colossians 2:12

Confession

The marks by which the true Church is known are these: . . . if it maintains the pure administration of the sacraments as instituted by Christ. . . .
Belgic Confession,
Article XXIX

123

Thomas Howard has pointed out how often we show that a thing is important to us by "acting it out." We perform a *ritual*. We not only say something; we also *do* something which says something. Thus, in one ritual two people approach each other, each extending his right hand. Then, shamelessly taking hold, the two people pump their locked hands quickly up and down through a six-inch vertical plane. They *shake hands*, of all things! Wordlessly, their ritual says "Hello!" or "Nice to see you!" or "Congratulations!" or "It's agreed, then!" or "No hard feelings!" or "That sermon was reasonably orthodox!" Sometimes people say the words out loud at the same time their hands are shaking. It is a kind of hand-mouth coordination.

Some rituals accompany present events which keep happening; for example, every day we shake hands when greeting people. Other rituals celebrate a past historical event of great significance; thus, we set off fireworks to recall a declaration of independence.

Sacraments do both. With certain words and acts we celebrate memorially a great past act of our Lord's. He once gave his broken body and shed blood for us. He once went down into death and came back up into life. Now by the Lord's Supper and baptism we not only remember these events; we also "act them out." We reenact, re-present these events with the "signs" of breaking bread, pouring wine, dipping in water. With words and with ritual acts we say to God and to ourselves: "We are the people of these Christ-events and of all they mean."

But, strangely and wonderfully, the very reenactment of these past events becomes for us a means of *present* grace. For by our breaking, eating, pouring, drinking, submerging, and washing, God himself acts here and now to refresh us for the way ahead. By giving us sacramental gifts and letting us use them, he says he is our gracious God. By receiving these gifts, we say we are his covenant people.

The pure administration of the sacraments is a main task of the institutional church and a mark of the *true* church. By these present ritual acts, we align ourselves with what Christ did in the past and are nourished for what he will do through us, his people, in the future. In other words, sacraments unite us to Jesus Christ—the same yesterday, today, and forever.

A Prayer

O Lord God, in your great mercy supply such gifts as are needful for the way ahead. Remind us that we are your people, that we are the people formed by all that was done in Jesus Christ, your Son and our Lord. Amen.

Scripture
For myself, I feel certain that you, my brothers, have real Christian character and experience, and that you are capable of keeping each other on the right road.
Romans 15:14 (Phillips)

Confession
The marks by which the true Church is known are these: . . .if church discipline is exercised in punishing of sin. . . .
Belgic Confession,
Article XXIX

124

Many of us have old, and somewhat uneasy, memories of the exercise of church discipline. We remember the terrible drama of "silent censure," the ominous public mention of a name, the embarrassment of meeting the offender, the hushed atmosphere in the congregation when excommunication occurred.

Churches are doing less and less of this cracking the whip over the backs of straying sheep. It is mostly because erring sheep amble out of range. They simply leave the fold. Or join some other flock. They do not care about our church discipline. As far as they are concerned, we may read our forms and go through our procedures as much as we like. They will just remove themselves from our reach.

Church discipline is an official task of the institutional church and a mark of the *true* church. It must not be neglected. But neither must it be seen too narrowly. We have long thought of church discipline as merely official—something which only church officers could do. We have thought of it as the narrow, punishing form of pressure brought to bear on an offender by a church council.

But, as John Kromminga rightly contends, church discipline is not mainly what the church council does to us, but rather what we do for each other. It is not just official "punishment of sin" but also mutual teaching, admonishing, helping, leading, guiding. Very often it is *encouraging!* What it is, in fact, is "keeping each other on the right road."

When a child is baptized among us, we promise "to receive this child in love, pray for him, help care for his instruction in the faith, and encourage and sustain him in the fellowship of believers."

We vow to help keep him or her "on the right road," to include this growing child of God in church discipline.

You see, it is not a threat but a *promise.*

A Prayer
Give us, O Lord, the maturity and kindliness we need to keep each other on the right road. Give us humility and love. Give us such discipline as will equip us to accomplish the work you have set out for us. Through Jesus Christ our Lord, Amen.

Scripture

"You shall receive power when the Holy Spirit has come upon you; and you shall be my witnesses in Jerusalem and in all Judea and Samaria and to the end of the earth."   Acts 1:8

Confession

To be reconciled to God is to be sent into the world as his reconciling community....Christ has called the church to this mission and given it the gift of the Holy Spirit. The church maintains continuity with the apostles and with Israel by faithful obedience to his call.

Confession of 1967 II, A, 1

125

There was a time when the church's foreign missionaries were regarded as a team of our best and bravest Christian soldiers. They were seen as an elite corps of shock troops. When they dispersed to their lonesome and difficult work, the Christians at home prayed with them, spoke encouragement to them, and assured them of their continued interest and support. When these troops returned home from Japan, Nigeria, Argentina, or the Philippines, they were warmly and gratefully received. Naturally, we were glad to hear about and see pictures of their work.

In some parts of the church there are signs of a dangerous shift. Some church members cannot even name their own missionaries. They don't know about them or care about them. When missionaries return, they are greeted with mild interest and a request to keep their program short. Some who offer to tell about their work are advised that it is not necessary. Missionaries who do not really fit in the foreign society to which they have been ministering return home to discover that they do not really fit among domestic Christians either. It can be deeply discouraging.

A lapse of interest in missions is a sign of decay in the church. Let us confess the truth: a church that does not extend itself and does not *care* to extend itself is diseased. A vital, healthy, exciting Christian church is always reaching, stretching, witnessing, adding on those who are being saved.

The institutional church does mission work. The extraordinary people who do this work represent Jesus Christ. But they also represent *us*. We must know their names, write them letters, pray for them with our children, deliberately take an interest in what they are doing.

For without mission obedience to Jesus Christ, the church will quietly dwindle and slowly begin to die.

A Prayer

O Lord, we confess that we know more about sports than about missions. We have neglected those who represent us in speaking the gospel in faraway places. Forgive us, we pray. And stir us today to begin a sharp new interest in the work carried on across the world. Through Jesus Christ our Lord, Amen.

Postscript

1. Do the forms and orders of the institutional church help us to praise God and be edified for doing the work of Jesus Christ? Or do they just get in the way? Wouldn't it be better to let the Holy Spirit guide us instead of man-made rules? Explain.

2. If it is true that the church needs not less preaching but better preaching, how can we get it?

3. Most Reformed churches baptize by sprinkling. Baptists, however, baptize by going down into water (immersion) and coming up again (emersion). Does it matter which mode we use? Why or why not?

Week Twenty-Six

What Is the Shape of Reformed Liturgy?

On Sundays we gather for public worship.
While gathered we and our ministers do
various things: greetings, hymns, prayers,
assurances, sermons, confessions,
sacraments, offerings, benedictions.

There is an *order* of worship. We do things in
order. But how did we get the order we
have? Was there specific planning and
hard thinking behind it? Is there rhyme or
reason to any of it?

The *liturgy* consists of "those acts done by
the church in its solemn assembly with
God."* Every church has a liturgy. All
churches are "liturgical churches." But
Reformed churches, like others, have a
distinctive shape to their liturgy. This
week we will be asking about that. What
do we do in our Sunday gatherings? Why
do we do these things? In what order?
What is the shape of Reformed liturgy?

---

*From the 1968 Report of the Liturgical Committee, the Christian Reformed Church. Most of this week's lesson represents or parallels the material and suggestions in this report. The "Confessions" this week will be from the Report as well.

Scripture

And they devoted themselves to the apostles' teaching and fellowship, to the breaking of bread and the prayers.

Acts 2:42

Report

Worship within the Old Testament was a two-laned avenue; in it God moved toward man and man moved toward God....The dialogue continues in New Testament worship....Worship for the people of the living God has always been a dialogue....The dialogue is the inherent structure of worship.

Report II, B and C

126

A dialogue is a two-way talk. Labor and management meet for "contract talks." These are dialogues. Protestants and Catholics discuss their differences. These discussions are ecumenical dialogues. Two people speak with each other over a telephone. They engage in dialogue.

Reformed worship is a dialogue. It reflects the shape of covenant life. God acts graciously in our lives to create and redeem. We respond with grateful acts of obedience. He does something. We do something back. God acts. We react.

So in worship. God speaks. Then we speak. God addresses us, his sons and daughters. Humbly and gratefully, we respond by addressing him, our Father.

Think over some of the things we do when we gather on Sundays. Near the beginning, God brings a "greeting" or "salutation": "Grace to you, and mercy, and peace...." Then we respond by singing a hymn of praise to this gracious, merciful, and peace-giving God. God

speaks his will for our lives through the reading of the Ten Commandments or some other biblical "call to penitence." We respond by confessing that we have sinned and fallen short of the glory of God. But a merciful God responds in turn by the assurance that he pardons, accepts, and forgives us. And we respond to *that* by singing our joy and thanksgiving. God speaks through a sermon. We reply with our offerings, or our confession of faith, or with a hymn of dedication, or with the faithful partaking of the Lord's Supper.

All of it is dialogue. That is the structure of biblical and Reformed worship. The gracious Lord of the universe condescends to meet and to speak with such as you and me. This is a special, exciting, dynamic *event*.

There are two attitudes toward this event. One is the dreary resolution to go through the motions again. The other is the expectant yearning once more to meet the living God.

A Recitation

Praise the Lord, all nations!
Extol him, all peoples!
For great is his steadfast love toward us;
　and the faithfulness of the Lord endures forever!
Praise the Lord!

—Psalm 117

Scripture

"Ho, every one who thirsts, come to the waters; and he who has no money, come, buy and eat!... Incline your ear, and come to me; hear, that your soul may live.
Isaiah 55:1, 3

The Lord bless you and keep you: The Lord make his face to shine upon you, and be gracious to you: The Lord lift up his countenance upon you, and give you peace.
Numbers 6:24-26

Report

God Himself...graciously calls His people into His presence.... The apostolic blessing is the proclamation of God's gracious intention.
Report V, A and E

127

Many dialogues are between equals. These equals "give and take." They thrust and counter-thrust. Each has a vote and (unless an arbitrator is brought in) there is no tie-breaker. Many dialogues are standoffs.

The dialogue in worship is not a standoff. And it is not between equals. It is a little like a dialogue between a parent and her child. A reasonable parent will dialogue with her child if the child is old enough. She will allow her child to speak. In fact, a good parent *wants* her child to speak openly, trustingly, freely, responsively. But there are times when a parent insists on having the last word. There are times when she talks and wants no back talk. That is, she doesn't want an *argument*. She is looking for obedience instead.

The worshiping dialogue with God is between unequals—the Creator and his creatures, the Father and his children, the Lord and his church, the covenant God and his people.

That is why a properly formed and Reformed liturgy begins with *God's* call to worship or with *God's* greeting. It is he who summons us to gather. It is not as if we roused ourselves to worship ("Come let *us* worship and bow down" or, worse, "Hi! I'm Jimmy. Welcome to..."). It is rather that God calls all of us who thirst to come to the waters and all of us who have ears to hear.

In the same way, after worship, it is God who dismisses us. The "benediction" is not a prayer *to* God; it is rather God's parting promise and gift, offered to people with their hearts—and even their eyes—wide open.

So the beginning call to worship or the salutation, on one side, and the parting benediction, on the other, frame our Sunday assemblies. In between we have dialogue with God. But it is dialogue between unequals. *God* has the first word.

He also has the last word.

A Prayer

I will extol thee, my God and King, and bless thy name for ever and ever. Every day I will bless thee, and praise thy name for ever and ever. Through Jesus Christ, Amen.
—from Psalm 145

Scripture
If we confess our sins, he is faithful and just, and will forgive our sins and cleanse us from all unrighteousness.   I John 1:9

Report
[The Confession and Assurance are] a liturgical preparation for the two cardinal phases of worship: the proclamation of the Word and the response of the people.   Report V, B

128

Confession and pardon are part of the rhythm of our relationship with God. Our confession; his pardon. Neither without the other.

The confession of sin is an act of the gathered people. "*We* have sinned." It is a prayer: "We have sinned against *you*, O Lord." The confession may be based on one of the ancient cries of desperation among God's people: "The harvest is past, the summer is ended, and we are not saved" (Jer. 8:20). Or it may be a pointed, existential, up-to-date confession of our very contemporary sin: "We have wasted your resources, fouled your creation, split your church."

Then comes the gracious assurance of pardon: a gift of God for the people of God. With the authority of representing God himself, the minister says something like this:

If you have indeed repented of your sins, and if you do seek your salvation in Jesus Christ and do wish to live the Christian life, I say to you, in the name of our Lord Jesus Christ, that God has forgiven all of your sins and accepted you as his beloved child, because of the sacrifice of his son.

The assurance of pardon is not "cheap grace." It is not offered to everyone dozing within earshot of the minister. It is offered to penitent people who attend to this grace of God with humility and with believing hearts.

Such people, renewed in their right relation to God—cleansed, restored, reassured—are now prepared to hear the word and to respond to it.

A Hymn or Recitation
Glory be to the Father and to the Son and to the Holy Ghost; as it was in the beginning, is now, and ever shall be, world without end. Amen, Amen.   —"Glory Be to the Father"

Scripture
Preach the word, be urgent in season and out of season, convince, rebuke, and exhort, be unfailing in patience and in teaching. **II Timothy 4:2**

Report
The sermon is the core of the Christian liturgy. Along with the reading of Scripture, it both anchors worship in the revelation of God and directs it toward life and its responsibilities in the present time. **Report V, C, 3**

129

Preaching, as we saw last week, is not just "twenty minutes to raise the dead." Nor is it a preacher's personal sharing of his religious experiences. It is rather a kind of Protestant transubstantiation: these ordinary words spoken faithfully from the lips of an ordinary human being may become for us, here and now, the very Word of God. The Second Helvetic Confession states it flatly: "The preaching of the Word of God *is* the Word of God."

But preaching is only part of the "service of the Word." There is first a "prayer for illumination." Here a preacher represents the people in asking for the testimony of the Holy Spirit as the Word is read: "Send out thy light and thy truth—let them *lead* us." This prayer reflects our conviction that unless the same Spirit who inspired these words now inspires us who read them, the words are empty and our preaching merely "the noise of solemn assemblies." Preaching the Word always needs first a right *hearing* of the Word.

Then there is the reading of Scripture itself. This is not just a preliminary to the sermon. It is a part of the liturgy in its own right, with its own importance. The Report concedes that "we do not have to ring bells, kiss the pages, or parade the book around in the fashion of Roman bibliolatry." Yet we should frame the reading not only with the prayer of illumination before, but with a short response *after* as well. Perhaps the congregation or the choir could sing "Praise be to thee, O Lord" after hearing the reading of the Word.

The sermon follows. Sermons are not for giving us a "blessing" so much as for building us up for service. A good sermon will "convince, rebuke, and exhort" us with reference to the whole shape of our lives *outside* the sanctuary.

In the sermon, God is using His freedom to address people, not as Israelite nomads or Jerusalem metropolitans, but as people of the demonically dangerous twentieth century.

(Report V, C, 3)

Even in this century, and through all its danger, God speaks through sermons. And his people hear.

A Prayer
Speak, Lord, for your servants are listening. Through Jesus Christ, Amen.

Scripture	Report
Through [Jesus] let us continually offer up a sacrifice of praise to God, that is, the fruit of lips that acknowledge his name. **Hebrews 13:15**	The shape of the liturgy is defined by the two main dimensions of the God-man relationship: the priority of revelation and the response of faith to it. **Report V, C**

130

After the sermon, many liturgies move quickly to an end. God speaks, the people respond with a hymn of dedication; God speaks the last word through the minister's pronouncement of the benediction, and the people go home.

In this sort of liturgy, the confession of faith (reciting of the creed), intercessory prayer, and offerings are scattered somewhere in front of the sermon.

But since these things are faithful *responses* to what God has done and what God now says, they may well be done *after* the sermon instead of before it.

God speaks through the sermon. Then the people respond by standing up to say strongly, "I believe in God the Father Almighty. . . ." I *believe* in the one who has just spoken. All of us—and I—say *Yes* and *Amen* to the promises and demands of the gospel.

Next comes the intercessory prayer—what has sometimes been called the "long" prayer. Except it needn't be so long. For praise and confession and the plea for illumination have already been prayed to God. Now, in intercession, we pray for the needs of the congregation, and for those in high places, and for unbelievers, and for all humankind. We become the priesthood of believers, offering before God some measure of the same gracious concern which God has first offered to us.

Finally, we bring our offerings—the fruit not only of our lips, but also of our hands and minds and lower back muscles. We return to the Lord a hearty share of the harvest of his land and the work of his people.

On many occasions the service will now climax with the celebration of the Lord's Supper—a celebration in which the whole movement of God's acting and our reacting blends into a harmony of the people's thanksgiving and God's gift of nourishing food for the days ahead. God gives and we "thanks-give."

Creed, intercession, offering, and supper—the "sacrifice of praise to God. . .the fruit of lips that acknowledge his name."

A Prayer
Now we offer, O Lord, not just our confession, prayer, money, and thanksgiving. We offer our hearts. We offer our very selves. Through Jesus Christ our Lord, Amen.

Postscript

1. Why do we call our meetings "worship services"? What is *worship?*

2. What do you think about beginning a liturgy with announcements of meetings, picnic suppers, births, cars with their lights on, and the like? How about beginning with the pastor's personal greeting: "Good morning! I'm Reggie, and I'd just like to welcome you..."?

3. In a "call to worship" sometimes used in Reformed churches, the minister quotes Psalm 95:6: "O come, let us worship and bow down, let us kneel before the Lord, our Maker...." Then instead of "kneeling down" the people all stand up! Why?

4. The meditations this week say little about the use of *music* in the liturgy. Yet this is an area of great liturgical sensitivity. Music as played and sung can greatly assist the liturgy—or it can become a stumbling block. Music is the "war department" in the church.

   Are there any guidelines to help us in this area? If people like it and get a "blessing" from it, is any hymn or chorus acceptable? Who decides?

5. *A Project.* Take a copy of last week's bulletin to class. Your leader will present a series of questions which should help you evaluate your church's "order of worship."

Week Twenty-Seven

How Is the Church Related to State and Kingdom?

We cannot leave this unit on the church without saying at least a word about two sorts of relations which the church maintains with entities outside itself. One of these entities is the state. The other is the kingdom of God. It should not surprise us that these are both *political* entities, for the Bible has much to say about our relationship to God and to the rest of his creation in political terms. *King, kingdom, Lord, sovereignty,* and many other biblical terms express patterns of authority and obedience which have become the basis of whole systems of theology oriented to the "sovereignty of God."

There are incredibly complex problems in the area of church-state and church-kingdom relations. Our format prevents anything but the briefest and simplest introduction. Still, we must at least ask: How is the church related to state and kingdom?

How Is the Church Related to State and Kingdom?

131

Robert Hudnut recalls one of President William Howard Taft's favorite stories. It concerned a man who had to give a dinner speech on the topic, "The Christian in Politics."

Well [said the President], the fellow rose at the invitation of the toastmaster, gazed out over the expectant audience, bowed and commenced. "Mr. Chairman, ladies and gentlemen. I was assigned the topic for tonight's dinner, 'The Christian in politics.' I did a great deal of research on the subject. I turned over half-a-dozen libraries. And my conclusion is simply this. There ain't no such thing." *(The Sleeping Giant)*

Sad to say, this cynic has his grandchildren in the church today. For them, politics and religion do not mix. Church and state are parallel tracks which never meet. The state is a necessary evil in a brutal world and is best left to brutal people to manage as they see fit. Meanwhile, the church's task is to save souls and dispense "spiritual" blessings—a safe concern for preachers, children, and other innocent folk. As the Nazi Goebbels said, "Let the churches serve God; we serve the people."

This is demonic propaganda. Christians may never simply abandon political power to the sons and daughters of this world. Reformed Christians are *political* Christians, actively taking an interest and role in government and always seeking to reform it according to the will of God.

Part of our political responsibility is obedience. So long as the state does not order what is "repugnant to the Word of God," we obey it as a divine institution. We obey even stupid rulers and inconvenient rules. We pay taxes. But we also do more: we vote. We run for office. We encourage justice and discourage injustice. We pray for judges, lawmakers, and executives.

That is, we do everything in our power as the church to give the state what it has coming from us. We "pay our dues." We render to Caesar the things that are Caesar's.

A Prayer
Forgive, O Lord, our political fear and cynicism. Raise up among us strong and visionary leaders to show us better ways of fulfilling our responsibilities as Christians in politics. Through Jesus Christ our Lord, Amen.

How Is the Church Related to State and Kingdom?

Scripture
And Jesus said to them, "Whose likeness and inscription is this?" They said, "Caesar's." Then he said to them, "Render therefore to Caesar the things that are Caesar's, and to God the things that are God's".
Matthew 22:20, 21

Confession
We reject the false doctrine [that] the State, over and beyond its special commission, should and could become the single and totalitarian order of human life.
The Theological Declaration of Barmen, II, 5

132

A recently published hymn offers a number of stirring and vibrant stanzas. The words are strong. They are colorful. They are deeply reverent. Listen:

Washed in the blood of the brave and the blooming,
Snatched from the altars of insolent foes...
Vainly the prophets of Baal would rend it,
Vainly his worshippers pray for its fall;
Thousands have died for it, millions defend it,
Emblem of justice and mercy to all.
(*Liberty*, Sept.-Oct. 1978)

What is the object of this high praise? What is being venerated in these breathless words? Salvation through Jesus Christ? The church? The gospel? The holy Bible?

None of these. The last stanza shows its true colors: "God bless the flag and its loyal defenders...."

The flag! This is a hymn to the American flag!

Now patriotism is a good thing. You do not like to hear a citizen of a free country speak with malice toward his own land any more than you like to hear him speak that way toward his own college or his own mother.

But there is a deadly idolatry here for Christians who get their love for country confused with their love for God. These Christians want to sing national anthems at hymnsings, fly national flags in church sanctuaries, identify The Way with the American Way, and obey the government no matter what it tells us to do!

Against this sort of temptation it may help some of us to remember the reign of terror and murder which nationalistic idolatry permitted in Hitler's Germany. It should help all of us to recall that one day our Lord took a coin in hand and used it to make a distinction between the things that are Caesar's and the things that are God's.

Someone once put it neatly. Caesar's coin had Caesar's image on it and belonged to Caesar. We have *God's* image on us and belong to him.

We must never get these images mixed up.

A Prayer
O Lord, let us give thanks for national gifts and national freedoms. But let us remember that our only comfort is that we finally belong to you and to your Christ. From all civil religion deliver us through Jesus Christ our Lord. Amen.

Scripture
"Therefore, O king, let my counsel be acceptable to you; break off your sins by practicing righteousness, and your iniquities by showing mercy to the oppressed, that there may perhaps be a lengthening of your tranquillity."   Daniel 4:27

Confession
The members of the church are emissaries of peace and seek the good of man in cooperation with powers and authorities in politics, culture, and economics. But they have to fight against pretensions and injustices when these same powers endanger human welfare.
Confession of 1967 I, C, 1

133

We who make up the church have a particular relationship to the state. On the one hand, we may not simply assume that the state is a dangerous beast. It is, after all, an institution of God to protect freedom and pursue justice. Neither, on the other hand, may we bow in final reverence before the state, worshiping its symbols and power. Our help is in the name of the *Lord*, who made the heavens and the earth—and the state.

We owe our government thoughtful obedience and active cooperation in the disciplining of society. We owe our governors respect and the regular office of prayer to God on their behalf.

There is something else we owe. The Old Testament shows us a number of instances in which the prophets of God spoke not only to the leaders of their own nation-church of Israel, but also to the kings of heathen countries. Knowing both God's righteousness and the nation's unrighteousness, a daring prophet such as Daniel would stand squarely before a powerful king and witness to the godly requirement for justice and "mercy to the oppressed."

The church today has this same prophetic mission. In one of his sermons Ernest Campbell offers an analogy:

For years it was common practice in mining to take a canary down into the pits. The canary with its sensitive breathing mechanisms could detect early any poisonous gasses that might be seeping in. When the miners stopped hearing the canary sing and saw its body topple to the bottom of the cage, they knew that they had to get out.

("The Church and the Common Good") When we, the church, speak strongly to our government about abortion, civil rights, war, prison reform, pornography, freedom of education, and other issues, we perform the "canary function." We act as a kind of early warning system.

Are we usually early enough?

A Prayer
Forgive, Lord God, the indifference and scorn which has often kept us from banding together and speaking out. Make us a strong, prophetic church. Through Jesus Christ, Amen.

Scripture
Then comes the end, when [Christ] delivers the kingdom to God the Father after destroying every rule and every authority and power.... When all things are subjected to [God], then the Son himself will also be subjected to him who put all things under him, that God may be everything to every one.
I Corinthians 15:24, 28

Confession
Thy kingdom come means... **destroy the devil's work; destroy every force which revolts against you and every conspiracy against your Word. Do this until your kingdom is...complete.**
Heidelberg Catechism,
Answer 123

134

Toddlers sometimes play with a number of plastic boxes which fit inside each other. One box fits inside a bigger one, which, in turn, fits inside a still bigger one, and so on. All the boxes fit into the biggest one.

In God's creation and his dealing with it, the highest, widest, vastest reality is what the Bible calls "the kingdom of God." It is the biggest box. Into it fits everything God has made and under it lies everything we have made—all our groupings, associations, relations, "structures." In fact, the kingdom includes not only *what* God rules, but also the ruling itself. "Kingdom" suggests both realm and reign, both domain and dominion.

The church is related not only to such other created realities as the state, but also to the greatest political reality of all—the kingdom of God.

How so? The church is an instrument, a tool, a vehicle of God's ruling. God uses the church to proclaim the reconciling events of Jesus Christ; to bring about this reconciliation by preaching, disciplining, praying, celebrating; and to embody the reconciliation in its own life as a restored people who love each other, pray for each other, work with each other. In this way the church becomes a test model, a "preliminary replica" of the final perfection of God's people.

Let us admit that talk of the kingdom often becomes theological jargon—the kind of talk which both puzzles and bores lay people. Perhaps we do best, then, simply to say what Jesus said. "Thy kingdom come," he said. At once he gave his meaning: "thy kingdom come" means "thy will be done on earth as it is in heaven."

On earth the church is an instrument of God's will.

A Prayer
Our Father who art in heaven, thy kingdom come; thy will be done on earth as it is in heaven. In Jesus' name, Amen.

How Is the Church Related to State and Kingdom?

Scripture
I tell you, you are Peter, and on this rock I will build my church, and the powers of death shall not prevail against it. I will give you the keys of the kingdom of heaven, and whatever you bind on earth shall be bound in heaven, and whatever you loose on earth shall be loosed in heaven.
Matthew 16:18,19

Confession
What are the keys of the kingdom?
The preaching of the holy gospel and Christian discipline toward repentance.
Heidelberg Catechism,
Q & A 83

135

The fall left a cosmic disarray. Some of the divine reordering is now being accomplished outside the church. God has his ways and means beyond the scope and knowledge of his people. This is a dimension of God's universal sovereignty and a part of the Lordship of his Christ. God's rule extends even to the depths of hell and the outposts of atheism and the farthest reaches of space.

But on earth the people of God are an instrument of God. They are not just one among many, but the *main* tool in God's reestablishment program. Thus, in medicine God's people work not merely at a lucrative business, but rather in the service of the kingdom, recapturing territory lost to disease. In business and industry God's people work not merely to amass capital, but deliberately to provide goods and services so that other creatures of God might live better. In education God's people seek not merely to stimulate and satisfy intellectual curiosity, but also to deepen their knowledge of and usefulness to the God who commands that we love him with all our *mind*. So in politics, in the arts, in the family. The people of God are a mighty, flourishing organism, organized according to several strategies to do law, business, medicine, education, science, and the arts in a way that retakes a part of creation formerly lost to the enemy. Here the church is the body of Christ, moving across the kingdom, reclaiming old ground, refurbishing a tarnished creation.

But within this people of God there is also the *institutional* church. It too is not just one Christian institution among many. It is the central institution. For it has been entrusted with the "keys of the kingdom." Through its preaching and disciplining, ultimate human allegiance and destiny are ordinarily determined. These are large keys. And they open to us a reality of incredible greatness and wonder.

A Prayer
Give us, O Lord, love for your church and awe at the height and depth, the power and reach of your kingdom. Make us instruments of your peace. For Jesus' sake, Amen.

Postscript

1. Meditation 131 says that Christians and the Christian church must take political responsibility and show thoughtful obedience to government.

   Why? Shouldn't preachers preach the gospel instead of getting mixed up in political issues?

2. The Belgic Confession, Article XXXVI, lists four duties of citizens. What are these? Can we still perform these duties today? Does it matter that the persons and institutions toward whom we perform these duties are sinful?

3. Meditation 132 suggests some danger signs of "civil religion" or the confusion of the things which are Caesar's with the things that are God's. Do we see any of these danger signs in our own land? Our own province, city, church? Do our members have "My country—right or wrong!" bumper stickers? How about the attitude expressed by "love it or leave it" slogans?

4. In Daniel 3:1-18 we find an account of civil disobedience. Three men with wonderful names disobey King Nebuchadnezzar.

   There are apparently times when a godly person must disobey. When? And by what standards?

5. A minister praying before his congregation asked God to "help us bring in your kingdom." Comment.

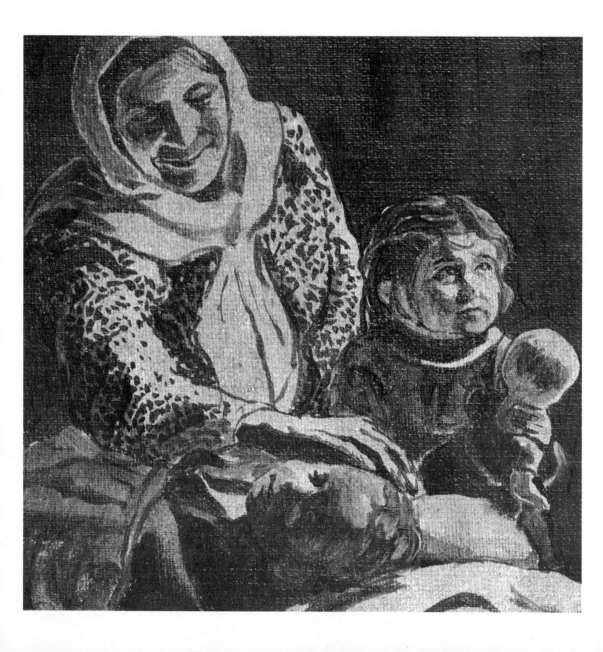

Week Twenty-Eight

How Do We Look at the Future?

We turn, finally, to the "last things." We have asked some questions about God, about humanity, and about the God-man. We have asked about our salvation and about the church.

But the church is on her way toward the future—a future, so the Bible tells us, which comes to a climax at the end of history with the return of our Lord. What is the shape of that future? What *sorts* of things come last? Indeed, how do we face our own "last thing"—our death?

These are some questions we shall raise in this concluding unit. We begin by asking about our general posture as Christians in facing what lies ahead: How do we look at the future?

Scripture

He delivered us from so deadly a
peril, and he will deliver us; on
him we have set our hope that he
will deliver us again.
II Corinthians 1:10

Confession

We confess...that God has
fulfilled the promise which He
made to the fathers by the mouth
of His holy prophets, when He
sent into the world...
His own only-begotten and eternal Son. Belgic Confession,
Article XVIII

136

One of the cruelest of Christian popular illusions is the belief that the biblical saints were always mightily secure and hopeful. Take Paul. Didn't he sing joyously even in prison? Didn't he stand chin-deep in trouble and still shout down the ages that nothing can separate us from the love of God? Isn't it Paul who assures us that "the sufferings of this present time are not worth comparing with the glory that is to be revealed to us"?

It is. But here in II Corinthians we learn that Paul has known some of the same discouragement which weakens and immobilizes the rest of us. In fact, says Paul, "we were so utterly, unbearably crushed that we despaired of life itself" (1:8).

Some of us know what Paul is talking about. We know the terrifying feeling that life is demanding from us far more than we can ever give. We know that powerless sinking to a place where only fear, darkness, and paralysis dwell. We know despair.

Paul talks of despair—the bottom of the soul and the essence of hell. Over the gates of hell, so Dante writes, are these words: "Abandon all hope, ye who enter here." Put off hope. And put on despair forever and ever.

Against that looming hopelessness Christians throw every weapon God gives them. There is "the encouragement of the Scriptures." There is "the power of the Holy Spirit" (Rom. 15:4,13). There are Word and Spirit.

There is one more thing—the knowledge that God our Father may be trusted to keep his promises. He has delivered us before. He will do it again. Thus, with shaking hands and weak knees, we try *again* in the wilderness to prepare the way of the Lord. In this desert we try once more to make straight a highway for our God.

So Paul, who has met the Christ lifted up in the wilderness, stares despair in the face, sets his jaw toward the future, and speaks for us and the whole Christian church:

He delivered us from so deadly a peril, and he *will* deliver us; on him we have set our hope that he will deliver us again.

Christians look at the future with *hope.*

A Prayer
O Lord our God, we do not grieve as those who have no hope. We hope for what we do not see and wait for it with whatever patience you give us. Through Jesus Christ our Lord, Amen.

Scripture
We rejoice in our sufferings, knowing that suffering produces endurance, and endurance produces character, and character produces hope, and hope does not disappoint us, because God's love has been poured into our hearts.   Romans 5:3-5

Confession
We can be patient when things go against us...and for the future we can have good confidence in our faithful God and Father that nothing will separate us from his love.
Heidelberg Catechism,
Answer 28

137

Certain Christians in the Middle Ages regarded despair as one of the "deadly sins." But foolish optimism is just as deadly and the attempt to pass it off as Christian hope just as sinful.

Some people seem to have been born sunny-side up. They whistle at seven in the morning, enraging everyone in their car pool. They smile in dentists' offices. They are *naturally* optimistic. Their motto, someone has said, is "Don't worry! It may not happen."

Fair enough. But let them—and let us—never suppose that simple optimism is what the Bible means by hope. Optimism says, "Don't worry! It may not happen." Hope says, "It may happen. But God will keep us." Optimism says, "Things will become better." Hope says, "By God's grace *we* will become better—and better able to deal with things until the end." Optimism says, "Cheer up." Hope says, "*Look* up. Your redemption is drawing near."

Christian hope comes to us as a gift in the wilderness, in the desert, in exile. It is not a "waking dream." It is "faith on tiptoe," straining toward a future which must be faced with complete realism. It is able, like Abraham, to "hope against hope" and to settle, in suffering, for that "endurance which produces character" and that "character which produces hope."

Let us be frank. Many of the things we hope for never arrive. We hope for excellent health, marriage to a particular person, stable faith and homes among our children. We hope to be respected by our peers and to go down to our graves happy and full of years.

Some of these things never come. We have our share of trembling hopes, faint hopes, and dashed hopes. A novelist once said that to live is to bury some hopes. We have all done some of this burying, often long after our hopes were dead.

Yet, in this graveyard of hopes, we who are Christians take a firm grasp on a central hope which alone "does not disappoint us." For this is the hope which is centered in him who loves us beyond all deserving—and even beyond all hope.

A Prayer
Give us the wisdom, O Lord, to abandon our dead hopes wherever you move us away from them. While we may regret the passing of old dreams and opportunities, help us to live in the present and to look toward your future, through the power of the Holy Spirit. Amen.

Scripture
Why are you cast down, O my soul, and why are you disquieted within me? Hope in God; for I shall again praise him, my help and my God.   Psalm 42:11

Confession
Nothing can befall us by chance, but [only] by the direction of our most gracious and heavenly Father; who watches over us with a paternal care.
                    Belgic Confession, Article XIII

138

NBC's morning television program "Today" reported on a woman who had taken Assertiveness Training. She was so impressed with what she had learned—how to make one's desires known and one's demands understood—that she decided to help those who still lacked this sharp new tool.

She set up a commercial service called *Assertion*. People could call her and hire an asserter to do their asserting for them. It worked! People called! Some wanted to ask for a raise, but did not wish to do the asking themselves. Others wanted anonymously to inform their friends of their breath quality. A few wanted *Assertion* to complain to neighbors about the noise level of their parties.

For a time the woman and her co-asserters were busy and happy. Moreover, all around town, people enjoyed higher wages, sweeter breath, and quieter parties.

But then things changed. One woman wanted *Assertion* to call her husband's company and tell them he was a manic-depressive. A number of customers requested that selected friends and strangers be insulted. Several wished the *Assertion* staff to call them back and talk dirty to them.

The woman gave up and got an unlisted number. She had hoped to help others. But her hope was lost in the sheer perversity of human nature, a perversity which is famous for turning human hope to disillusionment.

You do not have to hate humanity to believe a main biblical truth about hope. Our hope—like our help—is in the name of the *Lord*, a Lord who seems to visit us with hope especially when we are "sadder but wiser." Over and over the psalmists cry out of the depths to a guilty and weary people: "O Israel, hope in the *Lord!*"

So for us. Slowly at first, one quiet act of obedience at a time, we learn to withdraw our hope from the shaky places where we have invested it and to turn again to him whom we trust and for whom we long:

Why are you cast down, O my soul,
    and why are you disquieted within me?
Hope in *God*; for I shall again praise him,
    my help and my God.

A Prayer
Vindicate me, O God, and from deceitful and unjust men deliver me! Oh send out thy light and thy truth; let them lead me, let them bring me to thy holy hill and to thy dwelling, O God, my God. Amen.
                    —from Psalm 43

Scripture
Blessed be the God and Father
of our Lord Jesus Christ! By his
great mercy we have been born
anew to a living hope through
the resurrection of Jesus Christ
from the dead.   I Peter 1:3

Confession
Unto Almighty God we commend
the soul of our brother departed,
and we commit his body to the
ground; earth to earth, ashes to
ashes, dust to dust; in sure and
certain hope of the Resurrection
unto eternal life, through our
Lord Jesus Christ.
Episcopal *Book of Common
Prayer,* "The Order for the Burial
of the Dead"

139

Certain philosophers, ancient and modern, teach the acceptance of hopelessness as a virtue. Ancient stoics, for example, said that everyone loses the game of life, that all hope is an illusion, and that we should learn to lose without whining about it. Some modern French atheists echo the belief that hope is a *curse!* Hopeless pagans.

But more typically and familiarly human are such claims as "hope springs eternal in the human breast" (Alexander Pope) and "the word God has written on the brow of every human being is 'hope' " (Victor Hugo). Most people hold out some hope for the future.

Yet, to hear them talk, they do not hold it out very far. They play their hope close to the breast and express it with furrowed brow:

"Hope I'll feel better soon."

"I hope this ink stain will come out of your shirt!"

"Hope we don't run out of gas!"

"Hope you come and see us again real soon!"

The world is full of false hopes, dubious hopes, little hopes. The hope on human brows is written in small letters.

But Christian hope lodged in our Lord and his salvation is said with a resolute voice and written in capital letters across the New Testament. We have a "living hope," a "blessed hope," a "steadfast hope" in which we may "rejoice." It is a hope given by the power, the dynamite, of the Holy Spirit—a hope in which believers may abound. Biblical hope is large, aggressive, confident.

We do not get it so much from urging each other on: "Believe! Trust! Hope! Believe more! Trust more! Hope more!" We gain hope by looking to Jesus, the author and perfecter not only of our faith but also of our hope. Through his powerful resurrection we have hope not only for this life, but also for the life to come.

The Episcopal *Book of Common Prayer* has exactly the right tone when it talks of "sure and certain hope of Resurrection unto eternal life."

A Prayer
Lord, let us know our end, and what is the measure of our days.
Let us know how fleeting our life is! Surely everyone stands as
a mere breath. Surely for nothing are they in turmoil. And now,
O Lord, for what do we wait? Our hope is in thee. Through
Jesus Christ, Amen.   —from Psalm 39

Scripture
For to this end we toil and strive, because we have our hope set on the living God.   I Timothy 4:10

Confession
Such as truly believe in the Lord Jesus...may in this life be certainly assured that they are in a state of grace, and may rejoin in the hope of the glory of God.
Westminster Confession, Chapter XVIII, 1

140

Most of us know what a *placebo* is. Suppose a medical scientist wants to test the effectiveness of a new drug. In her test, she divides a number of ailing volunteers into two groups. One group is actually injected with the new drug. The other group, without being informed, receives only a placebo; that is, an inactive substance used only as a "control," or basis of comparison, in the experiment.

The scientist is pleased when her new drug helps some of the volunteers. But then she discovers that a number of those who receive only a placebo also improve—some of them quite dramatically. In effect, as Karl Menninger points out in one of his articles, these people have had not a drug but rather *hope* injected into them. They have been inoculated with hope. And they begin to feel much better.

"While there is life there is hope," says Becky Sharp in *Vanity Fair*. Accordingly, where there is no hope, there is no life—at least, not for long.

Observers in wartime have often noted that we need hope to survive. Victor Frankl confirms this with his report of experiences in a concentration camp. Frankl tells of fellow prisoners whose hope of release began to wither.

They reached a stage of almost complete apathy. They would just lie in their bunks, refusing to answer roll call or go out on a rock squad. The threat of a beating, the prospect of being shot—none of it would get them up and on their feet.

Then, in 1944, word got around that the war would be over by Christmas. Tired men, dangerously sick men, struggled to their feet and attempted their tasks with a new light in their eyes. Some of them even laughed for the first time in months.

But Christmas came and went. The war went on. And in the week after Christmas prisoners died like flies. No epidemic raged. Conditions got no worse. There was simply a loss of hope.

We need hope to live. And we need hope in Jesus Christ to live eternally. "If for this life only we have hoped in Christ, we are of all men most to be pitied," said St. Paul. Interestingly enough, those who have hoped most confidently for the next life have often lived most exuberantly in this one. For where there is hope there is life and zest and willingness to spend oneself for him toward whom we are moving, and who keeps our going out and our coming in from this time forth and forever more.

A Prayer
To this end we toil and strive, O living God, because we have our hope set on thee and on thy Christ. In his name, Amen.
—from I Timothy 4

Postscript

1. It is often said that a person's view of the future is determined by his or her view of *history*. One can find such historically conditioned views of the future in hymns, for instance. Take this stanza from "It Came Upon the Midnight Clear":

   > For lo! the days are hastening on
   > By prophet-bards foretold,
   > When with the ever-circling years,
   > Comes round the age of gold.

   What view of history do you find here? Is it Christian? How does a Christian look at history—and therefore at the future?

2. Meditation 137 states that despair was sometimes regarded in the history of the Christian church as one of the deadly sins—like pride or sloth. Apart from pathological despair born of depression, how do we sometimes sin not only in lovelessness, say, but also in hopelessness?

3. One of the most persistent of secular—especially Marxist—criticisms of the Christian hope for complete salvation in the future is that this attitude fosters social inactivity in the present. It blunts the pain of the poor and the oppressed. To what extent is that true?

Week Twenty-Nine

How Do We Face Death?

Marshall and Hample's *Children's Letters to God* includes a few simple sentences about death from a young boy:

> What is it like when you die? Nobody will tell me. I just want to know; I don't want to do it.   Mike

Most people do not want to die. They fight to live. But they are curious about this question of the ages: "What is it like when you die?" They think "nobody will tell" because nobody knows.

Yet followers of the resurrected Jesus Christ know at least something about death. What we know and how we should practice what we know will engage us this week. We take up a powerful and sensitive question: How do we face death?

Scripture
The living know that they will die.
Ecclesiastes 9:5

Confession
Our death does not pay the debt of our sins. Rather, it puts an end to our sinning and is our entrance into eternal life.
Heidelberg Catechism, Answer 42

141

Until about 1970 our contemporary Western society tried to keep a secret. The secret was that we will all die. Till the avalanche of "death and dying" literature buried it, a "conspiracy of silence" surrounded human death.

Thus, we used to avoid the words *dying*, *death*, and *dead*. We did not say, "He died." We said, "He passed away." Life insurance brochures have been especially careful: "If anything should happen to you. . . ." (Like what? Like inheriting a million dollars?) In some cases relatives have tried to get a person to decline and die without his ever noticing. Thus we have had physicians lie to dying people about their condition. We have had funeral cosmetologists prettify dead bodies so they appeared to be taking a nap. A Boston minister reports that relatives of the deceased once objected to his reading the twenty-third Psalm at the funeral on the grounds that it contained the morbid word *death*. These relatives knew a funeral was no time to raise *that* subject!

But even through the years of silence, people knew the truth. "The living know that they will die," as the Preacher says. At any rate, once past forty they know it. Someone has suggested that early in their forties most people psycho-logically try on their shroud. It is a "farewell to innocence." You know that when your own parents die, you move to the head of the line. As you grow still older, the conclusion is eventually unmistakable. Your friends die, one by precious one, and you know that you too are thoroughly mortal. The streets toward death are all one way. And you have already been traveling for some time.

Even children think about death. During a day of play, they may do a fair amount of "shooting" each other and playing dead. Then, at night, they may pray: "Now I lay me down to sleep. . . . If I should die before I wake, I pray the Lord my soul to take." Researchers have observed that even some apparently innocent children's games and songs have an old and eerie significance:

Ring around the rosies, pocket full of posies,
Ashes! Ashes! We all fall down!

A dying unbeliever once asked for "terminal candor." No Christian will face death the way he did—as a wall rather than a door. But the candor we can use. Unless our Lord returns first, we will all die. We will all fall down. And we all know it.

A Hymn or Prayer
O God, our help in ages past,
Our hope for years to come,
Our shelter from the stormy blast,
And our eternal home. Amen.

—"O God, Our Help in Ages Past"

Scripture
The wages of sin is death.
                                        Romans 6:23

Confession
By death we understand not only bodily death, which all of us must once suffer on account of sins, but also eternal punishment.
                    Second Helvetic Confession,
                                        Chapter VIII

142

One of the Grimms' fairy tales, recalled by William May, is about a young fellow who cannot *shudder*. He is particularly incapable of shuddering at the sight of death. Instead of recoiling from a corpse he encounters, he attempts to play with it. Deeply ashamed of his son's inability, the boy's father sends him off "to learn how to shudder." Obviously the boy is not yet fully human if he is so comfortable with death.

There is a "death with dignity" movement in America which has at least something to recommend it—"terminal candor," for instance. Be honest with dying people, says this movement. Tell a person what ails her and call the disease by its right name. Do not isolate a dying person or treat her like a thing without human and civil rights.

So far so good.

But many of the "let there be death" enthusiasts are still telling lies about death in spite of themselves. They suggest that death is somehow just a part of life, that it is quite "natural," that it is indeed a sort of chum. Formerly only stoic philosophers and English romantic poets talked pagan nonsense about death as a naturally kind friend. Now secularized Americans are doing it.

In a brilliant article on "The Indignity of 'Death With Dignity,' " Paul Ramsey suggests that the same program which gave us "calisthenic sexuality" is now promoting "calisthenic dying." For some secularists dying has become the latest exotic art or the newest indoor sport. Dying, for them, is as chic as ballet. You *train* yourself to flutter gracefully to your end, like the star of *Swan Lake*.

Thus, the technique manuals for secularists: *Death Is All Right, Living Your Dying, To Die with Style*, and the like. Experts remark that the burden of these manuals is that a properly dying person must not inconvenience anyone else. Go ahead! Do it! Die—and die with style! But slip away. Die discreetly. Die *"pianissimo."*

Here are people who need to be sent off to learn how to shudder. One place to send them would be to the Bible. The Bible does not see death as natural or as a kind friend, but rather as an *enemy*—"the last enemy to be destroyed" (I Cor. 15:26). Death in the Bible is an alien, a stranger, an intruder, a prime misery of our fallenness. Human death is something which *never should have happened*.

Death is the wages sin pays and, without Christ, the last hopeless indignity of human life.

A Prayer
O Lord our God, we cannot face death alone and we cannot face it as those who have no hope. Now point us toward the Christ who is the pioneer not only of our faith, but also of the way through death. In Christ's name we pray, Amen.

Scripture
The wages of sin is death, but the free gift of God is eternal life in Christ Jesus our Lord.
Romans 6:23

Confession
By his resurrection [Christ] has overcome death...Christ's resurrection is a guarantee of our glorious resurrection.
Heidelberg Catechism, Answer 45

143

There are two main teachings in the Bible about death. One is that death is an enemy. The other is that because of the mighty work of Jesus Christ, death for a Christian is a *conquered* enemy.

Death is an enemy. As we saw yesterday, there are ancient and contemporary pagans who deny it. Death, they say, is a graceful and natural free-fall from the tree of life. Like an autumn leaf we ripen and finally twirl slowly to the ground. The beauty of death!

But surely we know this is contrary both to the clear teaching of the Bible and to all clear-eyed experience. Death is always a separation; often it is a painful ripping and tearing. There is often suffering for the dying person and always for those who are left. The grief which is like fear, the terrible emptiness, the flood of memories stimulated by a scent, a discovered hat, an old bit of writing—for years these things probe in us a brokenness too deep for telling.

When Lazarus died, Jesus did not lead a chorus of joyous hymns. Jesus wept. He was acquainted with grief. And when our Lord turned to face his own death, he acted not with stoic calm and quiet resignation, but with struggle, revulsion, and prayers for reprieve. Jesus Christ *hated death like sin.*

Jesus wept. Then he called Lazarus out of the tomb. Jesus suffered under Pontius Pilate, was crucified, dead, and buried. Then God called *him* out of the tomb. Death could not hold him. God led his only begotten Son clear through death to the other side. Now he offers in some unimaginable way the same triumph of passage to his adopted sons and daughters.

The women who came to Jesus' tomb, says G. K. Chesterton, found that their Lord was alive; it was *death* which had died in the night! For all of us who are moving twenty-four hours a day toward our deaths, there is a blended truth, a bittersweet truth, to believe with all our heart:

Death is an enemy, but—thanks be to God who gives us the victory—it is a *conquered* enemy. Weeping may stay for the night, but joy comes with the morning. The wages of sin is death, *but* the free gift of God is eternal life in Christ Jesus our Lord.

A Prayer
Thanks be to you, O Lord, for your unspeakable gift. Amen.

Scripture
He himself likewise partook of [human] nature, that through death he might destroy...the devil and deliver all those who through fear of death were subject to lifelong bondage.
Hebrews 2:14, 15

Confession
For the future we can have good confidence in our faithful God and Father that nothing will separate us from his love.
Heidelberg Catechism,
Answer 28

144

Douglas Nelson retells in a sermon the sequel to the story of Lazarus—a sequel which comes from an early Christian tradition. The legend is that after being brought back to life Lazarus was asked about his experiences in the interim. People begged him to tell what he had seen or heard in the life beyond the grave. Instead, very quietly and very joyously, Lazarus laughed.

It is only a legend. But the laughter is medicine for what ails us when we face death. We know about eternal life. We have heard of joy in the morning. We believe Jesus Christ has conquered death. We really do. And yet...we are *afraid*. Fear of death, as Hebrews says, can enslave us not only when we are about to die, but also for a whole lifetime.

We are afraid of dying—of operations and chemotherapy, of suffering and helplessness, of pain and paraphernalia. We are afraid of becoming a burden. We fear losing our self-control and self-esteem. We are afraid of being separated from those whom we love and from the life which, in all of its thunder and busyness, has often been so sweet and good. We are secretly afraid of meeting him who knows every shabby thought, every graceless act which has ever cheapened our lives.

Yet we must die—and not as those who have no hope. Someone has compared the dying of a Christian to the movement of a child down a flight of stairs to a basement. It is late. There is an emergency and the lights have all gone out. From the basement the child hears his father calling to him. The child cannot see anything. He is thoroughly afraid. He doesn't want to descend those stairs. He doesn't know what's there.

Yet he knows *who's* there. And so, perfect love casting out fear one step at a time, the child slowly moves and reaches toward his waiting father.

Even for children of God death is a valley of shadows and darkness. But, as Richard Baxter put it, "Christ leads me through no darker rooms than he went through before." And in that darkness it is not God but only death which comes as a stranger. He who stands beyond death will be the loving Father for whom we have been longing all these years.

A Prayer
Dear Father in heaven, it is only when we see the valley of shadows that we look to the hills from whence our help comes. It is only when we fear and fight death that we see the long, sure reach of your amazing grace. Through Jesus Christ our Lord, Amen.

Scripture
Teach us to number our day ;
that we may get a heart of
wisdom.   Psalm)0:12

Confession
Because I belong to him, Christ,
by his Holy Spirit, assures me of
eternal life and makes me whole-
heartedly willing and ready from
now on to live for him.
Heidelberg Catechism,
Answer 1

145

We shall die, and we shall try to meet death with faith and hope. But, meanwhile, how shall we *live*? How shall we live "toward death"?

Paul Ramsey mentions two responses to the realization that we will die. Play-persons number their days to apply their hearts unto eating, drinking, and being merry—for tomorrow they die. That is the response of today's sad and earnest hedonism.

The other response is from those who know they are held by the everlasting love of God not only in this life, but also in the life to come. These are Christians who have resolved to live fully, but not frantically. These are people who number their days so as to get a heart of *wisdom*.

The numbering of one's days begins when the "sense of transience" awakens. It becomes instantly more precise when a person comes back from a brush with death. One of the people who survived the incredible "death-dive" of a passenger airliner over Michigan in 1978 later said how much each new day meant to him. Colors were more vivid, smells more savory, music and laughter more delightful.

So it is. So every day should be for Christians who believe they have been rescued from eternal death and will be guided through physical death. We are to number our days, reckoning each one as a gift. With deepening wisdom, we are to see which things in our lives really count and how much of what now occupies us is merely trivial.

For Christians human life is not a waiting game or a spectator sport. We are given our days as a gift from him who intends us to use them well. Sloth, or laziness, used to be thought a deadly sin. People do not ordinarily find it so deadly any longer. But it is. It is a premature death. To spend vast amounts of one's life waiting, drifting, drumming one's fingers, and watching one's television set is wasteful sin.

Admittedly, there are Christians who drive themselves wild trying to achieve. But there are also many who go down to their grave early in life and lie there, waiting for death to come. They never even *try* to live the lives God gave them.

"Teach us to number our days that we may get a heart of wisdom."

A Prayer
O Lord: support us all the day long, until the shadows lengthen and the evening world is hushed, and the fever of life is over, and our work is done. Then, in your mercy, grant us a safe lodging, and a holy rest, and peace at the last; through Jesus Christ our Lord. Amen.
—from the Presbyterian *Worshipbook*

Postscript

1. In these meditations we have tried to see how we *Christians* face death. But how would a secularist face death? Do secularists have *secular* ideas of immortality?

2. What happens to us when we die? Are we conscious afterwards? Or do we "sleep" till the resurrection at the end of history?

3. Is it permissible for a Christian to *want* to die?

4. It is becoming more common these days to have private family viewings of the body of a dead person, followed by early burial or cremation and a memorial service in the church. Is this to be preferred, do you think, to viewings and services centered in a funeral home? Does it matter?

Week Thirty

What About The Consummation?

We come, now, to the end. This last chapter
deals with those attitudes, events, and
final things which attend the end of history. One day our Lord shall bring all
history to its completion or perfection. He
shall *consummate* history. A number of
important questions surround our belief in
this. We end by asking them under the
general question: What about the consummation?

What About the Consummation?

Scripture
Watch therefore—for you do not know when the master of the house will come...lest he come suddenly and find you asleep.
Mark 13:35, 36

But know this, that if the householder had known at what hour the thief was coming, he would not have left his house to be broken into. You also must be ready.
Luke 12:39, 40

Confession
We believe...when the time appointed by the Lord (which is unknown to all creatures) is come...that our Lord Jesus Christ will come from heaven.
Belgic Confession,
Article XXXVII

146

The second coming has always held a particular fascination for certain Christians. Here they are—Christians with their charts and graphs, their Bible prophecies and pocket calculators, trying to figure the day and the hour of our Lord's return. Some have made confident predictions, including not only the time but also the *place* Jesus has chosen to land. So far they have always found it necessary to revise his schedule.

Surely the New Testament ripples with certainty about Jesus' reappearance. As Anthony Hoekema points out, the theme is sounded one way or another in every one of its books. But the New Testament—indeed, our Lord himself—tells us we do not know the time. It is none of our business. Our task is rather to *watch*. Stay alert! Be on the lookout for the unexpected Lord!

The images for his coming are remarkable. He is either a householder or a household thief! The Son of man is like a householder who comes home suddenly and catches his servants in bed. Or, incredibly, the everlasting Son of God is like a thief who comes silently in the night.

What is the point? There is, of course, good reason why a thief does not announce his coming. It would spoil all the fun. A thief wants his visit to be a surprise. He doesn't want you to fuss and bother and go to the trouble of preparing a welcoming party.

Is that it then? Does the sudden God delight in catching us off guard? Is he like a welfare officer who makes surprise calls on his clients? Is he like a minister who drops by before you can get your Bible out onto the coffee table?

No. The point is not that our Lord hopes to catch us napping. Just the opposite. He hopes to catch us wide awake, on the job, eager, expectant. Readiness is all.

Yet Jesus' prediction is that we will be surprised. He will come when we least expect him.

Perhaps one day when we are in church?

A Hymn or Prayer
Come, Thou long-expected Jesus,
Born to set Thy people free;
From our fears and sins release us;
Let us find our rest in Thee. Amen.
—"Come, Thou Long-expected Jesus"

What About the Consummation?

Scripture
The Lord Jesus [shall be] revealed from heaven with his mighty angels in flaming fire, inflicting vengeance upon those who do not know God...and [being] marvelled at in all who have believed.
II Thessalonians 1:7, 8,10

Confession
Our Lord Jesus Christ will come from heaven, corporally and visibly, as He ascended, with great glory and majesty to declare Himself Judge of the living and the dead.   Belgic Confession, Article XXXVII

147

In one of his sermons, Wallace Alston retells a story by the great Dane, Søren Kierkegaard. Kierkegaard describes a theater in which a large crowd was attending a play. A fire started backstage. With desperate urgency an actor rushed upstage to shout the warning to the crowd: "The theater is on fire! Get out!"

But the people did not get out. They nodded and giggled and stayed right where they were.

The acter became more frantic. He gestured and shouted louder. He pleaded with the people to believe him. And the people were impressed. Truly this was a fine actor. They rose to their feet and began to *applaud!*

Alston wonders whether the end of the world might come thus—prophets feverishly announcing it and people applauding their act.

One of our profoundest problems is that we *see* so little. We cannot see God. We cannot see heaven or the things of heaven. We cannot even see much of what God is doing in our world. We walk by faith, not by sight. And, to be honest, our faith often fails to grasp the reality of what it confesses. These things seem remote, unreal, airy—such things as dreams are made of. Thus, when a preacher gestures and shouts and pleads about them, we feel like congratulating *him!* What a rendition! What a performance! What a good act!

And one day there will be a stirring and commotion *outside*—an incredible breakthrough. Jesus Christ returns with power, fire, and the hosts of heaven. The play is over. The lights come on and we are confronted not just by a solitary Lord, but by a whole heavenly *community!* It is an invasion. A whole new world— "something," says C. S. Lewis, "it never entered your head to conceive—comes crashing in."

In this invasion each believer will experience a moment of terrible beauty and recognition, a moment of astonished stammering and then of final confession: "I have heard about this day, but I *never* thought....I had heard of thee by the hearing of the ear, but now my eye *sees* thee."

A Hymn or Prayer
Beautiful Savior!
Lord of the nations!
Son of God and Son of Man!
Glory and honor,
Praise, adoration,
Now and forevermore be Thine! Amen.

—"Beautiful Savior"

What About the Consummation?

Scripture
When he was at table with them,
he took the bread and blessed,
and broke it, and gave it to them.
And their eyes were opened, and
they recognized him.
Luke 24:30, 31

The trumpet will sound, and the
dead will be raised imperishable,
and we shall be changed.
I Corinthians 15:52

Confession
Christ's resurrection is a guaran-
tee of our glorious resurrection.
Heidelberg Catechism,
Answer 45

148

Peter Eldersveld used to tell the story of Albrecht Dürer's masterwork, *Praying Hands*. At a time when Dürer and a friend were both young and struggling artists, the friend gracious-ly undertook manual labor to support both of them. Gradually his own hopes for artistry fad-ed. Years later Dürer wanted somehow to repay the friend who had sacrificed himself so kindly. At last he decided to paint the hands that had toiled for him—hands stiffened and calloused by years of heavy work. He called his painting sim-ply *Praying Hands*. Those hands have since become famous across the world.

Hands are among God's choicest gifts. Most of us have a brace of hands—a matched pair. They are ingeniously made tools, capable of ex-traordinary speed, power, and accuracy. We are reminded of this whenever we see one of the world's great pianists at work on a truly wicked passage. But all of us use our hands in countless ways every day. Indeed, some of us who have a particular way with things are rightly called "handy."

Artists, as someone has remarked, have made several attempts to paint the hands of our Lord. These are the hands that once reached for lep-ers, blessed children, touched unseeing eyes, broke bread. These are the hands that washed the feet of disciples who would not dream of doing the same for each other. Artists have done their best with Jesus' hands, picturing them as strong, experienced, sensitive.

But, in fact, all we know about those hands is that at the end they were bloody, punctured, and torn. These are the hands that one Friday were opened to be wounded for our transgres-sions and bruised for our iniquities.

The next Sunday two men on the road to Emmaus talked with a stranger about their dead Lord and their dashed hopes for a Messiah. And then, over a small meal in a lamplit room, there was an astonished recognition. "He was known to them in the breaking of the bread" (Luke 24:35). A certain turning of the wrist, perhaps, and the movement of the hands! They had seen those very hands *before*!

Jesus Christ was the firstfruits of the resurrec-tion. It is a resurrection of the body. And an implication of this for all eternity is that one day we shall have hands again.

Will we use them? Will the new heaven and new earth include vocations more than vaca-tions? Very likely. But with a difference from our present situation. For the first time we shall pray without shame and without irony:

Establish thou the work of our hands upon us, yea, the work of our hands, establish thou it.

A Prayer
God our Father, we have no clean hands and no pure hearts. But we look to Jesus Christ through whom you have given us the victory both for hands and heart. Amen.

Scripture

Then the King will say to those at his right hand, "Come, O blessed of my Father, inherit the kingdom...for I was hungry and you gave me food...." Then he will say to those at his left hand, "Depart from me, you cursed, into the eternal fire...for I was hungry and you gave me no food."
Matthew 25:34, 35, 41, 42

Confession

The books (that is to say, the consciences) shall be opened, and the dead judged according to what they shall have done in this world, whether it be good or evil. **Belgic Confession, Article XXXVII**

149

The parable of the sheep and the goats tells us a day of judgment follows the resurrection of our bodies. We will be there.

One gets the impression from this parable that our judge will not ask us first how often we have read the Bible or prayed, nor how many times we have endured a church service, nor how eagerly we cultivated the sort of personal piety which allows us to say "Lord, Lord" all the time. Some of these things do nourish our faith, but Jesus Christ will want to ask what good works have *come* from faith. As always, he will judge the tree by its fruits.

Two sorts of trees—that is, two groups of people—are before him. Two groups of *surprised* people. One group consists of do-gooders. They have graciously welcomed representatives of hunger relief committees and then taken upon themselves the same financial burden to relieve hunger (perhaps taking out a loan) as others do to take a luxury vacation. They have adopted Oriental orphans, enlisted for prisoner visits, used their business skill to provide loans and housing for low-income people. They have acted politically in the interests of those little people who lack political power and savvy. They have spent money, time, emotional energy—they have spent *themselves*—ministering to the least of Jesus Christ's brothers and sisters.

These are people whose level of self-conscious piety may be low. But they are amazed to hear the kindest words of heaven directed to *them*: "Come, O blessed of my Father, inherit the Kingdom...."

And the others? They too are surprised. In fact they are stunned and then banished. Their record shows plenty of good works, but all of these good works seem to have been done for themselves and their equally comfortable friends. The record shows little or nothing done for "the least of these."

To conservative people all of this sounds so—well, so *liberal*. The disturbing truth is that no liberal theologian made it up. This terrible parable presents a social gospel, in fact, our *Lord's* social gospel. It is in the Bible. We cannot explain it away. And it ought to scare us.

It is true, of course, that all who trust Christ may face judgment without fear. But the parable says this trust is expressed and measured by ministry to the least of these. And by *that standard*, how many of us can really say we have put our trust in Jesus Christ?

A Prayer

O Father God, we have owed mercy and justice which we have not paid. We have ignored the haunted lives of the least of these while securing life for ourselves. Truly there is no health in us. Now forgive and heal us by the mercy of Christ. Then set us to work in the exciting task of doing good for Christ's sake. Amen.

Scripture

Then I saw a new heaven and a new earth; for the first heaven and the first earth had passed away, and the sea was no more.
Revelation 21:1

Confession

Even as I already now experience in my heart the beginning of eternal joy, so after this life I will have perfect blessedness such as no eye has seen, no ear has heard, no man has ever imagined: a blessedness in which to praise God eternally.
Heidelberg Catechism, Answer 58

150

The great twenty-first chapter of Revelation presents an incomparable vision of the homeland toward which the people of God have been moving for centuries. The resurrection of the body allows God's people to inhabit "a new heaven and a new earth." At the beginning we were banished from the garden, but at the end we shall be welcomed to a city—a *garden* city where rivers flow and the foliage is for "the healing of the nations." Once again "the desert shall blossom as the rose" and "the mountains drop sweet wine." Once again the creative God shall look upon what he has made and call it "very good." Once again the earth—*this* earth, renewed—shall be the scene of unbroken harmony between God, his children, and the rest of creation.

The vision of John is remarkable not only for what it includes: the great city, the gold and jewels, the transparent streets. It is also remarkable for what it banishes from the city of God. There shall be no more tears, no death, no mourning, no crying, no pain. There shall be no *night*. Interestingly, there shall be no temple—no going to church.

One other thing: the sea shall be no more.

Douglas Nelson suggests that this may be "one of the most haunting verses in the whole Bible." Perhaps he is right. But what does the verse mean? Why no *sea*?

For John, as for so many other biblical writers, the sea is a symbol of *chaos*. There it is, stretching out turbulently and mysteriously toward the horizon. This is the home of Leviathan, of the great sea monsters, of the human dead not yet yielded up by the wash and roll of the waters. Restless, heedless, incredibly powerful—such is the sea. The sea reminds us of every chaos which borders, and sometimes overwhelms, human life.

And one day the chaos will be gone. Into the disharmony of our world, our society, our own nightmares, God will bring harmony. Our disorder—his glorious new order. Our worldliness—his brave new world. Our chaos—his cosmos.

That, for all the ages, is how the story is to end—this story and this world. "For the former things have passed away." But the same Lord who closes his book on this life then turns to open another. For he who sits upon the throne says, "Behold, I make all things new."

A Recitation
He who testifies to these things says, "Surely, I am coming soon." Amen. Come, Lord Jesus! The grace of the Lord Jesus be with all the saints. Amen.   —Revelation 22:20, 21

Postscript

1. Meditation 146 emphasizes the fact that no one knows when the Son of man shall return. But don't we have some help with this? How about the "signs of the times"?

2. Much debate among conservative Christians has centered around the proper interpretation of the "millennium" or thousand-year reign of Revelation 20:4. You may have heard of "a-mil," "pre-mil," and "post-mil" views. What do these terms refer to? Does any of this debate matter particularly?

3. Mark Twain once noted that people think of heaven as going to church a lot, sitting around plunking harps, and the like. He wondered why anybody would picture *heaven* as consisting mainly in the performance of activities he now neither can nor wishes to do.

   How about that?

Bibliography

Allen, Diogenes. *Finding our Father.* Atlanta: John Knox Press, 1974.

Alston, Wallace M. "Facing Life's Incredible Demands." Sermon, Nassau Presbyterian Church, Princeton, N.J., 17 September 1978. (Mimeographed.)

—————. "The Gift of Sleep." Sermon, Nassau Presbyterian Church, Princeton, N.J., 8 January 1978. (Mimeographed.)

—————. "God and the Golden Rule." Sermon, Nassau Presbyterian Church, Princeton, N.J., 28 September 1975. (Mimeographed.)

—————. "When We Are Most Vulnerable." Sermon, Nassau Presbyterian Church, Princeton, N.J., 22 January 1978. (Mimeographed.)

And He Had Compassion on Them: The Christian and World Hunger. Grand Rapids: Christian Reformed Board of Publications, 1978.

Baillie, Donald M. *God Was in Christ: An Essay on Incarnation and Atonement.* New York: Charles Scribner's Sons, 1948.

Baillie, John. *And the Life Everlasting.* New York: Charles Scribner's Sons, 1936.

—————. *Our Knowledge of God.* New York: Charles Scribner's Sons, 1959.

Barclay, William. *Ethics in a Permissive Society.* New York: Harper & Row, Pubs., 1971.

Berkhof, Hendrikus. *Christ the Meaning of History.* Translated by Lambertus Buurman. London: SCM Press, 1966; reprint ed., Grand Rapids: Baker Book House, 1979.

Berkhof, Louis. *Systematic Theology.* 4th ed. Grand Rapids: Wm. B. Eerdmans Pub. Co., 1949.

Berkouwer, G. C. *Man: The Image of God.* Grand Rapids: Wm. B. Eerdmans Pub. Co., 1962.

Blamires, Harry. *The Will and the Way: A Study of Divine Providence and Vocation.* London: S.P.C.K., 1957.

Boesak, Allan A. *Farewell to Innocence: A Social-Ethical Study on Black Theology and Black Power.* Kampen: J. H. Kok, 1976.

Boggs, Wade. *All Ye Who Labor: A Christian Interpretation of Daily Work.* Richmond: John Knox Press, 1961.

Brown, Robert M. *The Significance of the Church.* Philadelphia: Westminster Press, 1956.

Buechner, Frederick. *The Hungering Dark.* New York: Seabury Press, 1969.

—————. *The Magnificent Defeat.* New York: Seabury Press, 1966.

Bunyan, John. *Grace Abounding to the Chief of Sinners.* Edited by Roger Sharrock. Oxford: Clarendon Press, 1962.

Buttrick, George A. *Prayer.* New York: Abingdon Press, 1942.

Calvin, John. *Commentary on a Harmony of the Evangelists, Matthew, Mark, and Luke.* Translated by William Pringle. 3 vols. Grand Rapids: Wm. B. Eerdmans Pub. Co., 1956.

—————. *Institutes of the Christian Religion.* Edited by John T. McNeill. Translated by Ford Lewis Battles. Library of Christian Classics, vols. 21, 22. Philadelphia: Westminster Press, 1960.

Campbell, Ernest T. "Can We Survive Our Extravagances?" Sermon, The Riverside Church, New York, 19 October 1975. (Mimeographed.)

—————. "The Church and the Common Good." Sermon, The Riverside Church, New York, 12 October 1975. (Mimeographed.)

—————. "It All Began in Antioch." Sermon, The Riverside Church, New York, 13 June 1976. (Mimeographed.)

—————. "Questions Jesus Asked: III 'What is the Kingdom of God Like?' " Sermon, The Riverside Church, New York, 21 March 1976. (Mimeographed.)

—————. "Questions Jesus Asked: VII 'Have You Come Out as Against a Robber?' " Sermon, The Riverside Church, New York, 11 April 1976. (Mimeographed.)

—————. "The Saddest Saying in the Gospels." Sermon, The Riverside Church, New York, 11 January 1976. (Mimeographed.)

—————. "Thomas Muenzer—The Reformer We

Tend to Forget." Sermon, The Riverside Church, New York, 26 October 1975. (Mimeographed.)

Carlozzi, Carl G. *Death and Contemporary Man: the Crisis of Terminal Illness.* Grand Rapids: Wm. B. Eerdmans Pub. Co., 1968.

Chesterton, G. K. *The Ball and the Cross.* New York: John Lane Co., 1910.

—————. *The Everlasting Man.* New York: Dodd, Mead & Co., 1925.

Coffin, William Sloane Jr. "The Parable of the Last Judgment." Sermon, The Riverside Church, New York, 18 March 1979. (Mimeographed.)

—————. "On Winning Defeats." Sermon, The Riverside Church, New York, 1 October 1978. (Mimeographed.)

Curtis, A. Kenneth. "A New Apostasy." *Eternity,* September 1978, p. 21.

Daly, Mary. *The Church and the Second Sex.* New York: Harper & Row, Pubs., 1968.

Dart, John. "Woody Allen, Theologian." *Christian Century,* June 22-29, 1977, pp. 585-89.

DeBoer, Willis P. Review of *The Christian Looks at Himself,* by Anthony A. Hoekema. *Calvin Theological Journal* 12 (November 1977): 209-17.

DeJong, Peter, and **Wilson, Donald R.** *Husband and Wife: The Sexes in Scripture and Society.* Grand Rapids: Zondervan Pub. House, 1979.

Dickens, Charles. *David Copperfield.* Introduction by R. H. Malden. London: Oxford University Press, 1948.

Dowey, Edward A. Jr. *A Commentary on the Confession of 1967 and an Introduction to 'The Book of Confessions.'* Philadelphia: Westminster Press, 1968.

Fairbanks, Charles B. ["Aguecheek"]. *My Unknown Chum.* Garden City, N.Y.: Garden City Pub. Co., 1912.

Feifel, Herman, ed. *New Meanings of Death.* New York: McGraw-Hill Book Co., 1977.

Forbes, Cheryl. "Judaism under the Secular Umbrella: An Interview with Chaim Potok." *Christianity Today,* 8 September 1978, p. 14.

Fosdick, Harry E. "The Importance of Doubting our Doubts." In *What Is Vital in Religion: Sermons on Contemporary Christianity,* pp. 89-99. New York: Harper & Bros., 1955.

Frankl, Viktor E. "Experiences in a Concentration Camp." *Man's Search for Meaning: An Introduction to Logotherapy.* Translated by Ilse Lasch. Rev. ed. Boston: Beacon Press, 1962.

Gallagher, Dorothy. "We Had Our Whole Lives Planned." *Redbook,* December 1978, p. 67.

Gilhuis, Cornelis. *Conversations on Growing Older.* Translated by Cor Barendrecht. Grand Rapids: Wm. B. Eerdmans Pub. Co., 1977.

Green, Michael. *Runaway World.* London: Inter-Varsity Press, 1968.

Hageman, Howard G. "Does the Reformed Tradition, in 1975, Have Anything to Offer to American Life?" *The Reformed Journal,* March 1975, pp. 10-18.

—————. "In No Strange Land." Sermon. *The Princeton Seminary Bulletin* 68 (Autumn 1975): 48-52.

Haley, Alex. *Roots.* Garden City, N.Y.: Doubleday & Co., 1976.

Handy, Robert T. *Members One of Another: Studies in the Nature of the Church as it Relates to Evangelism.* Philadelphia: Judson Press, 1964.

Heynen, A. James. "Covenant and Family." Speech given at Dordt College, 10 January 1979. (Mimeographed.)

Hick, John. *Death and Eternal Life.* New York: Harper & Row, Pubs., 1976.

Hoekema, Anthony A. *The Bible and the Future.* Grand Rapids: Wm. B. Eerdmans Pub. Co., 1979.

—————. *The Christian Looks at Himself.* Grand Rapids: Wm. B. Eerdmans Pub., Co., 1975.

Hoekendijk, J. C. *The Church Inside Out.* Edited by L. A. Hoedemaker and Pieter Tijmes. Translated by Isaac C. Rottenberg. Philadelphia: Westminster Press, 1964.

Holwerda, David E. "Liberation and Theology." *The Banner,* 23 March 1979, pp. 4-5; 30 March 1979, pp. 4-5.

Howard, Thomas. "The Idea of Sacrament: An Approach." *The Reformed Journal,* February 1979, pp. 9-13.

Hudnut, Robert K. *The Sleeping Giant: Arousing Church Power in America.* New York: Harper & Row, Pubs., 1971.

Huizinga, Johan. *The Waning of the Middle Ages: A Study of the Forms of Life, Thought, and Art in France and the Netherlands in the XIVth and XVth Centuries.* (London: E. Arnold & Co., 1948.)

Jewett, Paul K. *Man as Male and Female: A Study in Sexual Relationships from a Theological Point of View.* Grand Rapids: Wm. B. Eerdmans Pub. Co., 1975.

Kelly, Orville E. "Make Today Count." In *New Meanings of Death,* pp. 181-193. Edited by Herman Feifel. New York: McGraw-Hill Book Co., 1977.

Kierkegaard, Søren. *Attack Upon "Christendom."* Translated, with an introduction, by Walter Lowrie. Supplementary introduction by Howard A. Johnson. Princeton: Princeton University Press, 1968.

King, Martin Luther Jr. "Letter From Birmingham Jail." In *Symposium,* pp. 601-14. Edited by Arthur F. Kinney, Kenneth W. Kuiper, and Lynn Z. Bloom. Boston: Houghton Mifflin Co., 1969.

Kirkland, Bryant M. *Home Before Dark.* New York: Abingdon Press, 1965.

Klaassen, William. *The Forgiving Community.* Philadelphia: Westminster Press, 1966.

Kromminga, John H. *All One Body We: The Doctrine of the Church in Ecumenical Perspective.* Grand Rapids: Wm. B. Eerdmans Pub. Co., 1970.

————."Church Discipline as a Pastoral Exercise." *The Reformed Journal,* November 1974, pp. 12-15.

Küng, Hans. *On Being a Christian.* Translated by Edward Quinn. Garden City, N.Y.: Doubleday & Co., 1976.

Kuyvenhoven, Andrew. *Partnership: A Study of the Covenant.* Grand Rapids: Board of Publications of the Christian Reformed Church, 1974.

Leith, John H. *An Introduction to the Reformed Tradition: A Way of Being the Christian Community.* Atlanta: John Knox Press, 1977.

Lewis, Clive Staples. *The Four Loves.* London: Collins, 1960; Fontana Books, 1963.

————. [Clerk, N.W.]. *A Grief Observed.* Greenwich, Conn.: Seabury Press, 1963.

————. *Mere Christianity.* New York: Macmillan Pub. Co., 1952.

————. "Miracles." In *God in the Dock: Essays on Theology and Ethics,* pp. 25-37. Edited by Walter Hooper. Grand Rapids: Wm. B. Eerdmans Pub. Co., 1970.

————. *Miracles: A Preliminary Study.* London: Collins, 1947; Fontana Books, 1960.

————."Petitionary Prayer: A Problem Without an Answer." In *Christian Reflections,* pp. 142-51. Edited by Walter Hooper. Grand Rapids: Wm. B. Eerdmans Pub. Co., 1967.

————. *The Problem of Pain.* New York: Macmillan Pub. Co., 1962.

————. *Reflections on the Psalms.* New York: Harcourt, Brace & World, 1958.

————. *The Screwtape Letters & Screwtape Proposes a Toast.* New York: Macmillan Pub. Co., 1971.

————. "We Have no 'Right to Happiness.' " In *God in the Dock: Essays on Theology and Ethics,* pp. 317-22. Edited by Walter Hooper. Grand Rapids: Wm. B. Eerdmans Pub. Co., 1970.

————. *The Weight of Glory and Other Addresses.* Grand Rapids: Wm. B. Eerdmans Pub. Co., 1965.

Lifton, Robert J. "The Sense of Immortality: On Death and the Continuity of Life." In *New Meanings of Death,* pp. 273-290. Edited by Herman Feifel. New York: McGraw-Hill Book Co., 1977.

Lindskoog, Kathryn. "Defective Hearts Unlimited." *Eternity,* August 1976, p. 56.

Macbeth. In *William Shakespeare: The Complete Works,* pp. 999-1027. Edited, with an introduction, by Peter Alexander. New York: Random House, 1952.

MacDonald, John D. *No Deadly Drug.* Garden City, N.Y.: Doubleday & Co., 1968.

Marshall, Eric, and **Hample, Stuart, comps.** *Children's Letters to God.* London: Collins, 1967.

May, William. "Attitudes Toward the Newly Dead." In *Death Inside Out: The Hastings Center Report,* pp. 139-49. Edited by Peter Steinfels and Robert M. Veatch. New York: Harper & Row, Pubs., 1974.

————. "The Metaphysical Plight of the Family." In *Death Inside Out: The Hastings Center Report,* pp. 49-60. Edited by Peter Steinfels and Robert M. Veatch. New York: Harper & Row, Pubs., 1974.

Menninger, Karl. "Hope." In *The Nature of Man in Theological and Psychological Perspective,* pp. 183-200. Edited by Simon Doniger. New York: Harper & Bros., Pubs., 1962.

————. *Whatever Became of Sin?* New York: Hawthorn Books, 1973.

Mitford, Jessica. *The American Way of Death.* New York: Simon & Schuster, 1963.

Moltmann, Jurgen. *Theology of Hope: On the Ground and Implications of a Christian Eschatology.* Translated by J. W. Leitch. New York: Harper & Row, Pubs., 1967.

Moule, C. F. D. *The Meaning of Hope: A Biblical Exposition with Concordance.* London: Highway Press, 1955.

Mouw, Richard. *Political Evangelism.* Grand Rapids: Wm. B. Eerdmans Pub. Co., 1973.

————. *Politics and the Biblical Drama.* Grand Rapids: Wm. B. Eerdmans Pub. Co., 1976.

Nelson, Douglas E. Sermon abstracts, First United Presbyterian Church, New Haven, Conn., 1967-78. (Mimeographed.)

Newbigin, Lesslie. *The Open Secret: Sketches for a Missionary Theology.* Grand Rapids: Wm. B. Eerdmans Pub. Co., 1978.

Newman, Evelyn. "A New Look at Old Doubts." Sermon, The Riverside Church, New York, 10 September 1978. (Mimeographed.)

Niebuhr, H. Richard. *Christ and Culture.* New York:

Harper & Row, Pubs., 1951; Harper Torchbook ed., 1956.

Otto, Rudolf. *The Idea of the Holy: An Inquiry into the Non-Rational Factor in the Idea of the Divine and its Relation to the Rational.* Translated by John W. Harvey. Rev. ed. London: Oxford University Press, 1936.

Pannenberg, Wolfhart. *Jesus—God and Man.* Translated by Lewis L. Wilkins and Duane A. Priebe. Philadelphia: Westminster Press, 1968.

Pattison, E. Mansell. *The Experience of Dying.* Englewood Cliffs, N.J.: Prentice-Hall, 1977.

Phillips, J. B. *Your God Is Too Small.* New York: Macmillan Co., 1961.

Plantinga, Alvin C. *God, Freedom, and Evil.* New York: Harper & Row, Pubs., 1974.

Ramsey, Paul. "The Indignity of 'Death With Dignity.'" In *Death Inside Out: The Hastings Center Report,* pp. 81-96. Edited by Peter Steinfels and Robert M. Veatch. New York: Harper & Row, Pubs., 1974.

Read, David H. C. *Holy Common Sense: The Lord's Prayer for Today.* Nashville: Abingdon Press, 1968.

Report of Liturgical Committee (The Christian Reformed Church). In *Psalter Hymnal Supplement,* pp. 65-131. Grand Rapids: Board of Publications of the Christian Reformed Church, 1974.

Robertson, Edward D. "Funerals in a Presbyterian Congregation." Pamphlet, Wilshire Presbyterian Church, Austin, Texas, n.d.

Russell, Bertrand. "A Free Man's Worship." In *Why I Am Not a Christian,* pp. 104-16. Edited by Paul Edwards. New York: Simon & Schuster, 1957.

Sayers, Dorothy L. *Are Women Human?* Introduction by Mary McDermott Shideler. Grand Rapids: Wm. B. Eerdmans Pub. Co., 1971.

Scanzoni, Letha, and **Hardesty, Nancy.** *All We're Meant to Be: A Biblical Approach to Women's Liberation.* Waco, Tex.: Word Books, Pubs., 1974.

Scherer, Paul. *Facts That Undergird Life.* New York: Harper & Bros., Pubs., 1938.

————. *The Place Where Thou Standest.* New York: Harper & Bros., Pubs., 1942.

Schopenhauer, Arthur. "Of Women." In *The Essays of Arthur Schopenhauer,* pp. 72-89. Translated by T. Bailey Saunders. New York: Willey Book Co., n.d.

Shinn, Roger L. *Man: The New Humanism. New Directions in Theology Today,* vol. 6. Philadelphia: Westminster Press, 1968.

Sider, Ronald J. *Rich Christians in an Age of Hunger: A Biblical Study.* Downers Grove, Ill.: Inter-Varsity Press, 1977.

Smedes, Lewis B. *All Things Made New: A Study of Man's Union With Christ.* Grand Rapids: Wm. B. Eerdmans Pub. Co., 1970.

————. "God's Noble Lady." *The Reformed Journal,* January 1973, pp. 4-5.

————. *Love Within Limits: A Realist's View of I Corinthians 13.* Grand Rapids: Wm. B. Eerdmans Pub. Co., 1978.

————. *Sex for Christians: The Limits and Liberties of Sexual Living.* Grand Rapids: Wm. B. Eerdmans Pub. Co., 1976.

Steinfels, Peter, and Veatch, Robert M., eds. *Death Inside Out: The Hastings Center Report.* New York: Harper & Row, Pubs., 1974.

Stob, Henry. "Civil Disobedience." *The Reformed Journal,* April 1972, pp. 22-3.

————. *Ethical Reflections: Essays on Moral Themes.* Grand Rapids: Wm. B. Eerdmans Pub. Co., 1978.

Swinburne, Algernon T. "Hymn to Proserpine." In *Poems and Ballads, Atalanta in Calydon,* pp. 71-6. Edited, with an introduction, by Morse Peekham. Indianapolis: Bobbs-Merrill Co., 1970.

Tavard, George H. *Woman in Christian Tradition.* Notre Dame: University of Notre Dame Press, 1973.

Tennyson, Alfred Lord. "The Lotos-Eaters." In *The Poems of Tennyson,* pp. 429-38. Edited by Christopher Ricks. London: Longmans, Green & Co., 1969.

Thielecke, Helmut. *Our Heavenly Father: Sermons on the Lord's Prayer.* Translated by John W. Doberstein. New York: Harper & Row, Pubs., 1960.

Thomas George F. *Christian Ethics and Moral Philosophy.* New York: Charles Scribner's Sons, 1955.

Thomas, Lewis. *The Medusa and the Snail: More Notes of a Biology Watcher.* New York: Viking Press, 1979.

Thompson, Francis. "The Hound of Heaven." In *The Oxford Book of Modern Verse, 1892-1935,* pp. 54-9. Oxford: Clarendon Press, 1936.

Tournier, Paul. *Learn to Grow Old.* Translated by Edwin Hudson. New York: Harper & Row, Pubs., 1977.

Twain, Mark. *The Adventures of Huckleberry Finn.* New York: Heritage Press, 1940.

Tuck, William P. *Facing Grief and Death.* Nashville: Broadman Press, 1975.

Van Auken, Sheldon. *A Severe Mercy.* San Francisco: Harper & Row, Pubs., 1977.

Van Paassen, Pierre. *That Day Alone.* Garden City, N.Y.: Garden City Pub. Co., 1942.

Verkuyl, J. *Contemporary Missiology: An Introduction.* Translated and edited by Dale Cooper. Grand Rapids: Wm. B. Eerdmans Pub. Co., 1978.

Vos, Geerhardus. *The Teaching of Jesus Concerning the Kingdom of God and the Church.* New York: American Tract Society, 1903.

Vining, Elizabeth Gray. *The World in Tune.* Wallingford, Pa.: Pendle Hill Pubns., 1968.

"Washed in the Blood of the Brave." Hymn. *Liberty, September-October 1975.*

Williams, Clifford E. "The Other Side of State Street." *The Reformed Journal,* January 1977, pp. 4-5.

Wolff, Harold G. "What Hope Does for Man." *Saturday Review,* January 1958, pp. 42-5.

Wordsworth, William. "The Poet's Dream." In *The Poetical Works of Wordsworth,* pp. 72-4. Edited by Thomas Hutchinson. London: Oxford University Press, 1936.

Wolterstorff, Nicholas. "The AACS in the CRC." *The Reformed Journal,* December 1974, pp. 9-16.

————. "Covenant Keeping: The School." *The Banner,* 12 May 1978, pp. 10-11.

————. *Reason Within the Bounds of Religion.* Grand Rapids: Wm. B. Eerdmans Pub. Co., 1976.

Wolterstorff, Nicholas, and **Mouw, Richard.** "Are 'Bad Sermons' Possible? An Exchange on Preaching." *The Reformed Journal,* November 1977, pp. 8-11.